AF411475

A CONFISCATED MEMORY

Yfaat Weiss

Translated by Avner Greenberg

A CONFISCATED MEMORY

Wadi Salib and Haifa's Lost Heritage

Columbia University Press   New York

COLUMBIA UNIVERSITY PRESS
Publishers Since 1893
NEW YORK   CHICHESTER, WEST SUSSEX

COPYRIGHT © 2011 COLUMBIA UNIVERSITY PRESS
ALL RIGHTS RESERVED

LIBRARY OF CONGRESS CATALOGING-IN-PUBLICATION DATA
WEISS, YFAAT.
  [VADI SALIB. ENGLISH]
  A CONFISCATED MEMORY: WADI SALIB AND HAIFA'S LOST HERITAGE / YFAAT
WEISS; TRANSLATED BY AVNER GREENBERG.
    P. CM.
  INCLUDES BIBLIOGRAPHICAL REFERENCES AND INDEX.
  ISBN 978-0-231-15226-6 (CLOTH: ALK. PAPER)—ISBN 978-0-231-52626-5
(E-BOOK) 1. WADI SALIB (HAIFA, ISRAEL) 2. RIOTS—ISRAEL—HAFIA—
WADI—SALIB. 3. PALESTINIAN ARABS—ISRAEL—HAIFA—WADI SALIB—
HISTORY. I. TITLE.
  DS110.H28W4613 2011
  956.94'6—DC23

                                                          2011019705

CASEBOUND EDITIONS OF COLUMBIA UNIVERSITY PRESS BOOKS ARE PRINTED
ON PERMANENT AND DURABLE ACID-FREE PAPER.

PRINTED IN THE UNITED STATES OF AMERICA

C 10 9 8 7 6 5 4 3 2 1

REFERENCES TO INTERNET WEB SITES (URLS) WERE ACCURATE AT THE TIME
OF WRITING. NEITHER THE AUTHOR NOR COLUMBIA UNIVERSITY PRESS IS
RESPONSIBLE FOR WEB SITES THAT MAY HAVE EXPIRED OR CHANGED SINCE
THE BOOK WAS PREPARED.

CONTENTS

PREFACE

THIS BOOK OSTENSIBLY TELLS THE STORY OF A PARTICULAR PLACE in Haifa. Wadi Salib acquired its iconic status in the summer of 1959 when a protest on the part of immigrants from Arab countries, predominantly from Morocco, erupted into a series of riots directed against the authorities and the local urban, Ashkenazi, social-democratic establishment. It was this violent confrontation between the police and the residents of Wadi Salib that brought to public awareness the existence of intra-Jewish tension between immigrants and veterans, between those who had come from Arab countries and those of European origin in Israel. This tension would later be termed the *ethnic problem*. The events of Wadi Salib generated for the first time a political awareness of the existence of discrimination on the basis of ethnic origin among Jewish Israelis and of the sense of frustration and resentment that it nourished. While there is today no consensus as to the development of ethnic protest from that moment onward, nobody would deny that the events of Wadi Salib were a defining moment.

When Wadi Salib became an icon of protest by Jews from Arab countries in Israel, the fact that a mere eleven years previously it had still been a Muslim neighborhood was altogether forgotten. Located on Haifa's eastern fringe, during the British mandate the neighborhood was perceived as a threat to the continuity of Jewish settlement in the city. Like the other Arab quarters, it was overrun during the course of one day of fighting in April 1948. During the months of war and in the wake of the rout, like the vast majority of Haifa's Arab residents Wadi Salib's Muslim population fled for their lives. Of the approximately sixty-five thousand Arab residents, who constituted about half of the city's population, only some thirty-five hundred remained by the summer of 1948. Although it had retained its Arab name, when Wadi Salib became an icon in 1959 there was no trace of its former residents. Wadi Salib was now a deprived Jewish neighborhood in an Israeli city, planted in the present and without a past. How did it come to pass that the dimensions of the destruction of Arab existence in the city were erased and forgotten over so short a time span? My book seeks to provide an insight into the transformation of memory, the memory of Arab Haifa in Jewish Haifa.

This labor of memory seeks first and foremost to relate a different narrative of the city of Haifa. As such, it may be regarded as representing a general discussion of "mixed cities" in Israel. Coined by the British during the Mandate period to denote cities whose population comprised both Jews and Arabs, the phrase *mixed cities* evolved over time into a euphemism that conceals more than it reveals, encompassing a statement about a common existence that goes beyond yet ignores the cataclysm of the year 1948. This is particularly true of Haifa, whose leaders and institutions have always proclaimed a Jewish-Arab "coexistence," which they moreover market as a touristic consumption item throughout the year and as a commercial-folkloristic initiative during the period of the festivities of the three monotheistic religions toward the end of the calendar year. The relative calm that has characterized the lives of Haifa's Jews and Arabs since 1948 and the gradual rise in the number of Arabs living in the city, where they now comprise over 10 percent of the population, in many respects nourishes an inclination on the part of the majority to forget and erase the memory of the catastrophe of the Arab minority of 1948. *A Confiscated Memory: Wadi Salib and Haifa's Lost Heritage* strives to counter this amnesia.

This book does not proceed in a chronological manner, and its course may be likened to a spiral. From the small circle of time extending from 1948 to 1959, the book enlarges its circles, extending its reach to the initial settlement of Wadi Salib within the framework of the Ottoman Hejaz railway initiative up to the failed attempts at urban gentrification over the past two decades. The circular movement through time facilitates narration of the hundred years of Wadi Salib's rise and fall and its transformation into a ruin in the heart of the city of Haifa, while taking care not to succumb to the teleological pitfall of portraying a foregone conclusion. Had I followed the simple chronological path and related the annals of Wadi Salib from its promising beginning to its bitter end, this would have generated an expectation of revealing a direct relationship of cause and effect, an automatic congruence between chronology and causality. Yet the book does not assert a necessary causality that led to the destruction of Wadi Salib. Like the city of Haifa in general, Wadi Salib was destined for a bright future. There existed many visions about a possible future; the shelving of most of them, however, was by no means inevitable.

A circular narrative has additional merits. It enables one to point to a certain repetitiveness in urban development, particularly with regard to the reproduction of segregation in urban construction prior to and following 1948. Through all its various stages, Haifa was characterized by segregationist patterns of residence, which are clearly evident in the annals of Wadi Salib. During the Ottoman period, Wadi Salib was settled by Muslims. During the British Mandate period, the ethnic-religious segregation deepened into a national separation, while in the state of Israel, in contradiction to its integrative ideology of the Jewish melting pot, new intra-Jewish divisions evolved, as a result of which Wadi Salib became predominantly a Moroccan Jewish quarter. While the basis of separation changed with the transition from one period to the next, passing from religious affiliation to nationality and ethnicity, this segregation retained its exclusionary and discriminatory nature. Utilizing sociological conceptualization, the book discusses the changing lines of delineation and separation and their weight in the discourse on civil association and belonging. The linkage suggested in the book between concepts derived from the discourse on citizenship and the spatial perspective questions the accepted distinction between "internal" issues, namely, the question of interethnic relations within Jewish Israeli society, and particularly that relating to the discrimination of Mizrahi Jews on the part of the Ashkenazi establishment, on the one hand, and "external" issues, namely, the question of the Israeli-Palestinian dispute and its implications for the status of Palestinian Israeli citizens, on the other. Through the deciphering of the urban sphere of Wadi Salib in Haifa, it becomes apparent that the "internal" and "external" issues are inextricably intertwined.

Although the book refrains from generating simplistic and unequivocal causal explanations, it cannot evade a blatantly obvious and inconceivable phenomenon. This is the continuing presence over a period of several decades of an area of destroyed buildings in the heart of the city. The scar that runs along the entire length of Haifa's downtown from the port to the commercial center that, contrary to all proclamations about development, preserves the ruins of 1948 is partly interpreted through an examination of the juridical status of the former Arab properties in Haifa. As the book's title suggests, the archaeology of property forms an additional central axis of investigation. It addresses the shaky legal status of Arab property in Haifa and especially in Wadi Salib, known by the juridical definition "absentees' property," linking the restrictions on urban development, on the one hand, and the heavy burden of memory, on the other. The relation between loss of property and compensation and memory and identity crosses the length and breadth of Wadi Salib, connecting all its residents, Palestinian refugees and Moroccan Jewish evacuees. These conclusions have obvious relevance for many locations in Israel, and in this respect the book joins the "archaeo-logical turn" seen in Israeli research over the past two decades, which has engaged in exposing, reconstructing, and reviving awareness of the Arab past of cities in Israel.

The book is constructed as a tapestry of twenty-five vignettes, or frag-ments, that comprise the plot. They differ from one another and cover the relevant disciplines: history, architecture, literature, law, geography, sociol-ogy, and anthropology. This fragmentary structure also reflects the mate-rial condition of contemporary Wadi Salib, which is still a scene of desola-tion between mounds of rubble and bulldozers.

The narrative begins with the series of violent events that took place in the summer of 1959 and has imparted to the Wadi an iconic status in Is-raeli consciousness. Aware of the importance of Haifa, bastion of the Israel Workers' Party (Mapai), the party of the veteran Ashkenazi establishment, the prologue minutely traces the street fights in the alleyways of Wadi Salib. The topography that takes shape, grounded in Wadi Salib's past as a Mus-lim neighborhood, indicates the main thrust of the book, which shifts the events of Wadi Salib from the sphere of Israel's abstract socioethnic-class composition to the concrete Mandate period geographic-physical space or, in other words, from Jewish to Arab space.

Chapter 1, "War," reviews the transformation undergone by the city in 1948. Arab Haifa collapsed within a single day of fighting between April 21–22, 1948, some three weeks before the official declaration of the establish-ment of the State of Israel, following a protracted chain of violent occurrences that broke out in the city with the adoption of the partition plan as resolution 181 of the General Assembly of the United Nations on November 29, 1947. The chapter begins with the act of surrender of the local Arab delegation in Haifa, thereby marking the remnants of the Arab elite in the "mixed city." At the same time, it attempts to capture the confusion of the victors and the hesitation of the initial moments of appropriation of the newly emptied space, which soon gave way to political programs and outlines designed to consolidate and perpetuate the gains of war. Using the case of Haifa, the chapter demonstrates how ethnic homogenization became established as formal Israeli policy during the summer and autumn of 1948, relying on European and other precedents that served as ideological inspiration, on the one hand, and a source of legitimacy for the expulsion of Palestinians and the appropriation of their property, on the other. In both related and unrelated ways, initial cracks began to appear at this time in the status of the Jewish communities in Islamic lands. Within the burgeoning Arab nationalism that accompanied the decolonization process, their members found themselves torn between attempts to include the Jews and initiatives to exclude them. At the end of these processes, the Jews of Morocco, like many Jews living in Islamic countries, were to find themselves residing in the abandoned property of Palestinians in Israel in general and in Wadi Salib in particular.

Chapter 2, "Commotion," reconsiders the events of Wadi Salib through an institutional lens. The way in which the legal system dealt with the leaders of the Moroccan protest and the deliberations of the state commission of inquiry into the events reveal the web of intra-Jewish relations at the end of the fifties. The urban topography, which generates congruence between geographic location, ethnic affiliation, and social class on the slopes of the Carmel Mountain, likewise emerges from the discussions of the commission of inquiry. This topography has its origins in British Mandate times, during which the segregation that could already be discerned with Haifa's rapid development toward the end of the Ottoman period at the turn of the century became ever more entrenched. The British authorities' reluctance to invest in the city's development deepened the disparity between the Arab neighborhoods, which failed to mobilize outside capital for their development, and the Jewish ones, designed according to town planning principles and built with financial support mobilized by the Zionist movement. The antagonism between the Jewish garden neighborhood of Hadar ha-Carmel and Muslim Wadi Salib was stamped on the urban texture and exacerbated as the national dispute escalated. This antagonism was reproduced in the Jewish city, between the Mizrahi residents of Wadi Salib and the Ashkenazi dwellers of Hadar ha-Carmel, and was unloaded during the violent confrontation of 1959.

Continuing the institutional perspective, the chapter focuses on the settlement of Haifa after 1948 and the reproduction of urban segregation. The populating of Wadi Salib with Jewish immigrants, on the one hand, alongside the forced settlement of Haifa's remaining Arab population in Wadi Nisnas, on the other, constitute the defining moment of Israeli Haifa. The chapter simultaneously demonstrates how the creation of a legal foundation of appropriation, in the form of the Absentees' Property Law and the Development Authority, and the strikingly arbitrary nature of its application undermined trust in the legal system and belief in justice among both Jews and Arabs. By virtue of their status as tenants of abandoned Palestinian property, the Jewish residents of the Wadi found themselves in constant strife with the bodies administering the booty. The sense of umbrage and discrimination on the part of the Moroccan immigrants was exacerbated as a large section of European immigrants was able to ameliorate its economic condition in the wake of the reparations agreement with Germany, leave the abandoned property, and improve its standard of living.

The third chapter, "Evacuation," addresses spatial similarity and difference. It observes the Moroccan Jews prior to their immigration, concentrating on the poorest among them, the residents of the *mellah*—the Jewish neighborhoods in the large cities. While the Israeli authorities preferred to bring rural Jews to Israel, they were obliged to receive the urban population as well. Driven by the traditional antiurban bias predominant within social-democratic Zionism, from the early fifties onward Israel took steps to settle the immigrants on the rural frontier. Alienated from working the land, some began to abandon the Arab soil on the frontier and sought to settle in the abandoned Arab neighborhoods in the large cities. Once its original inhabitants were expelled, and contrary to the planners' intentions of emptying it of its Arab residents according to contingency plans drawn up as early as 1937, in the process turning it into a modern city, Wadi Salib was soon filled by impoverished Jewish residents. Rather than investing the paltry available resources in the development that Israel had constantly proclaimed, these were used primarily to effect a symbolic erasure of the Arab past by means of the Hebraization of the names of the streets of the neighborhood and the city.

The spontaneous settlement of Jewish tenants came to an end following the events of Wadi Salib. The conclusions reached by the commission of inquiry regarding the need to evacuate the Wadi initiated the process of its elimination. Institutional spatial oblivion is once again in evidence here. Rather than providing the inhabitants with alternative housing in the proximity of the Wadi, a solution they tended to prefer, the municipality chose to transfer them to housing projects. In so doing, it vacated the city center and left it a desolate place, while subjecting the residents to an isolated existence in suburbia. Moreover, in the name of an integrative ideology it ignored their cultural needs and destroyed their religious-community life. The chapter concludes with a general discussion of social integration, urban segregation, and civil equality through a broad observation of the city's Jewish and Arab neighborhoods prior to and after 1948. Notwithstanding the apparent similarity, the discussion reiterates the difference between Orientals and Arabs with regard to such issues as the link between urban residential patterns, identity, and civil equality, underlining the fundamental difference between discrimination and historical injustice.

The final chapter, *"Khirbeh,"* connects the two ends of Wadi Salib, its beginning to its ending. The construction of the Hejaz railway in the early twentieth century and the erection of the railway station at Haifa's eastern entrance constituted the first act of recognition of the city's economic potential, stemming from its topography and unique location. The transition to government by the British Mandate ushered in imperialist perceptions and colonial planning. Britain regarded control of Haifa Bay as part of the consolidation of its hold over the Middle East. The city held potential importance as a staging post on the way to India and to Mosul. This line of thought spawned the great British initiatives in the city: the harbor, the refinery, and the oil pipeline. These attributes, which marked Haifa as a city with a bright future, were lost with the transition to sovereignty. By breaking up the chronological order and ending the narrative with the beginning of the historical train of events, I offer the reader an account of Haifa in general and of Wadi Salib in particular as counterfactual history, as a future shelved with the transition from empire to nation-state. Faced with the accepted teleological interpretation of the annals of the State of Israel, which views sovereignty as an act of consummation and realization, the chapter, and, in fact, the entire book, offers a contrary reading. Just as Haifa in 1948 lost its importance and international prestige, it likewise lost the multinational milieu that had characterized it as long as it was a "mixed city." As a "Jewish city," Haifa was unable to compete with Tel Aviv, which had been thus from its inception and enjoyed additional advantages to those of Haifa. The epilogue ends with the novella *Return to Haifa,* written by the Palestinian author Ghassan Kanafani, in exile in Beirut, which deals with an encounter between the diachronic neighbors, between Said and Safiyya, former residents of the Hallisa neighborhood in Haifa, and the Holocaust survivor Miriam Goshen from Europe, who was housed in their former home.

Wadi Salib's first residents were wealthy people who built imposing Levantine Liwan houses on the slopes of the wadi in the 1880s. Following them, at the beginning of the twentieth century, Arab laborers on the Hejaz railway rapidly settled in the wadi in exceedingly cramped conditions. During the initial months after the Palestinian nakba, Jewish refugees, mostly from Europe, lodged themselves in the homes of the Muslim tenants. After them came immigrants from Morocco, who were evacuated to the housing projects in the city's suburbs following the Wadi Salib riots. Various conservation-minded bodies have attempted to save the remnants left after the process of evacuation and destruction and have failed time and again. These efforts bore partial success in the case of the railway complex itself, which, incidentally, was damaged by a missile strike during the Second Lebanese War in 2006. Today, on the margins of patches of ruin and rubble that cover most of the area of Wadi Salib, located on the territory of the old city destroyed in 1948, there stands a complex of courthouses serving Haifa and northern Israel. Some may find this ironic.

ACKNOWLEDGMENTS

I conceived the idea of writing this book after attending a lecture delivered by Dan Diner at the University of Haifa, in early 2000, in which he expounded on the connection between time, memory, and property in postcommunist Europe. He conjectured that the rights of the Palestinians would constitute a "sounding board" for the European debates, and it is to this that I owe the inspiration for this book.

My first opportunity to relate the place—Wadi Salib—to the issues of memory and property came during a lecture at a conference entitled "Memory and Restitution: On Historical Remembrance and Material Restitution in Europe," organized by the Simon Dubnow Institute and the Internationales Forschungszentrum Kulturwissenschaft (IFK) in 2001 in Vienna. A grant from the IFK in 2003 enabled me to devote several months to research on the topic. For this I thank the former head of the institute, Gotthard Wunberg, and Lutz Musner. From the outset, Yehouda Shenhav, editor of the series Theory and Criticism in Context at the Van Leer Institute in Jerusalem, showed considerable interest in the topic of the book and made it possible for me to publish it in Hebrew as part of the series. I thank him for his curiosity, friendship, and our professional discussions, which encouraged me to refine my arguments. The Hamburg Institute for Social Research enabled me to work on the manuscript over three summer breaks, placing at my disposal its excellent research facilities. For this I thank Ulrich Bielefeld and the head of the institute, Jan Philipp Reemtsma. In the context of two research groups, financed through the German-Israeli Foundation (GIF), titled Out of Place: Ethnic Migration, Nation-State Formation, and Property Regimes in Poland, Czechoslovakia, and Israel (2006–2008) and Property Reallocation and Symbolic Appropriation: Ownership, Ethnicity, and Memory in Twentieth-Century Czechoslovakia, Poland, and Israel (2009–2011), I was fortunate to discuss my thesis in a comparative and multidisciplinary framework. My thanks go to the GIF and to my colleagues. Elazar Barkan enlightened me about the debate on the role of writing the history of justice and reconciliation, and his influence is apparent in the overall structure of the book.

Students, colleagues, and many of my friends helped me by providing references, indulging in conversation, and reading sections of the manuscript. I wish to thank some of them in particular: Deborah Bernstein, Motti Golani, Yali Hashash, Sharon Livneh, Tamar Menashe, Alona Nitzan-Shaftan, Sandy Kedar, Gil Rubin, Dimitry Shumsky, and Natan Sznaider.

I have been greatly assisted by the Van Leer Institute in Jerusalem, which enabled me to publish the book in Hebrew in 2007 within the scope of its publications. I thank the former head of the institute, Shimshon Zelniker. Special thanks are due to Gabriel Motzkin, the present head of the institute, who facilitated translation of the Hebrew manuscript into English, thereby contributing decisively to the present publication. The English edition constitutes an update on the Hebrew edition: the preface and a large number of the explanations were added in the wake of the anonymous reader's enlightening comments, for which I am grateful.

This is a very personal book of nonfiction. Its writing was made possible by those close to me—Shira, Nussi, as well as my father and mother. Sadly, my mother did not live to read the final draft. I dedicate the book to her.

A CONFISCATED MEMORY

Prologue

"The Neighbors Who Get Rich on Our Account"

ON THE SUMMER EVENING OF JULY 9, 1959, CRIME SQUAD SERGEANT Yisra'el Walk was on a routine patrol in the Haifa area, accompanied by the driver of the police van, Said Abu-Sa'ada, from the village of Usfia.[1] Their patrol began at Shemen Beach and on their way back, toward ten at night, they paid a routine call at Ya'akov and Shalom Shitrit's coffee bar at 85 Shivat Zion Street, known as the Aviv Café. In the midst of an exchange of words with Shalom Shitrit regarding the running of the business and particularly on the matter of the brothers' application for a license to sell liquor, passersby entered the coffee shop, calling upon First Sergeant Walk to go out into the street. In the middle of the street lay a man struggling with a group of people who were trying in vain to remove him. Walk cleared the crowd, taking hold of the prostrate man's arms in an attempt to take him off the street, but was repulsed by him. "In a Moroccan dialect," Walk testified to the Public Commission of Inquiry Into the Events of Wadi Salib, the man, Ya'akov Akiva (Elkarif), said to him: "I have money more than Ben-Gurion. Give me a break, I have no one here and I don't want to live." Walk failed to persuade Akiva to accompany him. When the assembled crowd promised to take the man home, he relented.

As Walk continued on his patrol toward Hadar ha-Carmel and Mount Carmel, Akiva entered the coffee bar and asked for a glass of beer. The owner, Shalom Shitrit, refused to sell him beer. Akiva responded by grabbing an empty bottle, breaking it, and hurling it at a shelf full of bottles. At this point the damage sustained by the café owner amounted to eight bottles of liquor and a few glasses. Akiva's friend Avner Maman managed to take hold of him and began to drag him out of the coffee bar. At the exit Akiva grabbed a frying pan containing hot oil, poured it over Avner Deri, one of the patrons, and in so doing managed to topple the griller—"the hearth with the glowing embers"—as it is referred to in the police report. Maman and Akiva went out into the street and continued toward Wadi Salib Street. On the way, Akiva attempted to enter two further coffee bars in search of a drink, but Maman, so he claimed, dragged him off forcibly, saying to him "why go to prison, better come home."

According to the report of the Public Commission of Inquiry Into the Events of Wadi Salib, Haim First, proprietor of the coffee bar on 7 Wadi Salib Street, noticed "a Moroccan person" and a few moments later was told by a woman passerby "that the man was breaking bottles in the café because he was not allowed to drink." "He had better close the coffee bar," she advised, "so that the man will not enter." Isaac Weissler, owner of the coffee bar at 10 Wadi Salib Street, acted more promptly and, upon hearing that "there is a drunkard and they are coming to blows," hastened to close his establishment. Haim First likewise did not linger. He lowered a shutter and took in three of the four tables that stood outside. In any case Akiva had no intention of entering his café. He merely passed it by. "He didn't talk to me," First reported, "he was walking with another man. I didn't notice whether this man was supporting him, and they continued walking toward Iraq Street." At that moment a police patrol vehicle passed by, driven by Ya'akov Hayek and commanded by Asher Goldenberg. It was on its way to place patrolmen Yitshak Getenyu, Natan Edelstein, Nehemia Hochman, Shlomo Hinga, and Karol Segal in their positions. First signaled to the patrol vehicle to stop. "Must we close our businesses because of one man?" First, a new immigrant from Transylvania, complained in Yiddish to First Sergeant Goldenberg, who was sitting in the patrol car, "we pay our taxes." Goldenberg placated him, saying, "they've come to take the man away," and First indicated the direction in which Maman and Akiva had gone.

Maman and Akiva meanwhile entered the coffee bar belonging to Shlomo Rozolio at 24 Wadi Salib Street. As the patrol car approached the establishment, Karol Segal recognized Ya'akov Akiva, whom he knew from the time he had served as a policeman in the criminal section, some three to four years previously. Then, Segal recalled, Akiva had been a "pimp of prostitutes." Akiva was sitting with his back to the entrance and to the police patrol vehicle, which now parked at the front of the building. Sergeant Goldenberg pointed in the direction of Akiva. Maman, sitting opposite Akiva, leaped toward the policemen. Sergeant Goldenberg said to him, "Not you, the other one." Maman approached Goldenberg and said to him, "I promise I will take Akiva home safely; I'll calm him down." Goldenberg was unmoved and insisted that Akiva accompany him, "after what had happened." Akiva rose to his feet, came out, and leaned on the patrol car, asking Sergeant Goldenberg, "What do you want?" Maman, as Hayek, the driver of the patrol vehicle, recalled, tried to persuade Akiva in Moroccan, saying to him, "Go back to your place, they will not take you." Akiva said, "I'm not afraid, twenty policemen won't take me. I want to die, but not alone." Meanwhile, Hayek testified, "other people, Moroccan citizens known to Akiva, came up to him and tried to persuade him and move him away from the patrol vehicle."

From this point onward events unfolded rapidly: Akiva jumped onto the bar counter, took hold of a full bottle, and smashed it. The policemen leaped from the patrol car, Akiva began throwing bottles at them, one after another, and hit, among other targets, the windshield of the patrol car. The policemen took cover behind the patrol vehicle, and then several shots were fired from Sergeant Goldenberg's pistol through a hole in the windshield into the coffee bar where, at that moment, Akiva was standing some meter and a half to two meters from the door next to the bar. Further shots were fired from a different pistol. Akiva managed to say, "You are shooting at me, go on, shoot," continued to throw bottles, and then collapsed. The shooting stopped. Akiva lay recumbent on the bar, a bleeding wound open on his left hip. "We lifted him up," testified Hayek, "put him in the car, and immediately sped off in the direction of the hospital. We arrived at Rothschild Hospital and the policemen took him inside. I saw that he was still breathing." "Could you and Constable Getenyu have arrested Akiva as he was exiting the coffee bar?" Constable Karol Segal, who fired the second round of shots, was asked in his cross examination. "I think that we would not have succeeded in taking him in by force," he replied, "because he is a very strong, powerful, and tall man, and I and Getenyu are short. Compared to him we are like flies."

At ten thirty that evening a detective squad car with a civilian registration, driven by Constable Eliyahu Ashraf and alongside him First Sergeant

Haim Melekh, reached the corner of Shivat Zion and Wadi Salib Streets. They came across a gathering of some 100–150 people who surrounded the car yelling, "Our brother has been killed by the police." Ashraf testified that someone came running at him from the crowd, took hold of his shirt, tore it, and shouted: "You have killed our brother." He remembers that they pushed and pulled him and people began throwing rocks at the car where Sergeant Melekh was seated. Melekh remembers that "the driver Ashraf began talking to them in the Moroccan language; they at first indeed began to 'touch' him as well, but the language apparently had an effect on them, and they began throwing rocks at the side on which I was sitting." Once they had smashed the car's windshield they manhandled First Sergeant Melekh, forcibly pulled him from the car, and threw him to the ground. At the same time, some of them set out to overturn the police car. In the midst of this turmoil, shots were heard and in the ensuing uproar Melekh managed to escape. Meanwhile Ashraf got out of the car, taking cover from objects that were about to be hurled at him.

That same evening, Constable Kalman Haimowitz and his wife found themselves in the area of the disturbances. Haimowitz remembers initially noticing the prostitute Fariha entering Rozolio's coffee bar, intending to search for the patrolman in order to notify him of this. As this was happening, he heard the shots fired at Akiva and quickly sent his wife home to their apartment on 10 Wadi Salib Street while remaining on the street. He observed the crowd that formed around Melekh's and Ashraf's car. "The driver," he testified, "did not get out of the car. People began talking to the driver in the Moroccan language, which I do not understand; the driver got out of the car and they began pelting it with rocks." At that moment, a shot fired from the fourth floor of the building above the Aviv Café was heard. Three more shots were fired in the minutes thereafter, all from the pistol of a civilian employed as a guard at the National Bank with the aim of dispersing the "wild crowd." One of the witnesses remembers that when the shots were fired from the fourth floor one of the people in the crowd shouted "Nazi" at the person firing. "He was around one meter sixty five tall and looked about twenty-six years old." Haimowitz hurried to his apartment to get a pistol, returned to the scene of the event, stood in the middle of the street some three to five meters from the crowd, and fired one shot in the air. The people identified Haimowitz, the firer of the shot, as "the one with a nylon shirt." They turned away from the police car and from

Melekh, who had meanwhile slipped away, and some of them immediately attacked Haimowitz. One of Haimowitz's teeth was broken from the blows he received, but he managed to escape and ran toward Kibbutz Galuyot (Ingathering of exiles) Street. There he found Sergeant Melekh, and the two continued their flight until they came across a doctor in the street who helped them to telephone the police station and summon reinforcements. Patrol vehicles soon arrived on the scene, advancing along Independence Rise. "The policemen cleared the crowd around the car, Ashraf removed the car down Shivat Zion [Return to Zion] Street in the direction of Faisal Square." At 11 that night Yissaskhar Shefi, commander of the Haifa police force, appeared on the scene where he was greeted by an agitated crowd shouting, "You have killed a man! You have injured a man! They are selling arms to the Germans!" According to the report of the Public Commission of Inquiry, "a host of complaints of discrimination and wrongdoing, accompanied at times by the hysterical screams of women," was brought before Commander Shefi.

The first episode of the Wadi Salib riots began the following day. The tumult had subsided by the previous midnight, people returned home, and peace was restored to the Wadi. Early next morning, instructions were passed out in the neighborhood both by word of mouth and by means of "notes" calling upon residents to close the stores and to refrain from going to work. At seven in the morning some 150–200 people gathered at the Rambam synagogue in response to an appeal by the "Association of North African Immigrants." David Ben-Harush initially addressed the crowd, and from there they set out on a demonstration beyond the confines of the neighborhood on their way to police headquarters. The demonstrators waved black flags and placards with slogans such as "Where is justice?" "The police have killed an innocent man!" "There is no law in the land," and carried the national flag, its edges stained with blood—the blood of chickens, as the commission's report stated. Commander Shefi and Commander Bendel came out to meet the demonstrators in an attempt to calm them. The commanders explained to a delegation of the demonstrators that Akiva was not dead but injured and invited the delegation to accompany them to the hospital and verify this with their own eyes. They explained that the police were investigating the circumstances of the incident and deeply regretted it. From this time until the afternoon hours, some relatively limited incidents occurred. Around midday, some eighty to a hundred people gathered at the edge of the neighborhood, at Faisal Square, throwing rocks at patrol vehicles cruising the neighborhood. The crowd, noted the commission's report, comprised mainly children, youngsters, and women, among them pregnant women. When these had dispersed, the car of the manager of the local National Bank branch on Kibbutz Galuyot Street was set on fire and later the coffee bars belonging to Shitrit and First were damaged. The rioters then destroyed the club of the General Federation of Laborers in the Land of Israel (Histadrut), from where they proceeded to the Labor Party's (Mapai) club where they inflicted extensive damage.

From this stage onward, the situation escalated. At three in the afternoon a crowd of some two hundred demonstrators came across a police force and began throwing rocks at the policemen. The police began to arrest demonstrators and to advance gradually, while the demonstrators continued to pelt the policemen with rocks from the rooftops as they spread out through the streets of the neighborhood, some of which were narrow stairways, and in the alleys in the area. At this point Commander Shefi decided to try to calm the crowd, appealing to the people's conscience. By five o'clock that afternoon the situation appeared to be generally calm, the crowd dispersed, and the stores opened, but forty minutes later reports reached the police of a demonstration involving hundreds of people that was making its way toward Hadar ha-Carmel. While the police were sending reinforcements to the downtown area, two groups emerged from Wadi Salib in the direction of Hadar ha-Carmel, one running along Sokolov Street to Herzl Street and back along Yehiel Street, and the second along Yehiel Street to Syrkin Street, from there on to Shapira Street and back again. Each group numbered twenty-five to thirty people who smashed shop windows, damaged property, and quickly dispersed. At eight o'clock that evening some fifty people again tried to reach Herzl Street, but the police headed them off in time and they retreated to Wadi Salib while throwing stones. At eight thirty in the evening the incidents ceased. The tally of bodily harm came to thirteen injured policemen, two of them in serious condition, and damage to property estimated at twenty-five thousand liras. The police arrested thirty-four suspects, among them ten with a criminal record. Most were released the next day on personal surety with the aim of calming the tension.[2] A manifesto distributed that evening signed by David Ben-Harush expressed regret at the incidents and appealed for calm. A different manifesto distributed the same day stated: "Jews of North Africa, this past day has etched on our memory what lies in store for us in future from these neighbors who get rich on our account and then move into luxurious dwellings in Hadar ha-Carmel and into comfortable projects."[3]

As part of their efforts to placate the delegation of demonstrators, Commanders Shefi and Bendel expressed regret at the injury to Akiva and promised that a police investigation of the event would be conducted. And, indeed, an internal police inquiry was conducted over the following days. It exonerated Sergeant Goldenberg of blame. His shots, the committee concluded, had hit the inner rear wall of the coffee shop and the refrigerator at a height of ninety- centimeters, had thus been fired in different directions, and it followed from this that he had not attempted to harm Akiva and had not aimed his pistol at him. "Sergeant Goldenberg," the report asserted, "was, under the circumstances, entitled to fire warning shots as a means of deterring Ya'akov Akiva from hurling further bottles, but in so doing it would have been preferable had he fired into the air, actually toward the sky, rather than into the coffee bar, as he could have hit Ya'akov or the proprietor of the café." It was the policeman Karol Segal, the commission determined, who had fired two shots, one of which had hit Ya'akov Akiva. These shots were found to be unjustified, "both from the legal and the professional aspects." Segal had acted without receiving instructions to open fire, the commission concluded, and there had been no justification whatever to try and hit Akiva in the leg, since he had had been "alone" and not "in possession of a firearm." The commission therefore recommended arraigning Goldberg before a disciplinary forum and bringing Segal before a civil court.

The doctors were of the opinion that Akiva's condition at the time was too severe to enable him to testify. He was kept in Rothschild Hospital, suffering from a wound in his left side, damage to the large intestine and spine, and with a foreign body lodged in the spinal canal. Regarding the further event, the police commission concluded that no legal action should be taken against Constable Haimowitz, since "he had shown initiative and alertness even though he had not been on duty" and had played a part in rescuing Sergeant Melekh. The shots fired by the civilian from the fourth floor were likewise found to have been justified. "He who begins shooting at Mohammed will end up shooting at Rahamim," wrote Uri Avnery in his weekly *Ha-olam ha-zeh*. "He who incarcerates and exiles Suleiman without trial will end up incarcerating and exiling Nissim. He who today spits at Fatma will tomorrow spit at Mazal. What happened yesterday in Wadi Nisnas must of necessity happen today in Wadi Salib," wrote Avnery, expressing an opinion held by a minority of one at the time.[4] "Shots fired at a drunkard," Member of Knesset Aryeh Ben-Eliezer of the revisionist Herut Party teased the establishment, "we must admit that life in our society is not full of drunkards, nor full of rioters. If it is indeed necessary to shoot a drunkard on the rampage, I can imagine how many victims there would be every day and every night among nations in which drunkenness is an integral part of social life."[5]

1. *War*

Diachronic Neighbors

I could write a treatise on the transformation of civilization into archaeology.
—Zbigniew Herbert, "The Abandoned"

IN FORGING, AT THE END OF THE 1950S, A LINK BETWEEN WADI Nisnas, the Palestinian neighborhood of Haifa, and Wadi Salib, a former Muslim neighborhood and currently a residential area housing poor Jewish immigrants, Uri Avnery was alluding to the Israeli political milieu in general. Haifa served as a parable for him of the linkage and reciprocal ties between intra-Jewish ethnic tension and the Jewish-Palestinian conflict. When different normative systems exist side by side in a state, he warned, civil rights cannot be guaranteed. Israel, in which a section of its citizens—the Palestinians, to be precise—lives under military rule, operates under a dual administration that is bound to collapse, since under such conditions it is impossible to maintain the lines of demarcation. The norms created in the one context—the Jewish-Palestinian—he asserted, were destined to infiltrate and color the other, Ashkenazi-Mizrahi, context. Several decades were to pass before Avnery's observation was enhanced by others to arrive at a structural analysis of the multidimensional framework of Israeli citizenship, "which stratifies, rather than assimilates, its citizens."[1] Yet, beyond this incisive and discerning observation, which predated the Israeli citizenship discourse, explicit mention of the names of the Jewish slum Wadi Salib and the Arab neighborhood Wadi Nisnas in the same breath revived a suppressed memory. Avnery's words momentarily evoked the "mixed city," an image so shrouded in darkness that, despite Wadi Salib's Arab name, it seemed to have been completely forgotten.

One of the last to document the vanishing of the Arab Wadi Salib and the emergence of the Jewish neighborhood was Binyamin Halfon, head of the Jewish Agency's Department of Jewish Affairs in the Middle East, upon being summoned toward the end of 1948 to visit the living quarters of the North African immigrants in the eastern section of Haifa's downtown.[2] Halfon's visit was made in response to press reports and protest meetings that criticized and condemned the condition of the neighborhood's sanitation and the state of the apartments. Although the war had come to an end, its ravages were still evident in the city. These are Halfon's "impressions and observations of the visit":

> I left Haifa several weeks ago, and the old city was at the time a closed area that resembled a bubbling rubbish dump on which clumps of garbage, carcasses of pet animals, and remnants of unwanted articles were rotting at the mouth of the sewers. . . . It was difficult to imagine that in these streets—between mounds of rubble no one knew when or how would be removed, in houses whose windows and floors had been ripped out, in buildings half of which were designated for demolition and the remainder still standing by some miracle—people would soon be living. But hither, in fact, immigrants were indeed sent, and it is these buildings that they, of their own accord, invade.

Toward the end of 1948, Halfon was amazed to discover that the ruined area he had seen only a few weeks previously was beginning to pulsate with new life. Following the "great commotion," the Haifa municipality began to clear "the piles of rubbish and rot," leaving the ruins of the old city in place. "We now pass through alleys cleared of the piles of garbage, but the stench of mold and putrescence still emanates from adjacent yards," he wrote. "At times we are obliged to pick our way across remnants of rubble or to use paths going through yards and ruined buildings in order to bypass some huge mass towering above us: the remnant of what was once a large house."

Halfon's visit to Haifa took place in the wake of difficulties that had arisen concerning the absorption of North African immigrants in the city. In Haifa, Halfon noted, one finds the largest concentration of those of North African origin in Israel, while on the slopes of Stanton Street and in Haifa's old city they are to be found en masse. It was not the concentration per se but rather the first buds of protest that brought him to the city:

> Well-intentioned and other individuals became involved with the matter, and there were also those who attempted to incite the Moroccans against the authorities with assertions such as "The place and the quality of housing were found unworthy of absorbing immigrants from Europe ("Yiddish speakers" as they termed them) and they therefore assigned them to you," or "After all, *they* think that in any case you are accustomed to such conditions from the *mellah* [ghetto] of Morocco" or "the housing authorities probably think that you don't deserve anything better." "The far-sighted" deduced further: "As they discriminated against you regarding housing, so will you be discriminated against in everything."

When Halfon met the new residents at the end of 1948, it seemed that there was nothing left of the previous inhabitants other than "clumps of garbage, carcasses of pet animals, and remnants of unwanted articles." During the course of the years following, they were entirely forgotten. While only eleven years separated Muslim Wadi Salib from the Wadi Salib riots, the neighborhood's recent Arab past was not mentioned at all in 1959. This pertains to the secondary literature addressing the riots as well. When Uri Avnery mentioned the names of Wadi Salib and Wadi Nisnas in the same breath, he not only exposed the parallel existence of the Jewish slum and the Arab neighborhood but also the erstwhile Arab character of the Jewish neighborhood. In so doing he challenged the tendency to externalize the Jewish-Palestinian conflict and to demarcate it, and indeed the Palestinians themselves, as a separate area rather than as one of the components of Israeli society, which is perceived as solely Jewish.[3] These established lines of demarcation, scrupulously preserved, obstruct not only our understanding of the conflict but primarily one's perception of the place, with its various ethnic and national components.[4] It is impossible to understand the story of Wadi Salib without breaking down the conventional divisions.

Arab Haifa faded in an instant, in the blink of an eye, within just a few days in April, no more. The rapid, fleeting nature of events may perhaps explain the disturbing disparity between Haifa as a Palestinian symbol of the *nakba* (disaster), on the one hand, and its conventional image among Jewish

Israelis as a shining example of Jewish-Arab coexistence, on the other. Years before Arab Haifa's past was consciously erased, its erasure had been effected by events, by the pace at which they occurred, by the unimaginable totality. The reconstruction of memory must, therefore, suspend the historical flow and replay it slowly so as to observe for a moment the previous residents who disappeared so suddenly, but who continue to cast a shadow onto the city that became a Jewish city in an instant.

The fate of the "mixed city" was sealed on several fronts. One of these, albeit secondary but nonetheless fascinating, occurred on the night between April 21–22, 1948, within the four walls of the home of the Haifa banker Farid Sa'ad. Here, against the background of the fierce battles raging outside and in the face of certain Arab defeat, a number of Arab notables had gathered for a prolonged deliberation. They were certainly not the ones to decisively determine the course of events, but the historic drama that played out during those days conferred upon them a minor role, within the thankless mission they had taken upon themselves as members of the "Arab Emergency Committee." The following morning they approached Major-General Stockwell, commander of British forces in Haifa and the north. It is not known whether they initiated discussion with the Jewish side and, if so, for what reason. They were perhaps nudged into taking this step by the realization that the battle for Haifa had been decided and that no Arab reinforcements could redress the situation. Once they understood that they could expect no British military intervention in their favor, they were in need of some other form of assistance. Stockwell passed on the message to Moshe Carmel, commander of the Haganah forces in the Haifa area, who responded by drafting a number of conditions for surrender. Subsequent to these preliminary moves, two delegations, Jewish and Arab, met on the afternoon of the same day. The meeting took place in the Haifa town hall, the mixed municipality located—as it is today—between the Hadar ha-Carmel neighborhood and the downtown.[5] At the time, this was the line of demarcation between the Jewish and Arab neighborhoods. The meeting was held under the auspices of British representatives and with no journalists present, and was meant to discuss the terms of surrender and amendments formulated by Carmel as a condition for a cease-fire in the city.[6]

Woe to the defeated. The Arab delegation made its way to the town hall in British armored vehicles. A large Jewish crowd gathered outside the municipality and began to cheer and clap at the sight of the members of the Arab delegation.[7] The Jewish delegates arrived under their own steam. Haifa had in fact already been conquered during the day by the Haganah. This was of course the primary and decisive front on which the city's fate was sealed. The members of the Arab delegation, most of whom were Christians, included Farid Sa'ad, who, as well as being a banker, was a member of the Arab National Committee in the city; the businessman and honorary Spanish consul in the city Victor Khayyat; the lawyer Elias Kousa; the district court judge Anis Nasser; the businessman Ahmed Abu Ziad, who was also a lawyer and a member of the Arab National Committee; the lawyer George Mo'amer and Sheikh Abed al-Rahman Morad, head of the Muslim Brotherhood in the city. The two sides discussed the terms, some of which were disputed. In their memoirs, the British observers note that the position taken by the Jewish side was conciliatory and generally flexible. The meeting in the town hall lasted approximately an hour and a half, and upon its conclusion the Arab representatives requested a period of twenty-four hours for deliberation. This request was rejected and they were asked to come to a decision within an hour.

This fateful evening in April in effect placed a seal on the drastic changes to the city's population over the preceding four months. When the partition resolution was approved by the General Assembly of the United Nations at the end of November 1947, the number of Jews and Arabs in the city was almost identical. Now, on the occasion of the surrender, after three and a half months of war, the Arab population of the city had been almost halved.[8] This process occurred in waves. Between the partition resolution and February 1948 those who departed Haifa, some twenty thousand people in all, were mainly residents of the neighboring lands—villagers from the periphery, but also wealthy local Christians who traveled over land to the adjacent countries or to inland areas of Palestine. During the months of February and March, they were joined by many of the Muslim residents, some of whom took advantage of a joint Christian-Muslim initiative to evacuate women and children from the city, in this case by sea. There was also an internal migration of population within the city, such as that of the residents of Wadi Rushmia, Wadi Salib, and the Hallisa neighborhood, who fled for fear of Haganah attacks to evacuated sites in the area of the Carmel bus station, which had been abandoned by Christian residents after the Haganah had exploded several buses in the area. The number of Arabs leaving the city continued to swell in April.

There were those who were driven to action by economic factors. Among them were families belonging to the local bourgeoisie, who fled to Lebanon and Syria, alongside simple laborers who lost their livelihoods owing to the war. Many laborers lost their jobs at the British military camps and with various British institutions, which were gradually being dismantled and scaled down. At the same time, the city's residents were experiencing a serious deterioration in their personal security, as acts of reprisal that constantly harmed innocent individuals became a regular occurrence.[9] The massacre of Jewish workers at the refinery following a provocation on the part of the Irgun (National Military Organization in the Land of Israel) and the Haganah's reprisal in villages adjacent to Haifa put an end to a series of efforts at calming the situation on the part of the Arab National Committee, on the one hand, and the situation committee of the Haifa Community Council, on the other.[10] After a temporary calm had nevertheless been achieved, it was broken once more by attacks and counterattacks during January 1948. "Altogether," as we are told by the *History of the Haganah*, "retaliation was regularly employed in Haifa, and following each incident in which a Jew was harmed in the city the Haganah people tried to harm Arabs in the area in which the incident had occurred."[11]

The local Jewish leadership enjoyed clear organizational advantages over the Arabs in the city, even if their control was not absolute, as evinced by the blowing up of the Muslim committee building, which served the separatist forces as a place for public, welfare- and health-related, and charitable activities.[12] Following an additional wave of violence, the situation escalated with the detonation of an Arab car filled with explosives alongside the Solel Boneh building on Ha-namal Street and the explosion of a similarly laden Jewish truck on Ha-bourge Street in response.[13] The erosion of personal safety in the wake of hostilities along the seam line in the city, the scarcity of essential commodities like flour and bread, and the severance from other parts of the country likewise exacerbated the sense of isolation and encouraged the exodus. From the end of 1947 onward, notes the *History of the Haganah*,[14] the Arab population was in effect under siege. The advantage held by the Jewish side in defending the line of positions along the seam was clear, since this defense had been carefully planned over a number of years and was based on lessons drawn from the confrontations during the period of the Arab revolt in 1936–1939.[15] Regarding the drafting of local forces, the advantage likewise lay with the Jewish side: "People who were able to take a leave of absence from their work, especially Technion students who had left their studies, were drafted into units of the field corps. Since this force was confined to the urban sector and its personnel were not far from home, there appeared no particular reason to see to the supply of food, blankets, and clothing or to pay them wages."[16] The attempts made by the Arab National Committee and the Arab Higher Committee to stem the exodus from the city by means of decrees and proclamations proved fruitless, and when the city was finally captured the number of Arabs had declined to half of what it had been at the time of the United Nations resolution. Cooperation between these two bodies in attempting to halt the exodus was particularly problematic owing to the clash of interests between the Arab National Committee, which sought to restore calm and preserve the cease-fire in Haifa, and the mufti, al-Hajj Muhammad Amin al-Husayni, who preferred to inflame the conflict. "There were cases of people leaving before the city's liberation," noted Moshe Carmel, commander of the northern front and the man who directed the conquest of Haifa, thirty years later. "The Jews did not leave. They had nowhere to go. Where could they have gone?"[17] A mass exodus from the Jewish area of Haifa did not, indeed, take place. Carmel's assertion, like the firm statement that "the mass of Jews had nowhere to flee,"[18] obviously goes beyond an objective historical description and is rooted in the Israeli discourse of legitimacy. It offers an unequivocal yet disputable version of the event. There were a few isolated cases of "desertion." Thus, for example, several young men "liable for the draft" who sought to escape the danger were discovered on the ship *Russia,* which called on Haifa from time to time. They had been harried by the recruitment office, some had sought assistance from the British authorities, and a few of them had succeeded in slipping away in the hold of the ship.[19] This exception, however, serves to indicate the rule. Most of Haifa's Jewish residents did indeed remain in the city, while Jewish institutions made a great effort to dissuade people from abandoning high-risk neighborhoods both by affording protection and by exerting moral pressure. The Haganah, for example, set up public committees for the prevention of desertion after noticing that Jewish shopkeepers and owners of businesses in the downtown tended to close their businesses on days of high tension and flee to Hadar ha-Carmel.[20] Alongside fortification of the seam neighborhoods, the Haganah exerted normative pressure on the city's residents. "In order to demonstrate good citizenship and thereby encourage others," relates Zadok Eshel in the

Haganah account, "the lawyer Ya'akov Salomon made a point of descending every day from his residence in Hadar to his office in the city. His assistants and clerks accompanied him. Many Haganah loyalists did likewise."[21]

Starting off with a distinct disadvantage, the Arab side made desperate efforts to dissuade people from leaving in face of the ever increasing incentives in the first months of 1948: in Wadi Salib the Haganah took up position in an abandoned Arab house from which fire had been directed at Hadar, fortified the building, and began sniping at Wadi Salib itself. Sporadic exchange of fire between the "foreign" Arab forces—the fighters of the Arab Liberation Army and the mufti's volunteers—and the Haganah, for example, during the month of February in Wadi Salib, along with the seizure of Arab buildings in these neighborhoods, certainly persuaded many waverers to leave the city.[22] The tension between the local Palestinian and national Arab leaderships was augmented by the schism between the Muslim committee members, who took orders from the Arab Higher Committee, and the Christian leadership—a minority among the committee members—which adopted an independent policy on these issues. Further tensions surfaced between the position taken by the Arab Higher Committee and that of the mufti. Once the Arab National Committee began to encourage and urge women and children to depart, it found it difficult to stem the departure of others. While the committee did finally succeed in exerting its authority on most of its members, it found difficulty in doing so, for example, with regard to the Arab members on the city council.

Arab Haifa collapsed prematurely, at least according to the Haganah's general plan, which assumed that Haifa's turn would come only at the end. Acting upon the informed assessment that the British would remain in the city until the summer of 1948, the Haganah preferred not to risk possible friction with these forces and to wait. And, indeed, the British did plan to evacuate the "Haifa enclave"—the territory extending between Atlit in the south and Kurdani in the north—with only a few exceptions. The evacuation of the Stella Maris neighborhood in Haifa, for instance, was postponed to the end of July 1948 so that it could serve the British soldiers at the time of their retreat. The British, in any case, had hoped to continue their supervision of Haifa port following the ending of the Mandate, when it was due to become a free port. Likewise apprehensive about the future of the refinery, they had an overriding interest in preserving their control over key positions in the city, such as the command headquarters adjoining the central railway station on Plumer Square, and at weak points along the seam line. In mid April, however, the situation changed, and along with it British deployment. Persistent attempts by Arab irregular forces to take control of Hadar ha-Carmel from the direction of Wadi Nisnas and Wadi Salib placed Haifa high on the Haganah's agenda. In parallel, as they observed the turmoil, the damage to property and loss of lives, the British likewise began to modify their assessment of the situation. Stockwell's appraisal led him to conclude that in the given situation he would have to make do with defending "only the Haifa enclave." He assumed that he would be unable to take action beyond it to separate the warring parties and thus would be unable to protect vulnerable sections of the population. In light of these new circumstances, he chose to give top priority to ensuring the orderly and secure evacuation of his forces.

These developments in Haifa did not, of course, occur within a vacuum. On April 14 Kaukji's army was defeated at Mishmar ha-emek. On April 16 the British departed from Safed, leaving behind the Jewish minority in the city, and on April 18 they vacated Tiberias, which was immediately captured by the Haganah. These developments sent a signal to both sides involved that the British were bent on evacuation rather than on maintaining order and that their intention of departing from Palestine was final. Realizing that under such circumstances it was able to operate quite openly without fear of British intervention, the Haganah initiated attacks throughout the country, including the eastern and western Upper Galilee. Without British cover, it was clear that the Arab side was unable to hold its own against the Haganah. The defeat of Kaukji's Army of Salvation at Mishmar ha-emek proved that the external Arab auxiliary forces were likewise unable to tilt the balance and that the end of resistance was in sight. Against this backdrop, Lieutenant General Gordon Macmillan, general in command of the Palestine forces, endorsed the decision to redeploy on April 19. This was put into effect the next day, and included a British withdrawal from outlying areas and a concentrated effort at securing the lines of transportation designated for evacuation. As part of this hasty redeployment, the British were quick to update the Haganah, thereby enhancing its advantage over the Arab side. In any case, since the partition plan stipulated that Haifa be included within the area of the Jewish state, in this respect the future of the city had been decided in advance.

In fact, as early as mid-February and again in mid-April several meetings were held between Stockwell and Harry Beilin, the representative of the political department of the Jewish Agency in the city, and Abba Khoushy, secretary of the Haifa Labor Council, at which Khoushy's demand that control of the city be transferred to him following the evacuation of the British forces was discussed. The decision pertaining to redeployment of the forces in the city, to which Stockwell acquiesced, was made after taking note of the Jewish side's statement of intent and on the strength of the assessment that this party was the more likely to cooperate with the British in maintaining calm, which was essential for their orderly evacuation. The redeployment came as a surprise to Field Marshal Bernard Montgomery, British imperial chief of staff, to the British cabinet, and particularly to Foreign Minister Ernest Bevin. They were apprehensive that this hasty step could endanger overall strategic British interests in the Middle East.[23]

The struggle for control of the areas being evacuated between Jews and Arabs began immediately upon the withdrawal of the British forces. While one may cast doubt on the description of the Arabs of Haifa by Walid Khalidi, the official historian of the Palestinian national movement in the 1950s and 1960s, as "the least warlike urban population in the eastern Mediterranean,"[24] the Jewish side clearly had the upper hand. The possession of prior information was augmented by other tactical advantages: the location of the Jewish neighborhoods on a hill overlooking the Arab neighborhoods as well as better concentration and coordination of the Jewish fighting force. In addition, the Haifa Jews enjoyed the advantages of a community with a developed political organizational culture, which was part of an autonomous framework comprising a central administration that exerted its authority from its center in Tel Aviv over the periphery in many spheres, among them the prosecution of the war.

At noon on April 21 the Haganah began its operation to take control of Haifa, preceded by preliminary fire that continued sporadically into the next day. The Bi'ur Hamets ("removal of leaven") operation, as it was called in the Haganah's jargon, was planned as a pincer movement, by which the Haganah intended to alarm and destabilize the Arab side without necessarily capturing Arab neighborhoods. While returning the fire of Arab positions in various vulnerable points of the city, the Haganah intended to breach major axes toward the lower part of town and the port, capture Wadi Rushmia, and secure access to the city from the north. It was the battles around Rushmia bridge and Wadi Hallisa, accompanied by the Haganah's public address system calling upon the residents to refrain from aiding the foreign forces, that led, on the night between April 21–22, to a panic-stricken flight on the part of the Arab residents toward downtown Haifa and Wadi Salib. As it passed through the neighborhoods, the fleeing crowd infected local residents with its panic and they joined in the escape. At the same time, other Haganah units took further vital points downtown opposite the railway station, in Wadi Nisnas and in the Arab market. From time to time the fighting was supplemented by salvos directed downtown—"bombardment intended to soften up Arab Haifa," as the Jewish sources termed it.[25] It is doubtful whether their objective was purely military—in itself a complex issue in the context of hostilities in an urban area—and in any case the war was waged in the midst of a civilian population and between one population and another. The panic was fanned by a public address system and radio broadcasts in Arabic exhorting the residents to denounce the foreign fighting forces but, at the same time, transfer the women, children, and elderly to a safe haven. This demoralization had the intended effect.

"It Was Better Without Arabs, It Was Easier"

And my uncle added: "What will happen now?"

The British man began searching for appropriate words that could impart to this peasant, armed with a rifle, the extent of his disaster. He had lost his homeland and he must emigrate. The thought of the United Nations resolution began to run through the British man's head, the resolution on the establishment of the State of Israel, about which my uncle had not heard and of whose existence he was completely unaware.

The Englishman mumbled something to himself, trying to express the essence of the situation and to simplify it at the same moment: "This problem is beyond you . . . a problem between nations, after all they have already concluded everything between themselves, and you have no option but to emigrate."[26]

That same day thousands of Arab residents began pouring into Haifa port, crowding against the entrances, seeking any kind of boat to carry them to the port of Acre or the shores of Lebanon. The tension was fed by rumors of British willingness to assist in sea passage to Acre. In the tumultuous flight, some of the escapees lost members of their families. On several occasions, women, children, and the elderly were trampled in the midst of the terrible panic. Britain did indeed agree to place boats at the disposal of the fleeing crowd, while others chose to take land transportation, passing through the barriers that the Haganah had erected at the entrances to the city on their way to Nazareth, Jenin, and Nablus. Some fifteen thousand Arab residents fled the city over the two days of battle.[27] It was against this dramatic unfolding of events, in the presence of the Jewish representatives—Shabtai Levy, the Jewish mayor; Ya'akov Salomon, lawyer and the Haganah's liaison officer vis-à-vis the British; Mordechai Makleff, deputy commander of the Carmeli brigade; and several officers—and under the aegis of the British commanders, that the members of the Arab Emergency Committee were compelled to accept the terms of surrender.

All that day, and in the hours preceding the meeting, the committee members had tried to establish contact with the external Arab leadership through the Syrian consul in Haifa, Thabet al-Aris, seeking clear-cut instructions as to their response to the proposal laid before them. They approached Syrian president Shukri al-Quwwatli, members of the Arab League responsible for Palestine affairs, and, apparently in the end, also the mufti through Beirut, but received no response. Some thirty local residents, among the most prosperous in the city, reconvened in despondent mood at Khayyat's home in an attempt to formulate a policy with regard to the new situation that had arisen. It was they who decided to dispatch the seven-man delegation to the town hall in the hope of ameliorating the conditions set by the Haganah. In his account, Walid Khalidi notes that Stockwell warned the Arab delegates that, should they fail to sign the document, he would not be held accountable for the possible deaths of three hundred to four hundred more Arabs on the morrow. Khalidi goes on to relate that Khayyat replied: "What are you trying to do? We know Shabtai Levy, Ya'akov Salomon and all these people. We are old friends."[28] Stockwell took this as an invitation to leave the room and to leave the two sides to themselves. When they failed to reach agreement, the Arab delegates were given a short extension of one hour.

The Arab delegation returned to Khayyat's home, where the other committee members had been waiting all this time. In all probability this was the moment at which those present agreed upon a position, stating that they had no right to sign the terms of surrender. It is interesting to note that precisely on this point the interpretations of historians as divergent in their outlooks as the Palestinian Walid Khalidi, son of Jerusalem, and the Jewish Ephraim Karsh, born in Haifa and generally identified with the right, are quite similar. Khalidi asserts that acceptance of the terms drafted by the Haganah would have relieved the English of their responsibility for the city's Arab residents. Were the local Palestinian representatives to have done so, they would in fact have put their fate in the hands of the Zionists. Karsh, on the other hand, maintains that since Haifa had been included in the territory of the future Jewish state according to the partition plan, acceptance of the terms in this city would in principle have denoted tacit acceptance of the principles of the partition plan, namely, acquiescence to Jewish sovereignty.[29] While they were now required to respond within the framework of local circumstances, it was clear to the delegates that the implications of the matter at hand extended far beyond the city boundaries.

Left to their own resources, and after the Muslim delegates had been instructed to reject the terms of surrender, the Christian delegates returned to the town hall alone. They announced that, since the Arab armed forces in the city were beyond their control, they would be unable to observe the contractual terms, even if they were to sign the document. Given these circumstances, they announced, the Arab population—men, women, and children—would be asked to evacuate the city. The Jewish and British officers were thunderstruck. Some of them, according to Jewish and British sources, attempted to dissuade the delegation from making this terrible mistake, but the decision was final. If we are to believe Ya'akov Salomon's testimony, the Arab delegates asked him to take them home in his car rather than returning in British armored vehicles as they had come.[30] In light of this retrospective account of Salomon's, these appear to have been the last remnants of civil society in the mixed city.

The British concept of a "mixed city," this conventional and congenial anachronism, blurs and conceals the clear boundaries that pertained in mandatory Haifa. It was not a mixed society but a "dual society" that existed in the city. The meeting ground, as Yosef Vashitz notes in his study,[31] was primarily of an economic nature. Political order was imposed by the British Empire, the political institutions were in perpetual conflict, while absolute separation was maintained in the areas of education and welfare. Vashitz, a member of Mapam (United Workers Party) and of the Committee for Arab Affairs established immediately upon the cessation of hostilities in the city, analyzes the disparity between the various layers by means of a conceptual division between the state apparatus, the political system, and civil society. True enough, in the absence of a sovereign state these categories have only partial validity, and it is even more difficult to use these distinctions in their classical meaning against the backdrop of the lack of separation between religion and state in the area. Vashitz, however, chooses to employ them as "ideal types," namely, as social phenomena that never appear in their pure form but are treated as though they thus exist in the interests of conceptual clarity and methodical analysis.[32]

The vigor of Jewish civil society and its close and beneficial association with the Jewish political leadership underlines the relative weakness of Arab civil society, which was overshadowed by the Arab political leadership. The slow pace of modernization processes in local Arab society did little to encourage institution building, which played a decisive role in nation building within Jewish society. Internal processes of integration were likewise all but nonexistent. Patterns of marriage and social organization indicate a remoteness, not to say separation, between veterans and immigrants and between the urban and rural populations.[33] Local Arab political society was indeed more developed than its civil counterpart. The city's cosmopolitan character exposed its Arab residents to other residents and to Arabs from other areas and of different religious affiliations and paradoxically stimulated Arab national awareness.[34] But this political society showed only scant interest in ongoing economic and social problems and, up until the forties, ignored both the poor and the laborers as well as the dualist reality of Jewish-Arab cooperation.[35]

The "dualist reality" described by Vashitz was entirely confined within the boundaries of civil society. It went far further than mere mutual cooperation and was in fact generally characterized by conflict and competition.[36] The fact that the residents belonged on the one hand to an antagonistic political society and on the other to a dualist civil society at times led to "peculiar phenomena," such as the participation of an Arab politician in the struggle against the sale of land while selling it himself simultaneously. Vashitz puts it thus:

> Haifa was characterized by a far-reaching separation between individual-economic activity on the part of the members of Arab society and their political activity. . . . As an individual, he assisted Jews to disembark from the ship, to find an apartment and a supply of food, he built houses for them, sold them land, and benefited from this. As part of Arab political society, he opposed Zionism and every now and again was seized by an

existential fear that the Jews were liable to take over the country and expel him from it. But the existential fear did not prevent the individual from cooperating with the Jews in various ways.[37]

Similar phenomena were evident on the Jewish side. Thus, for example, in the lives of the Jewish laborers in mixed workplaces: "During the day they worked shoulder to shoulder with Arab laborers and when they returned home put on their khaki clothes, grabbed a blanket, and went off to the base to which they had been summoned in order to do guard duty in outlying areas and secure the safety of the city's residents. At dawn they returned to their homes, put on their working clothes, and made their way to the bus station, and were transported in the buses to their places of work."[38] Apparent contradictions were to be found also among the Jews: a Histadrut (General Federation of Jewish Laborers in the Land of Israel) campaign for "Jewish labor" was waged in parallel to cooperation with an Arab capitalist in founding a shared economic enterprise.[39]

A perspective that concentrates on the economic sphere may lead to an interpretation slightly different to that of Vashitz and expose the inner logic of what appears at first sight to be a contradiction. The economy in general and the labor market in particular did not bring Jews and Arabs closer together, even though they created and strengthened mutual contact between them. Economic development was inevitably linked to the national struggle and, owing to its total mobilization, was subject to constant tensions and contests. The extent of this complexity is demonstrated by Deborah Bernstein with regard to the sale of land to the Zionist movement's institutions.[40] While the Palestinian economic elite was vilified and harassed on this account, these sales actually channeled capital to the Arab economic sector in the city and hastened its development. Given these circumstances it is hardly surprising that the local Arab economic elite identified with the Palestinian national struggle while refusing to bow to national dictates calling for an economic boycott of the Jews. Among the Jews, one may likewise discern differences in outlook shaped by social class. While the urban Jewish bourgeoisie did not oppose the idea of "Jewish labor" in general, it refused to cooperate in its sweeping application as demanded by the Histadrut,[41] which would have meant ignoring every economic consideration.

In any event, and notwithstanding the internal contradictions in both camps, power relations between the two communities were not symmetrical. Despite living under the same regime, the Jews were subject to the Mandate, while the Palestinians were subject to a "quasi colonial" regime.[42] As the historian May Seikaly writes:

> Both the town and its community were drastically transformed during the period under study. Haifa changed from a small roadstead with a promising commercial center into a congested modern harbour city with major industrial projects and sophisticated trading activities. This transformation reflected many features of the development of European industrial and commercial cities. In Haifa, however, the process was not the result of a natural development of the economic structure of the country or the social consciousness of the people; it was a transplanted phenomenon, in which the financial and human components were alien to the inhabitants.[43]

The element of foreignness is employed by Seikaly to question the legitimacy of the historical course that was, in the end, destined to determine the future of Haifa by overpowering its Arab community. Vashitz, whose historical account bears many similarities to that of Seikaly, does not share the position she represents in the discourse of legitimacy. He too is aware of the Mandate's discriminatory practices and points to the advantage enjoyed by the Jewish side in merging the process of building the various aspects of a civil society—economic, cultural, and social—with the political process of "nation building." Furthermore, the idea of separating the economic sectors was essentially Jewish rather than Arab and stemmed from the aspiration of establishing an independent Jewish society.[44] The Arab side may, argues Vashitz, have been able to contend with the Jew as an individual, but the latter was supported by a social system. Whatever his socioeconomic affiliation, the Jew enjoyed advantages denied to his Palestinian neighbor. "If the Jewish businessman had an advantage over his Arab counterpart in his ability to operate in conditions of a capitalist economy, the Jewish labor force on the other hand enjoyed the advantage of being organized according to socialist principles of collective enterprise and mutual assistance."[45] Above all, when the Jews came "to build and be built," they enjoyed the advantage of a national ideology that acted as a mobilizing force over those whose ideological weapon consisted merely of a belief in the undeniable right to and ownership of the country and the fear of its loss.[46] The constant tension between cooperation and conflict of interest reached its tragic end during those dramatic hours of April 1948.

Let us return to the members of the Arab Emergency Committee. We can only surmise as to why they rejected the terms of surrender. Perhaps they feared that acceptance on their part would render them liable to the accusation of treason. One may well imagine the terrible distress experienced by the committee members. Stunned by the military rout and left to their own devices by their political leadership, as the representatives of a population fleeing for its life they were required to come to a decision without having been authorized to do so. Under these circumstances refusal was perhaps paradoxically simpler than acquiescence. It is clear that their decision was made independently and only retroactively gained the support of the Arab Higher Committee. In the ensuing weeks, and up to the invasion of the Arab armies on May 15, the Arab Emergency Committee dealt with the coordination of the mass exodus of the city's Arab residents and organized the convoys, assisted during the first few days by the British army, which provided trucks and escorted the convoys. Of the thirty-seven thousand Arabs estimated by the British to have been in the city after its capture only six thousand remained by mid-May.

There are no essential differences between the Israeli and Palestinian historiography regarding those decisive days of the fall of Arab Haifa. True, Palestinian historiography, unlike the Israeli, emphasizes the importance attributed by the Jewish side to urgent, not to say hasty, clear-cut military gains, for fear that the U.S., Britain, and, in their wake, the United Nations would renege on the partition resolution. While there is no argument between Palestinian and Israeli historians over Haifa's supreme strategic importance to the Jewish state, some Israeli historians emphasize the effect of the unrest in the city in hastening the military operation. Walid Khalidi, on the other hand, attributes greater importance to the wider strategic consideration that viewed Haifa as the point of connection between the north-south and the eastern axes. And while Israeli historiography points to social tensions between the foreign Arab fighters who arrived in the city with the various forces and the local Arab population, Palestinian historiography tends to underline Arab unity and blur the tensions; Israeli historiography furthermore frequently emphasizes the flight of both the political and the military local leadership on the eve of the military confrontation, whereas Palestinian historiography minimizes the dimensions of this phenomenon.

While there is general agreement on the totality of factors that led to the Arab defeat in the city, differences of opinion may be discerned as to the relative weight attributed to each factor. A conspicuous example of this is provided by the absence of authority and civil institutions on the Palestinian side, noted by Israeli historians and also by Khalidi, who, however, attributes only secondary importance to this issue. Palestinian historiography dwells upon the fact that the Arab Emergency Committee submitted to Stockwell on the morning of April 22, 1948, a document of principles drafted at their nocturnal meeting the previous evening. This document contained clear demands of the mandatory government to exercise its responsibility toward the Arabs of Haifa, to halt the Jewish offensive, and to protect their interests. Stockwell refused to accept the document and went as far as proclaiming in writing, in their presence, his refusal to intervene actively in the struggle. Israeli historiography plays down the importance of this event, viewing it as a type of backing required by the Arab delegation to place them beyond any suspicion of treason. Historians agree that Stockwell provided the Arab delegation with a document of principles drafted by the Haganah. Many differences have narrowed over the years. There is, for example, an indication of general agreement that the British handed clear advantages to the Jewish side in the struggle for Haifa and, on the other hand, that the Arabs of Haifa did not abandon the city because they had been called upon to do so by external Arab and Palestinian elements in preparation for the great campaign. Even as to the question of responsibility for the escalation of hostilities in the city in March, Israeli historiography has desisted from the tendency to blame the Arab side and now lends some credence to the Arab account, which from the outset pointed out that the Haganah had played an active role in this matter.

The mass Arab exodus threw the local Jewish leadership into considerable confusion. Thus wrote Ya'akov Lublini, the commander of Haifa city: "[Haifa] is standing the test of the entire people of Israel. This is the first time that the people of Israel have captured territory in which it is required be the master of the fate of another people which is in the minority. In this matter the eyes of the entire world are upon us. We feel discomfort with all the Arabs of Haifa leaving . . . but we must help those who wish to remain to acclimatize among us."[47] Already at the town hall, on the occasion of the surrender, Shabtai Levy delivered an emotional address in which he asked the Arab Emergency Committee to remain and was joined in this by other

Jewish delegates. Over the following days, Ya'akov Salomon and the lawyer George Mo'amer went from house to house calling upon the residents of Abbas Street aged over forty to return home, in an attempt to counter the position of the Arab National Committee. Salomon also roamed the streets of Wadi Nisnas, probably in the company of Ya'akov Lishansky, a prominent member of Haifa's Jewish society, who recalls the embarrassment of the moment. "What will they say in the wide world," he wondered, "No doubt they will say—that's what the Jews are like, Arabs cannot live under their rule."[48] The Haifa Jewish Community Council was quick to appeal to the residents of Haifa to return.[49] In an initiative of its own, the Histadrut called upon its members among the Palestinian workers to return to the city. The British observers including Sir Alan Cunningham, the last British high commissioner, and the American vice-consul Aubrey Lippincott conjectured that the appeal to the Arabs to return stemmed from economic considerations, in other words, from concern on the part of the Jews for the city's economy once the Arab workers had abandoned the city. Maintenance of the factories and the basic branches of the economy by means of a Jewish workforce, observers claimed, incurred greater expense than employing cheap Arab labor. Lippincott further believed that the Jews sought the Arabs' return in order to preserve an appearance of democracy.[50] The position of observer adopted by the British in the circumstances that evolved is surprising, particularly in view of the central role they had played in the collapse of Arab society in Haifa. After all, it was they who transferred control of the city to the Haganah and assisted in the evacuation of the Arab population during the course of the hostilities. It transpired that the remaining two protagonists, the Haganah as leading actor and the Arabs in a supporting role, played their parts too well. The British had certainly not intended to empty Haifa of its Arab inhabitants. "It is a dreadful thing to see the dead city . . . ," thus did Golda Me'ir, head of the political department of the Jewish Agency, summarize the impressions from her visit to the city of Haifa only a few days after the fall of the Arab town.[51] "Next to the port I found children, women, the old, waiting for a way to leave. I entered the houses, there were houses where the coffee and pita bread were left on the table, and I could not but [reflect] that this, indeed, had been the picture in many Jewish towns." Lublini describes how he accompanied Me'ir on her visit to the city. She did not wish to see the ruins and the desolation, but only the area in which Arabs still remained. Lublini took her to Mukhalis Street in Wadi Nisnas. This is his description: "We went up the stairs; the apartments on the first two floors were abandoned. As we ascended to the third floor, an old Arab woman approached us, carrying bundles in her arms. When the Arab woman saw Golda, she stopped in front of her and broke into tears. Golda stopped, looked at her, and tears ran down her face. The two women stood there and wept."[52] This was an initial shock. Over the ensuing weeks, even before the British had left the country, the Jewish leadership retracted its appeal to the Arabs to return. A Jewish observer is quoted by Benny Morris as saying, one month after the event, "a different wind [began to] blow. It was good without Arabs, it was easier. Everything changed within a week."[53]

Local initiatives on the part of representatives of the remaining Palestinian population to promote the return of the others were firmly rejected through diplomatic obfuscation. Such, for example, was the fate of the attempt by the Greek Catholic archbishop of Haifa, George Hakim, to encourage a move toward the return of Christian refugees to Haifa upon his return from a visit to refugees in Lebanon.[54] During the course of May, agreement on this matter began to crystallize between Ben-Gurion and the commander of the city of Haifa and the members of the situation committee. The general Jewish confusion in the face of the Arab exodus slowly began to dissipate. From the military perspective of the Haganah, there were clear benefits to be gained from a general exodus. The small number of remaining Arabs enabled the Haganah to reduce the military force required to maintain calm in the city and to evacuate them should the need arise to defend the city from attack from the outside. Lublini moved faster than Golda: "I looked at the weeping Golda and was angry at her. While I dared not torment her, I thought to myself: 'We are elated and happy that we have prevailed. We have eradicated the Arabs and can now walk about the city without fear of being fired upon or attacked, and here she stands crying.'"[55] The disparity between the local and mainly civilian embarrassment and the military point of view is noted by Morris:

> The local Jewish civilian leadership initially sincerely wanted the Arabs to
> stay (and made a point of letting the British see this). But the offensive of
> 21–22 April had delivered the Arab neighborhoods into Haganah hands,
> relegating the civil leaders to the sidelines and for almost a fortnight rendering them relatively ineffectual in all that concerned the treatment of

the Arab population. At the same time, the attitude of some of these local leaders radically changed as they took stock of the historic opportunity afforded by the exodus—to turn Haifa permanently into a Jewish city.[56]

"True, They Once Used to Live Apart"

"Welcome to the Medinah ["state" in Hebrew] of Israel," said the truck driver. This made me think they had changed the name of my beloved city, Haifa, to the Medinah ["city" in Arabic] of Israel and I felt depressed.[57]

The synchronic existence of Jewish Wadi Salib alongside Arab Wadi Nisnas conceals another elusive and diachronic dimension. Haifa's Arab inhabitants—the residents of Wadi Nisnas, for our purposes—and its Jewish inhabitants in Wadi Salib are not mere neighbors in the conventional sense. The dictionary tells us that a neighbor is someone who lives in the same or an adjacent building. The residents of Wadi Salib lived not only alongside the Arab neighbor but also in his place. They lived in the neighbor's home. This state of affairs in itself is quite ordinary: it is in the nature of real estate to pass from one owner to another. However, unlike change of ownership in regular market conditions, the residents of Wadi Salib were not the product of market forces but of historical dramas. The force of history rather than that of the market had landed them in the apartments of the Arabs. The last residents of Wadi Salib, those etched in Israeli memory in the wake of the riots in 1959, did not live in apartments that they had purchased; they lived in "abandoned property." The diachronic dimension is thus not merely a preface and is mentioned not in order to trace the obligatory chronological order of events, certainly not for the sake of political correctness. The unobservable traces of the previous occupants, their very absence, remained imprinted there. The legal term *absentees' property* perpetuated them and preserved their presence. The property of the previous tenants remained "abandoned" even after it was occupied by new residents.

Wadi Salib was never meant to accommodate Jews. According to political and military planning it was the Arabs left in the city who should have lived there.[58] Already in early May 1948, on the occasion of Ben-Gurion's visit to Haifa, the intention was announced of concentrating the city's Christian inhabitants in Wadi Nisnas and its Muslim inhabitants in Wadi Salib, in accordance with the character of these neighborhoods before the outbreak of war.[59] At the end of May, the Committee for Arab Affairs, appointed on cessation of the hostilities to deal with the Arabs who had remained in Haifa and their property, designated the neighborhoods of Wadi Nisnas and Wadi Salib as areas in which Haifa's Arabs would be permitted to operate schools.[60] Mindful of the interests of the Arab population, the authorities appointed key local figures who maintained special ties with the city's Arabs and who were familiar with the matter at hand to serve on the committee.[61] It generally functioned as an advisory body and at times as an executive arm under the Haganah's command. During the course of the war, its working assumption was that a part of Haifa's residents would return once hostilities had abated. This was a reasonable assumption at the time, when Israel had yet to establish an official policy opposing the return of the refugees, as it would one month later.

As long as it remained impossible to estimate the future number of Arab inhabitants, there was no point in finally determining the boundaries of their living quarters in Wadi Nisnas and Wadi Salib.[62] No mention whatsoever is made of the Wadi Salib neighborhood in the census of the Arab population conducted in the city at the beginning of June 1948.[63] The census results indicate a concentration of Haifa's Arabs in the western neighborhoods, that is, mainly in the German colony, in Stella Maris, in the Abbas neighborhood, and on Jaffa Street. Muslims, who had not lived there in the past, were now to be found also in the west of the city. The tendency of Haifa's Arabs to congregate in the western neighborhoods stemmed from the assumption that the British did not intend to withdraw from them.[64] At a meeting between representatives of the city's Arabs—Victor Khayyat, Shihadeh Salah, and Tawfiq Tubi—and the commander of the city, Rehav'am Amir, in early July 1948, Wadi Salib was again mentioned as a location in which the remaining Arab population could be concentrated.[65] The number of Muslims in the city was estimated at this meeting at 174 families. At a meeting of the Committee for Arab Affairs held on the same day the name of Wadi Salib was also raised as a possible place of residence for Haifa's Arabs, "if takers are to be found for it."[66] Against the backdrop of uncertainty as to the steps to be taken by Israel, different interpretations regarding the resettlement of the city's Arabs surfaced at the time: the British Consul General Cyril Marriott presumed that the decision to concentrate the city's Arabs in Wadi Salib and in Wadi Nisnas indicated an intention to turn them into human shields in the eventuality of Arab aerial bombardment once the truce had ended.[67] Continuing his efforts, the consul tried to mobilize the British vessel *Ocean Vigour* to evacuate some one thousand of Haifa's Arabs who, he believed, would, under these conditions, attempt to escape the city. Less than a year previously, incidentally, this same vessel served the British government to return some fifteen hundred of the *Exodus* refugees to the port of Hamburg.[68] In any event, Marriott's plan was shelved after the British Ministry of Transport informed him that the ship was currently carrying "illegal Jewish migrants" to the shores of Israel.[69]

The intention of maintaining two Arab neighborhoods in Haifa did not in the end materialize and all the city's Arabs were in fact concentrated in the area of Wadi Nisnas and a few additional streets. The reasons for this are shrouded in obscurity. It would seem that the small number of Muslims left in the city did not justify allocating them a separate area.[70] The location of Wadi Salib at the city's eastern gateway certainly played a part in the authorities' reluctance to settle it with Arabs. It was perceived as a threat so long as hostilities continued, and this led to cancellation of the original plan.[71] "It transpires that there are not many Muslims and that those who have remained are prepared to move to Wadi Nisnas," wrote the Committee for Arab Affairs.[72] "True, they once used to live apart," concluded the committee members, "but we had no interest in forcing them to remain apart and in so far as they themselves wished to live together, we assisted them."[73]

The committee had intended to follow the guideline of granting "the full rights of Haifa citizens" to the Arab residents remaining in the city.[74] But the circumstances that developed over the initial weeks of its operation indicated the limitations of civil equality and the evolution of a "differential citizenship."[75] Owing to the state of war, the military command could simply override the decisions of civil bodies.[76] Furthermore, the committee's operation was beset by an internal contradiction between its efforts to promote the rapid restoration of public order, ostensibly in the general public interest—"restoring regular day-to-day life," in the committee's jargon—and the fact that it devoted a considerable part of its activity to furthering the Jewish cause at the expense of the remaining Arab inhabitants. Activity in the sphere of housing, as we shall soon see, clearly exposed the blatant conflict of interest between the two sections of the population.

Various tactics were employed to render the fruits of war irreversible: evicting and settling, dismantling and assembling, destroying and constructing. These included population of the abandoned Arab neighborhoods with immigrants, as in Wadi Salib, the concentration of the remnants of Haifa's Arabs in Wadi Nisnas, and the destruction of Haifa's old town.[77] In most cases the destruction of Palestinian houses and villages was not directly linked to the hostilities. Already during the initial months of fighting in early 1948, and certainly following the battle for the Kastel in April, the Haganah tended to destroy houses for the sake of deterrence and psychological warfare. "The Jews don't know how to fight—therefore [instead] they destroy houses," was the interpretation conveyed to the Israeli leadership by circles close to the mufti.[78] A general consensus as to the opportunity of turning the "miracle" of the Arabs' flight into a permanent gain by means of the destruction of Arab villages began to evolve among part of the leadership, and in particular among those who, during April, the month in which Haifa fell, appointed themselves to the "transfer committee," namely, Yosef Weitz, Ezra Danin, and Eliyahu Sasson.[79] The destruction of Arab villages continued over the following months, with the tacit agreement of the political leadership, and particularly that of Ben-Gurion, but without its official approval.[80] This activity culminated during the months of autumn. It was difficult to justify destruction of such magnitude by military considerations during a period of truce. At a certain stage a new and unexpected need arose for buildings in which to house the new immigrants who had begun to pour into Israel in ever increasing numbers. At the same time, the destruction of Arab property continued in the mixed cities: Tiberias, Jaffa, and Haifa. Destruction of the Arabs' property somewhat paradoxically served as an argument against their return. "Those who return will see the destruction of their property, and this is liable to affect them in many detrimental ways," noted Uriel Friedland, a member of the city's situation committee.[81] A similar view crystallized at the national political echelon.

The destruction of Haifa's old town, located between Wadi Nisnas and Wadi Salib, was in line with this general activity. Built toward the end of the Ottoman period and connecting the western and eastern parts of the city, the old town served as an Arab residential quarter on the eve of the war.[82] With a view to adapting it to the conditions of a modern city, contingency plans for the renewal of the neglected quarter had been prepared already in the period of mandatory rule. The planning subcommittee of Hadar ha-Carmel council, operating during the first half of the 1940s, likewise considered alternative housing for the residents of the Arab old town within the framework of plans for the expansion of Hadar.[83] Israel's actions during 1948, however, were not a direct continuation of these plans. In the shadow of the events of war, the Israeli army carried out an extensive program of demolition, explained in part by the shaky state of the property, but with the intention, as in other places, of preventing the return of the Arab residents. The demolition activity in Haifa was termed the Shikmona Operation and was authorized by Ben-Gurion, in all probability without specifying its projected scope.[84] Its implementation began in the third week of July 1948, immediately following the beginning of the second period of truce, and continued over a period of several weeks.[85] The truce enabled use of the army in carrying out the demolition, thereby hastening its course.[86] Protests against the extent of the demolition reached the government's attention via the minister for minorities, Bekhor Shitrit, only after considerable parts of the city had already been destroyed.[87] As a Mizrahi Jew born in the mixed city of Tiberias in 1895 and a fluent speaker of Arabic who spoke Hebrew with an Arabic accent, Shitrit's attitude toward the Palestinian minority in the new state was exceptional. However, his relatively weak position in the government enabled Ben-Gurion to ignore his remonstrations.[88] During the course of the demolition, misunderstandings surfaced between the municipality and the state and army bodies regarding financial responsibility and the issue of compensation for the original home owners.[89] So long as the matter of compensation had not been clarified, Mayor Shabtai Levy expressed stern opposition to the operation, but once the minister of the interior, Yitshak Greenboim, assured him that the demolition was being carried out as part of a military action and that there would consequently be no need to compensate affected residents, as is the case regarding demolition for purposes of urban development, Levy changed his position and began to regard the operation as a groundbreaking and decisive step for Haifa's future development.[90] There remained only the small issue of the mountains of rubble. Within a matter of a few weeks, the erstwhile old town was turned into three hundred thousand square meters of rubble and building debris. Responsibility for its removal remained a bone of contention between the various agencies.[91]

The forced transfer of population within the city, together with the destruction, did much to disrupt the communal-religious makeup of Haifa's Arabs. For the first time, Muslims entered a previously Christian quarter. Access to the former western and eastern Arab sections of the city was now severely restricted owing to the rubble and debris that had accumulated between them,[92] leaving the Muslim population separated from its religious-cultural infrastructure, from the mosques and the Muslim cemetery. There were no mosques within the confines of Wadi Nisnas. Two of the important mosques that remained standing in the old town, al-Jarina and al-Istiqlal, were gradually restored, with the latter opening only in 1971. The Muslim cemetery was damaged by the demolition activity in the old town, and construction of a new one at the southern approach to the city was delayed until 1957. The Christian cemeteries on Jaffa Street were likewise neglected and damaged by demolition activity. The Greek-Catholic and Greek-Orthodox churches, also situated in the old town, were rendered inaccessible to worshippers.

In contrast to the haste that characterized the transformation of the urban landscape, which was driven by political and strategic considerations, the processes at the symbolic level were slow, even tardy. The tradition of the Mandate outlived the city's Arab inhabitants. Changing the Arabic names of the city's streets and neighborhoods was a laborious matter. An orderly tradition of street naming in the city was first introduced during the Mandate period. A joint Jewish-Arab committee established by the Haifa city council in 1934 decided upon and authorized various initiatives, and in this spirit a mixed tradition of street naming and signposting was maintained. The street names in Jewish neighborhoods were determined by neighborhood councils, which submitted them to the municipality for official approval. Street names in the city's Arab neighborhoods were determined by the mixed city council, which had an Arab majority prior to 1948. The council itself named the streets in the commercial center in the old city alongside the port as well as naming the roads that it built. In parallel, it tended to accede to British requests regarding English names, particularly along the main arteries of transportation. This manner of naming, which granted considerable authority to the neighborhood councils, underlined the city's segregationist nature, while the street naming expressed its binational nature. On the street signs the Arabic script appeared at the top, below it the English script, with the Hebrew script at the bottom.

Like those of other Arab neighborhoods and quarters, Wadi Salib's streets naturally bore Arab names that commemorated well-known figures and places in the Arab and Muslim world. Upon conclusion of the war, these names, and likewise the English names and manner of signposting, were no longer appropriate to the new conditions. This began to trouble both the townsfolk and the city fathers. They began to lodge complaints, write letters, draft petitions, and offer suggestions. Thus, for example, did a local lawyer complain to David Hacohen, the acting mayor:

> It is now fourteen months since the establishment of the State of Israel, and Haifa, its principal port city, still displays in all its streets, other than those of Hadar ha-Carmel, signs carrying the names of the streets *in English* (above) and below the English—Arabic and Hebrew. This gives the impression to anyone coming into town and entering Kings Street, or another of the city's important streets, that the city's national affiliation is not yet an accomplished fact, as if there were still some sort of English or international dependence or semblance of dependence. Were this the case in Tel-Aviv, Rehovot or Rishon Letzion it would not be such a serious matter, but Haifa is different: Haifa is still coveted by others in one way or another, and it behooves the city's institutions to care for its Israeli complexion, at least in such elementary matters as the language of the street names, from the first moment. One gains the impression that we ourselves are as yet uncertain as to Haifa's status.[93]

As noted, the change was gradual, not to say tardy. Up until 1951 the municipality took no steps to change the names, while independent initiatives on the part of citizens were rejected outright. The Hadar ha-Carmel council, for instance, appointed a committee to decide upon names for streets in the neighborhood and its environs, which concluded that "with the changes that have occurred in our city over the past year, [there is a need] to also review the names of several streets in the vicinity of Hadar ha-Carmel and the downtown that are no longer appropriate to the new circumstances of Jewish Haifa."[94] The committee sought to change the name of Wadi Salib Street to Malakhi Street.[95] The unease expressed by Hadar ha-Carmel council was directed not only at the Arabic names but also at the German ones. The council proposed to change the name of the "German colony," "which is liable to arouse gloomy memories, particularly among the inhabitants of this place, most of whom are new immigrants who have experienced the torments of the Nazi hell," to Rehavia, which "expresses the feeling of consolation on the part of the people of Israel who have lived to see the defeat of the tyrannical rule of the Germans."[96] Private applications to the management of the city council indicate a general unease with regard to the Arabic names as well. The "daughters of al-Idrisi Street," for example, applied to the mayor with a request to change the name of the street on which they lived: "We offer three proposals, such as: 'Victory' street, 'Conquest' street, or 'Independence' street. But if the mayor is unable to change the street name according to our proposal we shall be happy if he calls it by a different name. We should like to receive the new name joyfully, on Independance Day [!]"[97] Some made applications against the backdrop of personal tragedy. A bereaved father, for example, wrote as follows: "I appeal to you to do me a kindness and to change one street of infiltrators and Arab murderers to be named after my son; when I pass along Iraq Saladin, Stanton, and other such streets my heart aches, as, to this day, their names have not been changed. On my behalf, and on behalf of my poor wife who lost her only son for the liberation of Haifa, we ask your honor for this kindness to change one street and name it after our son. And in so doing may you be spared from mourning for sons."[98] Through these individual applications for renaming, we may glimpse the varied lineaments of the residents of the town that had suddenly become Jewish. A member of the city council who represented the Communist Party was eager to rename downtown Kings Street as Gromyko Street, thereby demonstrating appreciation for the decisive assistance given by the USSR in the establishment of the state. "I feel certain," she wrote, "that I am expressing the opinion of the majority of the city's residents."[99] The Cracow Ghetto Fighters survivors group requested that due respect be paid to the fighters in the city, as was customary "in most European countries, and particularly in Poland."[100] The group's request was "to change the name of 'Mountain Street' to 'The Ghetto Fighters' or 'The Ghetto Fighters Way'." But for the first three years, during the tenure of Mayor Shabtai Levy, the municipality steadfastly adhered to its position that the change to names "that will express in their content and ring the political change undergone by our country and our city" could be made only after the next municipal council had been elected.[101] At this stage no change was made to the Arabic names. The naming tradition of the "mixed city" lived on, as if the Arabs still resided in it.

"Where Does Colonization End and Forced Transfer Begin?"

The events that unfolded at such dizzying speed in the Israeli-Palestinian space in general and in Haifa in particular were not unique. They had numerous historical precedents. Many leaders of the *yishuv*—soon to be-come a state—whose world was populated by a rich historical repertoire, discerned this immediately. Some of them were familiar with the precedents at first hand, others from hearsay. While Golda Me'ir visualized pogroms and expulsions from recent and ancient Jewish history, the imagination of others was fired by more recent, even immediate, world history. It was Moshe Sharett who frequently employed historical comparisons in a calcu-lated manner to substantiate his firm resistance to the Palestinian return. At a meeting of the provisional cabinet on June 16, during which he underlined the difference between a public declaration of a planned initiative to expel the Arabs—a move that he termed "madness"—and their fortuitous flight, Sharett contemplated two examples: the Turkish-Greek case[102] and the ex-pulsion of Sudeten Germans from Czechoslovakia.[103] In referring to the ex-pulsion of the Sudeten Germans, Sharett went a step further, adding: "The aggressive enemy brought this about, and the blood is on his head and he must bear [the consequences] and all the lands and the houses that remained . . . all are spoils of war . . . all this is just compensation for the [Jewish] blood spilled, for the destruction [of Jewish property]. . . . This compensa-tion is natural."[104] Sharett outlined a historical course that linked unrelated episodes into something akin to a chain of events that retrospectively justi-fied the expulsion of the Palestinians. According to this outline, the loss of property—in this case the loss of Palestinian property—became the final link in a chain that begins with the dispossession of the Jews by the Nazis and leads to the Middle East, passing on the way through the expulsion of the Sudeten Germans. The Israeli cabinet was party to the logic of this argument, except for a few members who voiced opposition to conferring the status of permanency upon what was thus far the temporary Palestinian expulsion. The Sudeten expulsion was utilized not only within the internal political discourse but also in Israel's response to international demands for the return of the refugees. In his attempts at mediation in the area during the summer of 1948, Count Folke Bernadotte, a member of the Swedish royal family who had served as president of the Swedish Red Cross and who was now the UN's representative sent to stop the fighting in Palestine, endeavored to explain to Sharett that world public opinion would reject the steps taken by Israel to prevent the refugees' return. Sharett responded by saying that "the world, which understood the uprooting of the Sudeten [Germans] from Czechoslovakia, would understand this."[105] Bernadotte clearly comprehended the refugee chain in terms that differed from those expressed by Sharett at the cabinet meeting: not as a consecutive course in which the Palestinian exodus indirectly compensated the Jews for the Nazi robbery, but rather as an unacceptable moral contradiction between the Israeli demand for recognition of the immigration and rehabilitation of Jewish refugees in the State of Israel and the Israeli leadership's uncompromising position toward the Palestinian refugees.[106] While Sharett and Bernadotte remained divided on the issues of legitimacy and international recognition, they both regarded the historic development in the Middle East in a shared context as a link in the chain of historic events that had occurred in Central Europe only two to three years previously; namely, as part of the greater course of ethnic cleansing in their time.

"Consequently, while ethnic cleansing affects people, what is really at stake is territory," asserts and emphasizes the scholar Jennifer Jackson Preece,[107] in determining that the prime consideration when shifting people is to "secure territory defined in ethnic terms."[108] Unlike genocide, which involves an unmistakable intention to eliminate and destroy parts of an ethnic, religious, or national group, ethnic cleansing—without diminishing the suffering of its victims—is intended to cleanse territory.[109] The turning point with regard to this practice, argues Preece, is the year 1948. In preceding years, ethnic cleansing was perceived as a legitimate practice derived from the logic of the right to self-determination, while from this year onward, and in fact from the beginnings of the cold war, a process of outright delegitimatization of such steps began to take hold, reflected in international conventions. The events of 1948 in the Israeli-Palestine arena are chronologically and phenomenologically located in the space of ethnic cleansing, which emerged toward the end of the Second World War and ended with the commencement of the cold war.[110] If we are to accept these distinctions, 1948 lies in the no-man's land between the former legitimacy and the present illegitimacy.

One of the conduits through which the European discussion of ethnic cleansing toward the end of the Second World War permeated Israeli discourse was the "transfer committee." Appointed by the Israeli government at the end of August 1948, this was essentially a follow-up committee to the unofficial transfer committee founded by Yosef Weitz earlier that year and comprised two former members of the first transfer committee, Weitz and Danin, who were joined by Zalman Lifshitz. The transfer committee was indeed an advisory body rather than a decision-making forum, but the importance of its proposals should by no means be underestimated. At the time of its operation during the course of 1948, the prestate institutions of the *yishuv*—the Jewish Agency, the Jewish National Fund, and the National Council—were still in a position to mold the complexion of the country. Governing of the country was finally due to pass to the institutions of the state—the government and the Knesset—only in 1949, and prior to that point Yosef Weitz in person and the transfer committee were able to exert considerable influence over the political echelon.[111] The theoretical platform for the committee's work was provided by a forgotten Zionist by the name of Joseph Schechtman.[112] Some may remember him as the biographer of Ze'ev Jabotinsky, but they are not, in all likelihood, aware of the other Schechtman. Having evaded the clutches of the Nazis upon his escape in 1939 from Warsaw to France and from there to the U.S., Schechtman began his research in the early 1940s. The results of this study were presented in his book, titled *European Population Transfers, 1939–1945,* published in 1946,[113] which to this day serves as a basic textbook in the study of ethnic cleansing.[114] On the strength of European experience between the world wars, Schechtman was adamant in maintaining the impracticality and pointlessness of minority treaties and regarded them as a failure. Aware that no future peace agreement would be capable of drawing a map of Europe that delineated ethnically homogeneous geopolitical entities, Schechtman adopted the position gaining ascendancy at the time, according to which the only practical solution in certain danger areas was the "ethnic shifting of the minorities."[115] Schechtman by no means regarded ethnic cleansing as constituting a universal method for the solution of the problems of minorities. In some cases fair treatment of the minority on the part of the state within the framework of international treaties would suffice. In other cases bilateral mutual agreements might provide a solution, while in yet further cases an international supervision mechanism might do so through the League of Nations.[116] Schechtman likewise did not reject Soviet solutions to the problems of minorities outright. Any possible solution other than transfer should, in his opinion, be accorded top priority. Transfer, Schechtman asserted, was the last resort, "not as an ideal solution but as a necessary evil."[117] Choosing to employ medical metaphors, he likened ethnic cleansing to the removal of a cancerous tumor from the patient's body. "Only false sentimentality or blindness to the best interests of the patient," argued Schechtman "would permit pity to outweigh sound medical judgment."[118]

A synopsis of Schechtman's book appears as appendix 2 among the working papers of the Israeli transfer committee.[119] This summary is one of many examples of the way in which European experience filtered through to the world of those who shaped Israeli policy. European influence on the Zionist project was not confined to the spirit of ethnic nationalism prevalent in the latter half of the nineteenth century, but found direct and immediate expression in the reproduction in Israel at the time of its establishment of the principle of ethnic homogenization as applied in Europe, mainly upon the conclusion of the Second World War.[120] Europe serves, for example, as a laboratory for the examination of the opportunities and risks attendant upon existing arrangements for refugees regarding the issue of the irredentist threat, namely, those national minorities living along the borders of countries in which their ethnic group constitutes the majority. "The irredentist minorities were bad and disloyal citizens of their countries," the summary proclaims.[121] "They constantly sought assistance from their mother countries and developed into a fifth column working for these countries." Such had been the behavior of the German, Hungarian, and Bulgarian minorities in Poland, Czechoslovakia, Romania, and Yugoslavia. In some cases the ruling majority had tried to conclude a reasonable arrangement with the minorities, but they had rejected these proposals. "Relations between the minority and the majority deteriorated considerably," writes A. Goren, who composed the synopsis of Schechtman's book, in the working papers of the Israeli transfer committee, referring the reader to the relevant pages in the book. He adds in parentheses: "Analogy—Arabs in Israel—fifth column."

Schechtman's book was perceived by the members of the transfer committee as a source of practical ideas for a solution to the Palestinian refugee problem. From the Turkish position on the population transfer between Turkey and Greece, the summarizer of Schechtman's book learned that it was wise to avoid territorial concentration of the minority so as to preempt future territorial demands and added parenthetically that there was "a danger that an Arab minority in Israel would work toward the imposition of a neighboring state or states on Israel."[122] The Turkish-Greek agreement of January 30, 1923, and the Bulgarian-Turkish agreement of November 1913 retroactively endorsed existing population transfers. From these agreements, Goren drew the "lesson" that "the countries to which their brother refugees fled were reconciled to the existing facts and did not regard the return of the refugees to the places from which they had fled as a solution."[123] Apart from Schechtman's book, the transfer committee had at its disposal documentation of historical precedents of settlement of compensation issues arising from the exchange of populations, which Schechtman had submitted directly to Ezra Danin, a former senior Haganah intelligence officer and now a senior adviser on Arab affairs with the foreign ministry.[124] On the basis of his familiarity with historical precedents, Schechtman clearly tended to support the official Israeli position, which proposed collective compensation, rather than the various Arab positions, which demanded individual compensation. "Wherever the country of departure attempted to compensate every resettler for the property left behind, on the basis of an evaluation of each individual property by a mixed commission representing the country of departure and the country of reception, the effort invariably failed," he concluded.[125] The individual investigation of each separate claim, he asserted in writing directly to Foreign Minister Moshe Sharett, is destined to drag on over a long period and in the end to be detrimental to the refugees themselves, as in the Turkish-Greek case of 1923. Collective compensation, as awarded in the population exchange between Bulgaria and Romania in 1940 or between Romania and Turkey in 1946, produced better results.

What, then, was the significance of all these precedents? Goren seemed undecided as to the moral implications of the comparative framework suggested by Schechtman's book. "The approach [of the book] is a humanistic one," he notes. "It seeks the minimum injustice to the suffering individual. It opposes in principle forced transfers, particular of peasants, since they are so closely attached to their land. The Arabs can exploit the book against us more than we can against them."[126] A few pages earlier he had in fact tended to find solace in the comparative framework:

Far fewer agreements pertaining to exchanges of populations and their transfer are to be found in history than the extermination and expulsion of entire populations, with no redress whatsoever. This is what happened to the Armenians in Turkey, to the Assyrians in the Hakkari mountains, Ormia, and Iraq. This is what happened to the Jews and other peoples in

Nazi Europe. Compare likewise the massacres and mass flights follow-ing the partition of India. It follows that a state's willingness to resolve a refugee problem, which arose by no fault of its own and through the aggression of the "protectors" of these refugees, indicates good will and accommodation.[127]

The "Memorandum on the Settlement of Arab Refugees" submitted by the transfer committee to Ben-Gurion in late October 1948 enumerated no less than twenty-five "migrations of nations."[128] It made a point of noting that the Israeli-Palestinian case differed from this long list.[129] The essential dif-ference in their view was to be found in the reasons for the migrations of nations. Whereas in other cases it was a matter of persecution of the minor-ity by the majority on the basis of their national affiliation, religion, race, or economic position, in the Israeli-Palestinian case "it was not that the Jews had declared war against the Arabs and had deported them from their lands as a result of their victory. It was the Arab majority in the country that had provoked and attacked the Jewish minority."[130] This version of the historic event, which remained undisputed within Israeli historiography for several decades, was formed and took hold not only on the strength of the course of the events themselves but also on that of the comparative aspect and the relevant insights as to the relation between expulsion and compensation. "We cannot assume responsibility for the exodus of Palestinian Arabs and the destruction of their property resulting from the war," state the gen-eral notes in the synopsis of Schechtman's book appended to the report of the transfer committee.[131] The illegitimacy of historical action, as they had learned from the historic precedents of population transfer, is translated into economic terms and may turn out to bear a heavy price. The authors of the report were aware of the refugees' wish to return:

It is no surprise that the refugees yearn to return to their homes and their lands and are prepared to recognize the State of Israel and its govern-ment . . . but they are unaware of, or do not wish to know, the condition of their abandoned property. And we should distinguish between mov-able property and real estate. The latter has been completely destroyed, both in the countryside and the city . . . the furniture in the houses has been destroyed and many houses too have collapsed owing to damage sustained in the war, and entire villages have been utterly destroyed owing to war damage. The entire urban, industrial, artisan, and commercial economy has likewise been undermined. And not merely the equipment—the machinery, the instruments, and the goods—has disappeared, but also the houses; many are damaged, many are destroyed, and many have collapsed down to the foundations. Thus this type of real estate—the buildings—has lost much of its value, and those that have survived—residential buildings—cannot serve as a sanctuary for the Arab refugees since they are occupied by Jewish refugees.[132]

The report was adamantly opposed to the possibility of the return of the Arab refugees.[133] Its authors had gained this insight, too, from Schechtman, who had reached the categorical conclusion that there is "no precedent for return" in the twentieth century.[134] In recent decades, Schechtman asserted, over thirty million people had been uprooted from their homes as a result of war or alterations of borders. "In none of these instances—each involving numbers far greater than in Palestine—was there any serious attempt to restore the status quo ante: that is, to return the displaced persons to their original home."[135] Schechtman was resolute in his assertion, which took no note of the details of each case or the political intentions involved: "Experience shows that exodus is irreversible."[136] There was nowhere to return to, Schechtman explained, because the place of those uprooted is immediately taken by new settlers. Insistence on restoring matters to their previous state is liable to lead to a never ending chain of uprooting with potentially calamitous consequences. This state of affairs should be accepted as having been decreed by fate, and responsible statesmen should direct their attention at solving the remaining problems.

Among all these cases, the authors of the report identified an international willingness to accept de facto the situation created by the war, something that had become apparent to the political leadership in the U.S. and Britain already in the early 1940s. Those at the time who expressed reservations about such a solution did so out of an aversion to "uprooting [people] from an entrenched place."[137] And yet, since the displacement had in any case occurred during the course of the war, the committee members sought a solution "more rational and fundamental than mere return." To this was added the fear that the Arab refugees would constitute a burden on the state's treasury and would, should they return, be condemned to a life of economic hardship. The authors pointed out the risk that the returnees may become disloyal to the Jewish state and concluded by insisting that "the return of Arab refugees would limit the ability to handle the return of not merely the equivalent but a greater number of Jewish refugees and immigrants." Given these circumstances, it was clear to those involved that "Jewish refugees must take precedence."

Population Exchanges

"Your uncle never had great faith in ethics, and when he found himself on the pavement like us, he lost it entirely. He made for a house occupied by a Jewish family, opened the door, threw his belongings inside and jerked his round face at them, saying very distinctly: "Go to Palestine!" It is certain that they did not go, but they were frightened by his desperation, and they went into the next room, leaving him to enjoy the roof and tiled floor."[138]

The political decision to deny the refugees the option of return came to fruition between April and June 1948. In July of that year it became official Israeli policy and was reaffirmed by the Israeli government in August and September. The memorandum of the "transfer committee" did not thus produce policy but merely accorded it a certificate of approval. While this policy was being formulated, some of the abandoned homes of the Palestinian refugees were already being repopulated. The first to be housed in the Arabs' homes were the Jewish residents along the seam line whose houses had been destroyed during the hostilities.[139] In its initial stages this repopulation took place during the course of negotiation with the Arab owners and in return for payment for use of the property, but later, when the housing shortage became acute, the Jews simply began to take over the abandoned property. In the spring of 1948, as ever greater numbers sought accommodation, this practice was adopted as the principal solution to their plight.[140] In the meantime, the authorities began settling recent Jewish immigrants to the country in the houses of the Palestinian refugees. This measure provided a speedy solution to the immigrants' acute need for housing, but was, at the same time, a deliberate initiative aimed at blocking the return of the Palestinian refugees.[141] The abandoned Arab quarters in the mixed cities were the first to be populated by Jews.[142] "Jaffa and Haifa," writes Benny Morris, "had the largest and also most modern concentrations of abandoned Arab dwellings, and so it was only natural that the first mass channeling of new immigrants was to those two towns. This project was facilitated by the close proximity to the abandoned neighborhoods in these cities of Jewish urban infrastructure and services that had not gone unscathed during the fighting."[143] In various areas the settlement was in part implemented street by street, in parallel and in close proximity to the battles being waged. There is evidence to show that this activity was undertaken with the aid of maps on which the rooms handed over to the immigrants were marked. The proximity to the battle arena, eyewitnesses reported, struck dread into the Holocaust survivors.[144] Research has failed to elaborate on this point, and there are only few references to it. Perhaps this silence derives from the fact that the course of events was self-evident given the circumstances, but its origin may lie in the sense of the breaking of a moral taboo, as one refugee took up residence in the property of another.[145]

Among the new tenants, mostly of European origin, were also immigrants from Morocco. This was a new phenomenon within the local demographics. The number of Moroccans who immigrated to the country during the Mandate period was extremely small and did not exceed nine hundred souls.[146] The establishment of the state did indeed arouse among them a longing for Zion, but their number within the "mass immigration" remained relatively small and did not exceed thirty thousand individuals or only some 12 percent of Moroccan Jews.[147] While the proportion of Orientals among the immigrants in 1948 was small, the Jews of North Africa constituted a majority among them. This is most probably the origin of the image of a "Moroccan immigration."[148] The immigration from Morocco was, from the outset, exposed to the constant tension of its coincidence with the arrival of the Jews from Europe. The fate of the Moroccan Jews was linked to the fate of European Jews in both essential and practical ways, which range from close ties to dependence and competition. The processes that led to the establishment of the State of Israel, first and foremost to the international recognition upon which its birth was conditional, were without doubt embedded in the Holocaust of European Jewry.[149] It was not only these external processes, however, but also internal dynamics that created ties between the Jewish Diaspora within the framework of the Zionist solution that was then beginning to gain momentum. Thus, for example, when some Jewish circles in Morocco became less enamored with France, the colonial power, in the wake of the cooperation between the French and the Vichy regime and the enforcement of anti-Jewish legislation in North Africa during the war, Jewish circles in France with influence in Morocco began to modify their assimilatory anti-Zionist position.[150] The Jews of Europe and North Africa were linked to each other not only ideologically but also on a practical level. The American Jewish Joint Distribution Committee—the largest worldwide Jewish welfare organization—began, for instance, to channel part of its resources to alleviating the plight of Moroccan Jews once it had completed its work in the displaced persons camps in occupied Germany. These ties were far more apparent within the Zionist movement. In the wake of the horrendous implications of the Second World War on Jewish demography, the Zionist movement had turned its attention to the numerical potential offered by the Jews of Islamic countries in general, and by Moroccan Jewry—the largest Oriental community—in particular. The war and the Holocaust created a link between Zionism, which had begun as a Western European movement devoted to the welfare of Eastern European Jewry, and the Jewish Diaspora in the Islamic lands. Not only the attraction to Zion but also the centrifugal processes that led to the rejection of the Jews by Moroccan society were indirectly connected to Europe. The evolution of Jewish nationalism in Morocco as well as its Arab counterpart was a by-product of the local process of decolonization that gained momentum following the Second World War and constituted a continuation of its results.

From its outset and throughout its course, the Moroccan immigration was directly related to the Israeli-Palestinian dispute. Moroccan society was initially fundamentally suspicious of Zionism, and its mainly Muslim leadership regarded the movement as competing with the burgeoning Moroccan nationality. The Zionists' loyalty toward the project of Moroccan independence was questioned, since they were linked to a different national project.[151] This cautious suspicion deteriorated into overt hostility with the escalation of the Jewish-Palestinian conflict and Morocco's growing relations with the Arab League.[152] Tension reached its peak in June 1948 when violent incidents, the most serious the Jews had experienced since the inauguration of the French Protectorate in 1912, occurred in two Moroccan cities, Oujda and Djerada.[153] With the active encouragement of Zionist functionaries, the violent outburst led to a hasty wave of migration, during the course of which twelve thousand Jews immigrated to Israel from Morocco between June 1948 and March 1949.[154] Among these was David Ben-Harush, destined to become the leader of the Wadi Salib riots.

Meanwhile, given the geopolitical conditions that had recently evolved, apprehension arose that the fate of the Palestinian refugees would become entwined with the fate of the Jewish migrants from Arab countries.[155] Already in early May 1948, in an initial report he presented to the provisional government, Bekhor Shitrit warned that "a large and considerable Arab minority is living amongst us, and our country is surrounded by Arab kingdoms and states and far-flung Muslim countries in which a large Jewish population lives."[156] These words contained a veiled warning about the way in which the fate of the Jews in Arab countries was liable to be bound up with that of the Palestinians.[157] Shitrit was not alone in his awareness of the fate of the Jews residing in Arab countries, although his perspective did indeed differ from that of others. He looked both toward the West and the East: toward the "nations of the world" and the universal values derived from the worldwide debate on minorities and their rights and toward the Jewish minorities in Arab countries. The official political echelon, and most prominently Foreign Minister Moshe Sharett, likewise linked the fate of the Palestinian refugees and their property with that of the Jews in Arab lands on numerous occasions. In a memorandum circulated to Israel's diplomatic representatives in July 1948, Sharett noted that "[the] question [of] Arab return can be decided only as part [of a] peace settlement with Arab State[s] and in the context of its terms, when [the] question [of] confiscation [of] property [of] Jews [in] neighboring countries and their future will also be raised."[158] In accordance with this guideline, Sharett assigned to the transfer committee the task of laying the foundation for the exchange of population, that is, Palestinians in exchange for Jews from Arab countries.[159]

And the committee members did indeed directly link the fate of the Palestinian refugees' property with the future of the property of the Jews residing in the Arab countries, in a manner that was to emerge within but a few years as a self-fulfilling prophecy. In the final memorandum they submitted at the end of October of that year, the members of the transfer committee had this to note:

> The absorption of the Arab refugees in Arab countries should not be conditional upon the transfer of the Oriental Jews from them within the framework of a population exchange. The Jews living in Arab countries are loyal guests who fulfill their duties with conviction. They should therefore enjoy all the rights of the Arab citizens of these countries.

Should they wish to leave and immigrate to Israel they shall exercise their right to free migration and will be permitted to take their property with them. If the Arab governments were to demand the exodus of the Jews in a population exchange, the Israeli government would agree to this, on condition that they be able to take all their property or that their property be fairly evaluated and deducted from the value of the assets of the Arab refugees in the State of Israel, earmarked for their settlement in Arab countries. And should the Arab governments take punitive measures against their Jewish subjects, the government of Israel will take this into consideration with regard to the Arab refugees.[160]

These words were in fact directed toward the Jews of Iraq, who had been designated as a primary objective for potential exchange of populations and who were destined to bear the brunt of this circular argument.[161] The situation of Moroccan Jews at the time differed from that of the Iraqi Jews. Morocco had yet to be granted independence and was subject to the rule of the French Protectorate. While Jewish migration was indeed influenced by the growing link between awakening Moroccan nationalism and the Israeli-Palestinian conflict, it proceeded in a gradual manner, without coercion and by way of cooperation between the Israeli government and the French authorities, both of whom sought to slow down the process. But in Morocco as well one could discern initial signs of a link between the status of the Jews and the process of decolonization, the nationalist leanings of which wavered between exclusion and inclusion of the Jews.

Let us return to Haifa. Between May 1948 and March 1949, 24,000 of the 190,000 immigrants who arrived in Israel that year were housed in the city.[162] On this matter Amiram Gonen writes:

The overwhelming majority of new Jewish residents in former Arab neighbourhoods were of a rather low socio-economic status, mainly because of the circumstances of their own uprooting, either from war-torn Europe or from Arab countries. Most came without any property or savings, equipped with low or irrelevant skills, and were plunged into an economy ridden with severe problems. They immediately occupied, at least temporarily, the lower strata of the evolving Israeli society. By settling en masse in former Arab neighbourhhods they had turned them into low-status segments within a newly formed ecology of cities, now inhabited predominantly by Jews.[163]

Independently of their former status or the quality of their buildings, these neighborhoods immediately became low-status areas.[164] The immigrants spread out in Haifa's downtown according to their countries of origin: those who hailed from Romania settled around Carmel Station and Iraq Street, which for a while was known as "Bucharest" in the local jargon.[165] The Moroccan immigrants were housed close by, in a part of Wadi Salib and its vicinity. Ben-Harush arrived too late to find a decent apartment. When he was released from military service, in November 1949, there was none available. He therefore had no choice but to occupy a room in Eglon Steps in Wadi Salib. This was an inauspicious starting point.

2. *Commotion*

"And I Wanted to Do Something Nice,

Like They Have Up in Hadar"

What provoked Fedukin's fury and dedicated hatred was precisely this sentimental egocentricity of the accused, their pathological need to prove their own innocence, their own little truths, this neurotic going around in circles of so-called facts encompassed by the meridians of their skulls. It enraged him that this blind truth of theirs could not be incorporated into a system of higher value, a higher justice which demanded sacrifice, and which did not and must not care about human weakness.
—Danilo Kiš, *A Tomb for Boris Davidovich*

ALL THAT DAVID BEN-HARUSH HAD WANTED TO DO WAS TO OPEN a modest café. He was thirty-five years old. During his eleven years in the country, after immigrating from Morocco by way of Algeria and the transit camp in Cyprus, he hadn't managed to establish a footing for himself. The café would, he hoped, put an end to his ongoing economic hardship.[1] To this end he had sold his small dwelling, bought a one-room apartment for himself and his family, and invested the proceeds in a new café. "I wanted to set up a café and snack bar in our neighborhood in Wadi Salib," he told the State Commission of Inquiry appointed to investigate the events following the shooting of Ya'akov Akiva.[2] "I thought to myself—there is no modern café in the area, and I wanted to do something nice, like they have up in Hadar, with an espresso machine, and I did everything, but I didn't check out the situation properly," he explained. Before Ben-Harush could convey to the commission how he had failed to assess the situation, Judge Etzioni, the commission chairman, was quick to comment: "Perhaps you weren't a good businessman?" "Possibly," Ben-Harush declined to disagree. He described his bar as "attractive and modern, with modern furniture, decor, pictures and also an espresso machine." Later on he added a gramophone and "Arab records." It soon transpired, however, that the clientele that visited Ben-Harush's place "comprised only fellow [North African] immigrants." "No one of European origin entered my place," he told the commission. They preferred the establishment opposite, frequented by those of

Romanian origin. "It is only natural that people frequent the shop to which they are accustomed," the committee member, Member of Parliament Jaacov Klebanoff, explained to him.

"Natural" or not, the financial means of those frequenting Ben-Harush's establishment were meager. Most were employed in relief works or in jobs connected to the port. "I didn't want to keep spirits," Ben-Harush told the commission, "but later on I had no choice." "The clientele demands this?" asked Klebanoff. Ben-Harush replied unwaveringly, "Yes, if the good sir wishes to note, of all things, that our ethnic group drinks liquor." Klebanoff backtracked, perhaps taken aback by Ben-Harush's directness. "I was referring to clients in general, not yours in particular," he quickly tried to make amends.[3] "A person who had had a drink sat there and talked, poured his heart out, and I began to get to know their problems," Ben-Harush continued. The café did not provide him a livelihood. "When they had money they drank and paid, when they had no money I had to give them credit." "In any event," he began to get to know "the members of his community."

Ben-Harush soon got involved in politics. "Several young men approached me and told me that Mapai intended to open a branch downtown, that a council belonging to Mapai would be formed there and also people from among us would be appointed to the Mapai assembly, and this time the intention was to choose members from among us so that they would be able to work within the community and assist the members of their community." Ben-Harush claimed that he had declined the offers. He required further persuasion. "I was bashful," he related. In the end he relented and arrived with his friends at the Mapai club on Hammam al-Pasha Street. "We crowded together inside and lo and behold, people of European origin appeared there, around fifteen people. I began to look around and to doubt whether the people here would choose candidates from our ethnic community. What are these people doing here [I thought]?" Ya'akov Tsorfati, from Mapai's Oriental sector department, got to his feet and began to read out Mapai's candidates for the downtown branch.[4] "And to our surprise we hear the names ending in *vitch* and *berg* and such like, many names of people of European origin, and no mention of my name. Then the entire audience got to its feet and began chanting 'Ben-Harush,' 'Ben-Harush!'" Pressured by the shouting, Tsorfati relented and added Ben-Harush's name, but the latter had been severely burned by his first political experience and demanded that his name be removed from the list. He retreated with his friends to his café. "I brought out some beer, we drank and began to consider what to do next," Ben-Harush related. "Then I said to them—let's set up an organization of our own, it will be nonpolitical and we will help one another, we will give guidance to those who can't write, we'll direct the perplexed to the right places, the organization will not be involved in politics at all." This was the moment, so he told the commission, when the Union of North African Immigrants came into being in Ben-Harush's café. The inaugural convention was attended by 130 people. Shmuel N. Eisenstadt, one of the five members of the public Commission of Inquiry appointed by the prime minister to investigate the events, asked why the members came only from the Wadi Salib vicinity. "Since it was the Sabbath eve they didn't manage to come," replied Ben-Harush.[5]

What occurred in Wadi Salib, compressed by historical memory into a single event, was in fact a chain of events that took place during July and August of 1959. These were preelection days, and the city's power brokers had no intention of allowing Haifa to slip from Mapai's resolute grip. In these circumstances the Union of North African Immigrants, which, contrary to Ben-Harush's account, had been founded prior to the shooting of Akiva, was viewed with repugnance by Haifa's rulers. For some weeks there had been tension between its members and Mapai activists in the city, and it appears that crude attempts at "buying off" the leaders of the union had come to naught.[6] The Mapai people believed that the union's activists had already been bought off by the Herut movement and, in any event, had evaded their clutches.[7] The Akiva shooting incident sparked a wave of disturbances across the country and gave notice of the potential national repercussions of the local event. Labor bureaus in Migdal Ha-emek and in Beersheba were set on fire. In Jerusalem the police succeeded in dissuading the residents of Musrara from demonstrating.

Tensions reached their peak on the night of July 31, 1959. An election rally organized by Mapai at Hadar Cinema, situated on the seam between Wadi Salib and Hadar ha-Carmel, developed into a riot. The account given by the police speaks merely of dispersing a violent demonstration. According to those detained and their lawyer, this was a provocation on the part of the authorities instigated by the Ha-poel Platoons, intended to provide the city authorities with an excuse for detaining those who had fallen out of favor with them.[8] The Ha-poel Platoons were a remnant from Mandate times, when Jewish laborers—members of the socialist founding generation—had organized themselves in self-defense against attacks by the Arab population of the city. Now these were Mapai stewards, armed with metal bars and batons, who had been put in charge of public order. As they violently dispersed the demonstration, the police charged into the heart of Wadi Salib from Hadar above. According to the neighborhood's residents, the police threw stones they had previously collected on the roofs of houses in the neighborhood.[9] In any event, stones were thrown from the roofs of houses on 'Umar ibn al-Khaṭṭāb Street.[10] The police eventually surrounded the home of Haim Maman, a prominent activist in the Union of North African Immigrants, who at the time was in an apartment at 1 Tariq Street together with his family and three other activists in the organization, Naftali Sabag, Yosef Shem-tov, and David Ben-Harush. An attempt by the police to break into the fortified house ended with a shot fired from an unlicensed Beretta pistol in Ben-Harush's possession. Luckily no one was injured. Ben-Harush and his comrades were arrested together with another fifty-nine Wadi Salib residents who were dispersed throughout the various detention centers in the country. Documents of the Union of North African Immigrants were confiscated by the police.[11]

Judge Miryam Starkman was chosen to preside over the trial of Ben-Harush and his comrades. Ben-Harush was in his late thirties, and the others were a few years younger. Arieh Marinsky, Ben-Harush's lawyer, described the judge in his memoirs:

> She came from Russia during the third immigration wave, a committed Zionist, and worked on road construction. She spoke with a thick Russian accent, and there was no better representative than her of the socially inspired immigration of the old *yishuv* in general and of Haifa in particular. Opposite her stood a new immigrant who had been a shoemaker's apprentice in Morocco and who now found himself on a life course that threatened to resemble frighteningly well a Moroccan ghetto. Miryam Starkman and David Ben-Harush represented, precisely, the extremes that were supposed to merge in this country.[12]

From a concise report given little prominence in *Haaretz*, one can discern additional disparities between the judicial establishment and the detainees: "The police minister has conveyed to the minister for religious affairs that, following his submission, an additional one of the weekdays has been designated for visits to the Wadi Salib detainees in the Jalameh Detention Center." "Thus far," the report continued, "one visiting day per week has been designated, falling on the Sabbath. Assigning an additional visiting day in midweek will allow observant relatives to visit the detainees as well."[13]

Starkman's brief was to try the four suspects according to the indictment that included, among other counts, conspiracy and incitement to riot. Ben-Harush was also accused of possession of an unlicensed pistol. The men were furthermore accused of threatening and insulting a police officer, assaulting policemen, and unlawful assembly. The trial of the other detainees did not evoke similar interest and proceeded outside the limelight.[14] The trial of Ben-Harush and his comrades was soon portrayed in vivid political colors. An attempt at invoking the help of the Supreme Court in transferring the case from Haifa to a different court was unsuccessful, since Justice Starkman, employing a type of "hijack," hastily read out the indictment to the accused and noted their plea of "not guilty."[15] Following these steps, any transferal of the trial was conditional upon the explicit agreement of the judge, who naturally refused, but agreed to expand the judicial forum to a panel of three judges.[16] During the course of the trial the judge provided ample grounds for her disqualification. It transpired that, for example, she had signed the warrants for the arrest of Ben-Harush and his companions before the Mapai election rally; that is, before the clashes themselves and the disorderly conduct that provided the official justification for the arrests.[17] The list of detainees for whom arrest warrants were issued, as police commander Yissakhar Sheffy testified, had been prepared in advance and was based on activities and transgressions perpetrated between July 9 and July 31, that is, on Ben-Harush's involvement in demonstrations held in the wake of the shooting of Akiva.[18] Attorney Marinsky describes in his memoirs the way in which the separation of powers reached a point of collapse when, during one of the court sessions, none other than the justice minister, Ya'akov Shimshon Shapira, appeared in the courtroom claiming that he found this to be "an important and interesting trial."[19] The minister, relates Marinsky, was given a raised chair to one side of the courtroom and sat at the level of the judges' podium. Marinsky's memory had, in fact, misled him, since Shapira became justice minister only at a later date, but as a member of parliament and former attorney general his appearance in the court room certainly challenged the principle of the separation of powers.[20]

While the prosecution continued to adhere to the police account, according to which the police had used force only after they had been pelted with stones, the line of defense in Ben-Harush's trial was based on the attempt to expose the planned provocation on the part of the ruling party designed to incriminate Ben-Harush and his comrades. The location of the election rally at Hadar Cinema on the edge of Wadi Salib when the invitees resided in neighborhoods far from Wadi Salib; facing the loudspeakers deliberately toward Wadi Salib; the prior deployment of the police in excessive numbers; and the issuing of arrest warrants for specified individuals even before the riots had broken out, all suggested evidence of a trap, not to say a provocation. The loudspeakers, asserted the defense, attracted the residents of Wadi Salib, while the time that elapsed between the police warning to the demonstrators to disperse and the attack upon them was too short to allow them to comply with the order.[21] The explanation of the search warrants issued prior to the riot offered by the officer, Singer, was that during the course of a patrol on the night preceding the arrests he had noticed the three accused and four other people emerging from the old Muslim cemetery on their way to Hadar Cinema and had assumed that they intended to disrupt the election rally. For this reason, he claimed, he had issued search warrants against them.[22] The prosecution had difficulty in producing civilian witnesses, and when the defense pointed out that all the prosecution witnesses were policemen it offered the alarmed testimony of an eight-year-old boy, Moshe Ohanna, who found himself trapped in Haim Maman's apartment during the riot.[23] Two other children were also called upon to testify. The *Al Hamishmar* daily noted that Justice Starkman had asserted, regarding one of the children, that "I think this child is lying!"[24] *Haaretz* noted that she had warned this child that he would not be allowed to return home until he told the truth.

The trial was held against the backdrop of the approaching elections and the attempt on the part of Ben-Harush and the Union of North African Immigrants activists to join forces with the Jerusalem Organization of North African Immigrants and to contest the elections as an independent party to be led by Ben-Harush. While the Mapai leadership was publicly dismissive of this initiative, repeated attempts were made behind the scenes to "buy off" Ben-Harush and his comrades.[25] The minister for religious affairs at the time, Ya'akov Toledano, visited Ben-Harush in prison and offered him a realistic seat on Mapai's list of candidates for the parliamentary elections. Ben-Harush declined the offer.[26] He asked to be released in order to present an independent list for election. When his request was refused, he was forced to run the election campaign from prison. In elections to the fourth Knesset, held about a week after the decision on his appeal to the district court, Ben-Harush's list was only a few hundred votes short of passing the cutoff point and gaining a seat in parliament.

The defense attorneys, Shmuel Tamir and Arieh Marinsky, succeeded in acquitting Ben-Harush and his companions of the grave charges of conspiracy and conspiring to damage property.[27] But on the remaining counts the court's decisions were extremely harsh. Ben-Harush was convicted of illegal possession of a pistol, of acting with intent to hinder a policeman, of firing a loaded firearm, and of threatening and insulting police officers. Shem-tov, Sabag, and Maman were even convicted of an offense that had not appeared on the original indictment: providing assistance to Ben-Harush. Acting with untoward harshness, the magistrate's court refused to release three of them on bail pending the appeal hearing in the district court. The sentences were likewise severe: Ben-Harush was sentenced to two years in prison, which represented the sum total of cumulative sentences rather than one concurrent sentence, even though the transgressions had been perpetrated as a chain of actions comprising a single event.[28] Shem-tov and Sabag were sentenced to six months in prison, and Maman to nine months. In a minority opinion, Judge Ya'akov Ziegelman favored a more lenient sentence, proposing that Ben-Harush receive eleven months and the other three only two months in prison. He declared that he saw no reason to adopt a policy of imposing particularly severe punishment on these defendants.[29] The defense appealed to the district court and was partly successful: Shem-tov, Maman, and Sabag were exonerated of any wrongdoing, even though the court rejected the contention that these three men had suffered an injustice owing to the amendment of the charge sheet. Ben-Harush was cleared of the charge of firing a loaded firearm according to section 100, and his cumulative sentence was modified to a concurrent one and thereby reduced from two years to only ten months in prison. "After a while," notes Henriette Dahan-Kalev, who has thoroughly researched the Wadi Salib events, "it became known that Ben-Harush had received a franchise to open a kiosk and that his comrades had received assistance in finding accommodation."[30]

This approach was to become an established method, whereby the establishment would buy off leaders of protest against discrimination and deprivation by means of tempting offers and benefits.

A month after the events and a few days prior to the publication of the commission's report, Prime Minister and Minister of Defense David Ben-Gurion met with a group of North African youngsters participating in a study program. "You are aware of what has been happening recently. I want you to tell me absolutely frankly whatever you think of what has happened, not merely as one Jew to another, but as someone would speak to his brother," he addressed the students, "What do you think about what has happened? Is it a chance occurrence, is this discrimination, is there bad blood between one ethnic community and another? Whatever you think, but give me the heartfelt truth."[31] One of those in the audience made the mistake of thinking that he had indeed been asked for his opinion and replied, "A person doesn't break windows just for the fun of it and not just for the sake of a political party, there is a different reason for it." Ben-Gurion begged to differ: "I was born in Russia. I have been to Wadi Salib, I entered a place above which I saw a sign: Land of Israel Workers Party Club (Mapai)! In Russia I saw something that is known by a Russian word—although many Jews throughout the world are familiar with this word—pogrom. What I saw there—that was a pogrom." A pogrom indeed? Was this a synonym for vandalism and hooliganism in Ben-Gurion's vocabulary? The logic of the events in Wadi Salib was, however, moving from the margins to the center. When the demonstrators destroyed the Histadrut club and the Mapai club in Wadi Salib they were not venting their frustration on a discriminated and defenseless, weak ethnic minority as they channeled hostile sentiments toward a threatening central authority. Precisely the opposite. As the weak link, they had marked the target with absolute clarity. These were the central regime's symbols of power.[32] Ben-Gurion, in any event, ignored this and remained trapped within the contradiction between ideological refusal to accept the notion that this was an ethnic dispute and the profound ethnic conditioning of his mental world.[33] There was no pogrom in Wadi Salib. There was also no massacre and fortunately no fatalities either. The members of the commission of inquiry, who concluded in their report that "while the background to the riots . . . was of a social and ethnic nature, they did not exhibit an interethnic element and in fact there was no case of one ethnic community harming another such community," likewise chose to play down the ethnic dimension.[34]

"The Lights of Hadar and the Carmel Wink at Them from Above"

"Desphina can be reached in two ways: by ship or by camel. The city displays one face to the traveler arriving overland and a different one to him who arrives by sea."[35]

It is not every day that a city or a neighborhood has the honor of finding itself at the center of a state commission of inquiry. The commission comprised five members and was headed, as mentioned earlier, by Judge Moshe Etzioni.[36] Born in Galicia and a member of Ha-shomer ha-tsair, Etzioni immigrated to Palestine as a jurist in the mid-thirties, with a doctoral degree from the Jagiellonian University in Cracow. At the time that he headed the commission of inquiry he served as deputy president of the Haifa district court. Ten years hence he would be appointed to the Supreme Court. The remaining four members were the lawyer Ram Salomon, member of parliament and lawyer Jaacov Klebanoff, the chief rabbi of Ramle, Yitzhak Abuhatssira, and the sociologist Shmuel Noah Eisenstadt. Klebanoff, also a jurist, was born in 1887 in the region of Minsk in Belarus and completed his studies at Petersburg University in 1912. He immigrated to Palestine in 1921 and was a member of the Haifa Community Committee and a founder of Kiryat Motzkin. He was also a member of the first, second, and third Knessets and a member of the law committee in the first and second Knessets.[37] Yitzhak Abuhatssira, known also as Baba Haki, was born in Tafilalet in Morocco, immigrated to Palestine in the mid-forties but returned to Morocco shortly thereafter. From there he moved to Oran in Algeria, which served as a transit point on the way from Morocco to Israel. In 1947 he made his way to Paris with his two wives and children and from there immigrated to Israel in 1948. He was soon appointed chief rabbi of the towns Ramle and Lod.[38] Eisenstadt, born in 1923 in Warsaw in Poland, immigrated with his mother in the early 1930s. He studied at the Hebrew University in Jerusalem and within a few years, in the late 1940s, became head of the new department of sociology founded by Martin Buber. When appointed to serve on the commission of inquiry he was a leading expert in the field of migration in Israel, following the publication of his book *The Absorption of Immigrants* in 1954. It is doubtful whether there is anyone whose work has done more than that of Eisenstadt to shape the study of Israeli society locally while at the same time bringing it to the attention of the international academic community.[39]

The commission of inquiry, appointed subsequent to the riots and following the shooting of Akiva, heard most of its evidence at the end of July 1959 and submitted its concluding report on August 17, 1959, under the impression of the events in Wadi Salib that had led to the arrest of Ben-Harush and his companions. Twenty thousand people live in the vicinity of Wadi Salib Street, of whom some one-third hail from North Africa, says the memorandum submitted to the commission members by the deputy mayor of Haifa, Zvi Barzilay.[40] The area includes 5,089 apartments with 7,599 rooms. Whereas the average number of rooms per apartment in the city is 1.9, stressed Barzilay, the average per apartment in Wadi Salib is 1.49. He had no precise data on the number of apartments that accommodated families with 8, 9, and 10 members, "but anyone who wanders around the neighborhood and sees the dark hovels, without air, without water and sanitation, can well imagine the degree of bitterness, disappointment, and despair that these families, lacking a livelihood and a decent existence, experience every day." Barzilay went on to describe the social conditions. Among Haifa's 170,000 residents, he explained to the commission, the municipality's social welfare department deals with 26,000 individuals, of whom 7,500 are of North African origin; 10,000 of these clients live in the area between Wadi Rushmiya and Hamra Square, with Wadi Salib at its center. Half of these, by the way, hail from North Africa. Barzilay continued by providing a statistical summary of the data: while only a third of the population of Wadi Salib is of North African origin, this section of the population constitutes 50 percent of those taken care of by the social welfare department, and, conversely, two-thirds of those in care of North African origin live in Wadi Salib. To this, Barzilay added the issue of education: whereas the general rate of children among Haifa's population in need of special education is 3 percent to 5 percent, in Wadi Salib and its environs the proportion of such children reaches 13 percent to 14 percent. Barzilay drew the attention of the commission to Haifa's distinctive structure, which "comprises a number of topographical layers, each of which corresponds to a particular social character. Each level on the hillside is superior to that below it both in topographical and social terms." In attempting to describe to the committee the sense of frustration felt by the residents of Wadi Salib in the face of the growing disparity between the development occurring around them and the "stagnation of the downtown," he forsook the dry tone of the report and used more poetic language: "The lights of Hadar and the Carmel wink at them from above while they are caught in the grip of unemployment in the gloom of the narrow, moldy alley and in the suffocating hovel."

Barzilay's explanation threw some light on the question why the Wadi Salib demonstrators had ascended to the Hadar ha-Carmel neighborhood to vent their anger on the display windows and shops altogether unrelated to the events in Wadi Salib. As a characteristic Ashkenazi neighborhood, Hadar symbolized both the middle class and the hated Mapai establishment and, owing to its proximity to Wadi Salib, presented a convenient and available target. This proximity provided a trigger for the riots, since it enabled Wadi Salib's residents to observe from close quarters the deepening disparity between them and their Ashkenazi neighbors.[41] While these explanations are indeed valid, they ignore the underlying antagonism between the two neighborhoods imprinted by decades of urban planning. Its roots preceded the ethnic struggle that took place in the city in 1959 and lie in the era of the mixed city. From beginning to end, during both the Arab and Jewish periods, the neighborhoods of Wadi Salib and Hadar ha-Carmel were alien to and alienated from each other. The social alienation and cultural gap between these two adjacent quarters made their mark on the urban topography already in the 1920s, when Hadar ha-Carmel emerged alongside, opposite, and in opposition to the poor downtown Arab neighborhoods.[42] The seam persisted, but whereas at the time of the Mandate it had divided the Jewish middle class from poor Arabs, in the 1950s it would separate upwardly mobile Ashkenazim from destitute Mizrahim.

At the bottom of the matter lay urban planning, or perhaps the lack thereof, and certainly the contradiction between the two. The planning of Haifa, like that of the other cities in the country, was entrusted to the countrywide British Planning Committee, which in turn appointed regional planning committees. For reasons that remain unclear the Haifa regional committee was appointed relatively late and produced a master plan only in 1930.[43] For about a decade, the city thus developed in a haphazard manner without an overall master plan. Furthermore, in the spirit of late imperialism, the British perception sought to reduce the financial burden placed on the British taxpayer and to promote British interests in Palestine by means of the local taxpayer while constantly reducing expenditure. The practical outcome of this policy was the transfer of responsibility for the establishment of an urban infrastructure to local bodies.[44] A senior official in the British Colonial Office, for example, rejected the municipality's application for a loan toward the construction of a central sewage system on the grounds that "I cannot understand why Haifa should have a plan for which it is unable to pay; Athens has no sewage, over a third of Marseilles is without sewage; Haifa should either pay up or make do without. . . . Haifa is not a particularly important city."[45] British policy thus actively contributed to the widening gulf between the various sectors of the city's residents in the years preceding the urban master plan, and this disparity continued to grow during the 1930s despite the plan.[46]

The Jews had arrived in the city from the sea, whereas the Arabs had come overland. Employment opportunities, first and foremost the projects initiated by the British government—the railway, the port, and the refinery—brought the Arab workers to Haifa.[47] To these were added several large-scale enterprises—the "great mills," Shemen and Nesher—the private and public business sectors, the construction industry, Arab industry, and various jobs provided by the Jewish economic sector. The time of the British Mandate witnessed accelerated migration to the city. Arab migration to the city was motivated by a combination of many factors. Among these was the hope of improving one's economic circumstances by working in the city during slack periods in agriculture, the wish to elevate oneself socially and economically, and, in some cases as well, the aspiration to free oneself from village life with its social control and family coercion and authority.[48] Those migrating from the villages preferred the mixed cities—Haifa, Jerusalem, and Jaffa—to the Arab cities, which lacked developed economic resources. This state of affairs drove some of the residents of these cities themselves to move to the mixed cities.[49] The quest for employment, then, formed the basis of the migration to Haifa on the part of Arabs and Jews alike.[50] Workplaces, and in particular positions with the British administration, created a mixed employment market. Even though Haifa was considered a "mixed city" with regard to the employment market, clear restrictions applied. The city's development in its three sectors—the Arab economy, the Jewish economy, and the mixed governmental economy—took place amidst tension between the political and the civil realms, the contradiction between partnership and competition, and against the backdrop of contingent economic crises, and was directly linked to the contradictory and conflicting Arab and Jewish national goals.

A similar pattern evolved in the residential sphere. Apart from isolated islands of partnership, an ongoing segregation between Jews and Arabs was maintained in the city. Whereas Arab Wadi Salib developed haphazardly, with no direction whatsoever, Jewish Hadar ha-Carmel was built according to strict principles of urban planning. Since the founding of the neighborhood on land made available by the Jewish National Fund in the early 1920s, it was administered by a cooperative association that succeeded in appropriating for itself wide-ranging powers as a municipal body in every respect. Taxes levied on its residents financed ongoing needs the municipality failed to meet. In 1921, for example, these taxes were used to pay for "repairs to the road alongside the fence of the Technion . . . where the coaches tended to sink into the mud; laying of a two meter-wide pavement along the same road, planting trees on the pavement; installation of five street lamps and the hiring of two guards [who] were also responsible for lighting the lamps, tending the trees on the street and watering them, as well as cleaning the neighborhood's two streets."[51] Hadar ha-Carmel neighborhood was established on the model of the English "garden city" and was considered a shining example of urban planning at the time.[52] This was clearly evinced by the ample provision of public areas for general benefit. Only two months after the neighborhood committee was formed, it decided upon the construction of several public buildings including an assembly hall, library, and a neighborhood committee meeting place.[53] Binyamin Garden, laid out on an eight-dunam plot allocated for this purpose from the outset, became the apple of the neighborhood's eye. Ten benches were installed in the garden for use by the residents, and it became "a place where young mothers congregate, [who] lead their children in strollers to breathe fresh air in the heat of the day, and a place of rest and conversation for the elderly in the evening."[54] In the mid-twenties the committee initiated construction of a stone wall to encircle the garden, within which a "handsome stone kiosk" was built, planned by the architect Alexander Baerwald.[55] Uniformity of form and insistence on aesthetic values characterized the neighborhood. When, for example, paving of the roads had been completed, the neighborhood committee ordered uniform road signs from Bezalel (the first school of arts and crafts in Palestine, established in 1905 at the Seventh Zionist Congress in Basel) to signpost the neighborhood's main thoroughfares.[56] During Hadar ha-Carmel's initial years, before the national dispute had begun to impinge on it, development of the neighborhood was subject to the principles laid down by the general city plan, which assigned it the distinct character of a residential quarter and insisted that the downtown area, and it alone, would continue to provide the commercial and industrial infrastructure of the entire city. This separation accorded with the taste of a European observer. "The Jewish suburb of *Hadar ha-Carmel*," says a 1929 British tourist guide, "is now one of the pleasantest residential quarters in Palestine."[57] The contrast between the adjacent neighborhoods—the Arab downtown and Hadar—was clear for all to see. "Old Haifa," wrote New York businessman Julius Schwartz in the mid-twenties, "has all the characteristics of an Arabian town—narrow, dirty streets the buildings of which are huddled together and kept in a highly unsanitary condition. Now, however, a new Jewish suburb called Hadar ha-Carmel is being developed about half-way up Mount Carmel. Here the streets are wide and clean, the houses modern and provided with garden space."[58] The dichotomy of the neglected Arab city opposite the developed Jewish one is likewise reflected in the description of Haifa in a mid-thirties English tourist guide: "Higher up the slope is the residential suburb (mainly Jewish) of *Hadar ha-Carmel*, which, with its villas, blocks and flats, hotels, shops and cafés in European style, offers a remarkable contrast to the older town below."[59]

The differences, however, were not merely aesthetic in nature, and their significance went far beyond the personal taste of this or that external observer. May Seikaly, who has studied the Arab Haifa of the Mandate period, points out the link between economy, welfare, and national dispute. The topography of the place revealed the underlying strata, the tension between the nationalities, and the economic disparity. And, indeed, the circumstances of the rural Arab migrants in Haifa had steadily deteriorated during the thirties.[60] Many of them found it difficult to keep up the monthly rental payments on their homes, which bore no relation to their modest wages as laborers and could constitute as much as one-half of these. During the 1920s, they had still been able to share rented rooms through family connections or through fellow villagers. Already then, however, and to a greater extent in the mid-1930s, many of the rural migrants found improvised solutions, living on the streets in sacks or in the covered area of the market, in the large caves of Wadi Rushmia, in tents, and in tin shacks erected by house owners on the roofs. Approximately half of Haifa's Arab population resided in slums, mostly in the eastern part of town.[61] "The Arabs live in shanty towns without sewage and water . . . the Jews live in pretty houses," concluded the British governor of the region, Edward Keith-Roach, in 1936.[62]

Seikaly traces the process of pauperization of Haifa's Palestinian society, distinguishing between the haves and have-nots. She maintains that the "have-nots felt the political and economic deprivations most keenly and now retaliated in the mid-1930s by militant activities."[63] Some found solace in their Muslim identity, which was reinforced with the migration from village to city and provided a religious answer to their material distress, as, for example, in the sermons of al-Shaykh 'Izz al-Din al-Qassam in the al-Istiqlal mosque on the edge of Wadi Salib.[64] The Jews were soon to become aware of the Arabs' distress. The well-being of the residents of Hadar, which had from the outset been intended to provide a standard of living different from that of the local Arabs, was suddenly threatened as the national dispute intensified and began to impinge on the relations between the communities. The clear distinction between residential quarter and commercial district, which Hadar ha-Carmel's first settlers had found so attractive and that was attuned to the taste of the European tourist, had already eroded by the time of the violent clashes of 1929.[65] In the wake of these events, the Jews living in the isolated neighborhoods of Harat al-Yahud and Ard al-Yahud—Haifa's first Jewish neighborhoods located east of the old city—retreated to the confines of Hadar and were temporarily accommodated in tents and in the grounds of the Technion and Reali High School.[66]

The year 1929 saw the end of the original plan to separate the Jewish residential area from the downtown commercial and industrial district when it transpired that under the circumstances created by the growing national dispute it was impossible to ensure a regular supply of food and water to the Jewish residents. The logic of the isolationist Zionist enterprise recoiled against the Jewish settlers as the voluntary seam and separation lines were suddenly transformed into lines of confrontation. Under these new circumstances the few stores in the neighborhood were unable to provide for the needs of residents and refugees, and the supply of milk and vegetables was cut off owing to the severing of transportation routes. It was now obvious that the plan for establishing a Jewish residential neighborhood without its own retail commercial and artisanal center that would be utterly dependent on the Arab downtown could no longer provide adequate solutions. The residents of the neighborhood were thus forced to modify the "garden city" vision of "green plots in front of the houses." It is, of course, quite possible that the violent events merely served to hasten processes that would have evolved gradually as part of the natural course of migration and urban growth.[67] In any event, as the refugees from the isolated neighborhoods began to close down their businesses and trade in vegetables, fish, and fowl in the open air, the institutionalization of commerce and business in the areas of Hadar ha-Carmel gained greater acceptance.[68] As the population grew from a few hundred in the early 1920s to thirteen thousand residents in the 1930s, and when the first two-story buildings gave way to three- and even four-story structures, the neighborhood lost its original suburban character.[69] "Hadar ha-Carmel is over-built and totally ruined as a desirable suburb," complained the British town planner Clifford Holliday in 1933 when engaged in planning Sri Lanka's capital city.[70] From the perspective of the garden city, this was certainly a valid assessment, but up to the 1960s and 1970s, when Wadi Salib's Jewish residents would be evacuated, Hadar preserved its image of a spacious middle-class residential neighborhood.[71]

By the mid-thirties, then, the various parts of the city were already functioning as separate systems maintaining their distance from one another. The escalation of the national dispute reinforced the existing trend toward segregated residence on the basis of religion and place of origin. The tension between the two nations took the form of clearer lines of demarcation between Jews and Arabs, both among veteran residents who had lived in mixed neighborhoods at the turn of the century and among the new migrants. The two trends—increasing segregation and the growing disparity in urban planning—were intertwined: the nationalist tension led to separation within mixed areas and to an increasingly segregationist tendency in the new Jewish precincts. Their decision to free themselves of economic and financial dependence on the Arab quarters exacerbated the distress of the Arab neighborhoods, thereby generating increased hostility among their residents.[72] While the Jewish neighborhoods had enjoyed a measure of independence from the early 1920s onward thanks to their professional and organizational capabilities in urban planning, the Arab neighborhoods achieved a certain degree of self-organization only in the 1940s. This development was perceived by the Arab population as the product of a deliberate policy of discrimination.[73] The new districts, notes Seikaly, referring to the

Jewish residential areas, initially brought considerable economic benefits to the city in general. In time, however, and in parallel to the worsening national conflict throughout the land, these neighborhoods began directing their activity solely toward their separate commercial and financial needs.[74] In the forthcoming years, the water supply and sanitation, education, and health systems in the Jewish areas were installed and institutionalized by virtue of donations provided by local residents and the national Jewish institutions. From the mid-1940s onward, the bourgeois Jewish circles in the city tended to divest themselves of commitment to the impoverished Arab precincts in the city. "We live in a mixed city. This is not the same as life in a neighborhood," warned David Hacohen, one of the leaders of Haifa's Jewish community and a city councilor: "The home is indeed in the neighborhood, but the business is located in the Arab street. People spend ten hours a day there, the port is there, the market is there, that is where those children live, who are liable to get illnesses and from whom my children in the Jewish neighborhood will contract the illnesses."[75]

Mismatch

The antagonism imprinted on Haifa's urban texture—between Downtown and Hadar, between the traditional Arab quarters and the modern Jewish quarters—was among the invisible ingredients of the riots. The overt and central ingredient touched upon general aspects of recognition and distributive justice. The sense of discrimination and deprivation was centered on the topic of housing and stemmed from the lack of transparency and obscurity of the principles by which it was distributed. "The whole neighborhood is complaining. It is plain to see that none of the institutions handle people appropriately. There is discrimination," complained Ben-Harush to the commission of inquiry, "when the immigrants arrived in '48 and there was mass immigration, the most attractive houses were in the possession of the Haganah, and when it evacuated it handed them over to people from Europe and they are occupied by them now or have been passed on by them to others."[76] 1948 was the year of the great division, the year in which the apartments were divided. When Ben-Harush in 1959 raised the matter of the terms by which the "abandoned property" had been distributed before the commission of inquiry as a contributing factor to his distress, it seemed as though this chapter of history had already been forgotten. And now it transpired that the distribution of the property of the Palestinian refugees continued to throw a dark shadow over those who benefited from the booty. The first action taken by sovereign Israel embodied from the beginning an arbitrary element that desecrates every principle of the sanctity of private property and which left its mark on the totality of intra-Jewish relations, as the events of Wadi Salib exposed.

Wadi Salib and Wadi Nisnas were thus two aspects of the same process, whose delayed effect was in retrospect seen to transcend relations between Jews and Arabs in the young state and reflected also on intra-Jewish relations. As Wadi Salib was emptying of its original Muslim residents, Wadi Nisnas was being densely populated by the remnants of the Arab residents in Haifa. It was the military echelon that, without consulting the civilian authorities, made the decision to concentrate Haifa's Arab residents in Wadi Nisnas. This decision was met with criticism and evoked resentment. Its implementation began as soon as the British troops had departed from the city on June 30, 1948.[77] Members of the Committee for Arab Affairs warned that this was a decision that ignored the "civil consequences," but the critics were powerless to halt the move that was implemented against the backdrop of the war and with the authority of the military level. Given these circumstances, the members of the Committee for Arab Affairs had no choice other than to cooperate, if only to alleviate the sense of unease and the suffering of the civilian Arab population.[78] They opened an office in Wadi Nisnas in which Arab and Jewish representatives jointly decided upon distribution of the apartments.

Initially it appeared that the populating of Wadi Nisnas would present the thornier problem.[79] The military government did not bother to prepare an adequate infrastructure for the operation, failed to ascertain which of the house owners were present in the city and which were absent, failed to arrange the apartments in advance or to connect them to the power and water networks, and neglected to provide means of transportation.[80] The Haifa Arabs who moved into Wadi Nisnas when the forced population began early in July fared better than those who were transferred at a later stage. "On the whole," reported Committee for Arab Affairs member Vashitz, "the distribution of apartments went well. There was no difficulty at first since the apartments were good. The apartments that remain now are less good and this will present difficulties since those arriving are among the residents of the German Colony who lived in more modern apartments." Vashitz reported that residents were seeking a solution by exchanging apartments once the operation neared its conclusion. There was a problem regarding furniture in the houses being occupied, maintained Vashitz, and inspectors were required to handle this. The dynamic that developed stemmed from economic and social class disparities. From some houses there was nothing at all that could be removed, but "there are a few houses that contain very beautiful furniture on a par with that in the most respectable homes even in Hadar ha-Carmel," he wrote.[81]

Some of these luxurious houses, by the way, lost their splendor very rapidly upon their transfer to new tenants. In some of these houses, originally designed for a single family unit, three and even five families were now accommodated owing to the pressing needs of the hour. During the course of the coming years the tenants were obliged to add toilets, washrooms, and kitchens in passages and areas that had originally been designed as public spaces and to improvise other additions. In any case, they lacked the means for ongoing upkeep of the expensive buildings. "Mismatch" is how Amiram Gonen describes the disparity between the high quality of these buildings and the low economic status of the new occupants.[82] This description also applies to some of the more spacious buildings of Wadi Salib. Construction of the neighborhood's buildings commenced toward the end of the nineteenth century. They closely followed the course of the wadi, which is still discernible along present-day 'Umar ibn al-Khattāb Street. Initially, small houses were erected close to the wadi itself, housing people of meager means, while the spacious houses were constructed later, above and at some distance from the wadi.[83] A network of steps connecting the upper parts to those adjacent to the course of the wadi was constructed on both its banks. If one's eye can still today make out some vestige of beauty amidst the total destruction, these are the remnants of the special character that the stonework and design of the entrances lent to the houses of Wadi Salib, and to the spacious houses in particular.[84] The thick stone walls were hewn by hand. Some of these were built by the double-wall method, that is, two hewn stone walls containing smaller stones and mortar in between, with the outer wall left as natural stone while the wall facing inward to the house was covered with white plaster on a quicklime base. The main design effort was put into the apertures, the most common being a triangle of arches, an ancient motif in Muslim construction that was generally located on the building's main facade. A headstone was placed at the top of each arch, brought into relief by a distinctive texture. The breadth of the arched facade generally corresponded to that of the main hall and allowed it to bathe in light. The arched openings led on to marble balconies laid on stone extensions, surrounded by iron balustrades with stylized fixtures, as were the entrance arches themselves. Construction of a later period reveals an attempt to simplify the shape of the arches to render them more modern and functional. The architectural component in which the greatest decorative effort using stone and iron was invested was generally the entrance, at which a heavy wood door was installed.

The most prominent of Wadi Salib's luxurious houses was the House of Arches, situated on the topmost strip, where the urban villas were placed within walled gardens containing a fruit orchard.[85] To this day this is one of the few buildings that remain intact within the sea of rubble that once was Wadi Salib. It was built by the Jarrar family, a Muslim family among the largest property owners in the Jenin area, whose sons migrated to Haifa in the 1870s in the wake of the economic growth.[86] It was Hassan Jarrar, a senior member of the family married to a Lebanese woman, the daughter of one of Beirut's most esteemed families, who built the house, most probably between the years 1870–1874. At this time he was already involved in the institutions of the city's administration, maintained contacts with consuls and foreign merchants, and kept servants and Negro slaves. His decision to construct a house in Lebanese style, known in the profession as a central hall house, or Liwan house, indicates his inclination to follow the dictates of fashion. Close to one-third of the building's considerable area was devoted to hospitality functions and evinced the owner's elevated public stature.[87]

At the center of the House of Arches is a space surrounded on both sides by rooms that make up residential wings. In the past the breeze blowing from the sea could be felt in the space. The house was specially adapted to the humid climate of the coastal region, and the coolness of the space was maintained also by its insulation from the heat outside, provided both by the residential wings and the tiled ceiling. The most impressive and dominant element, which gave the structure its name, was the *riwaq*, the arcade of columns and arches on three sides of the building that mediated between its interior and the outside and gave it its decorative appearance. Three entrances led into the structure, one of which was added at a later date. One of the original pair led through a long passage to the foyer and on to the hospitality space, thereby preserving the customary separation between the private and public spheres. An additional separation, between the genders, was in all probability maintained by means of the wings, one reserved for men and the other for women.

The character of the House of Arches was dictated by its users and their needs rather than by architectural whims. This construction style, which had spread from Lebanon to other countries with similar climate and in particular to Palestine, combined local construction materials and building traditions that had evolved in the East with the topographical conditions and the local, liberal way of life. In the wake of the development of commercial ties with Europe, the pace of import of building materials—tiles, glass, and wood beams—quickened and made its mark on the architectural style. The thin wood beams imported from Turkey and Romania enabled construction of a light tiled roof, completed with flat tiles brought from Marseilles. These materials did not allow for domes and massive walls. It became customary to build thin walls only some thirty centimeters thick, which could not accommodate the traditional niches. The articles previously stored in these niches were now placed within mobile closets imported from Europe. The European style also found expression in the introduction of beds, which determined, to some extent, the use of certain rooms as bedrooms and detracted from the previous flexibility in the use of the residential spaces.[88]

The House of Arches is distinctive for the richness of its materials and the profusion of decorative elements. An example of these is provided by the various kinds of floor paving: the formal spaces were paved with large grayish-white and black-veined marble tiles and the living rooms with ceramic tiles, while the passageways and storerooms were made of limestone. Careful attention was likewise paid to the design of the ceilings. In the spaces open to visitors the wood ceiling was covered with several layers of thin plaster on which still-life motifs of flowers and fruit were painted. Samples of wood taken in later days reveal that the European ceiling was made of tall spruce, white fir, deciduous cedar, and forest pine. These woods were imported from Europe, which indicates that the ceiling was probably built at a later stage, when steamships had been introduced as a means of transportation from Europe to the shores of Palestine. The roof construction, on the other hand, the arched windows, and the shutters were all made of cedar of Lebanon and *Pinus brutia* (Calabrian), imported from Turkey. These belong to the early stages of the structure. Baroque and Rococo motifs adorned the ceiling. These had filtered down from eighteenth-century Europe to Istanbul and from there on to the provinces. The meeting of ceiling and wall was covered in decorative wood cornices, ordered, so it seems, from a catalog containing a limited number of patterns.

Hassan Jarrar's two wives, engaged in an inheritance feud, continued to live in the building up to 1914 with their sons. Their subsequent fate is unknown, and they may have fled the city only in 1948. In 1950 the building passed into the hands of the Shikmona company and its many rooms were divided among several families. The Baydoun family was accommodated on the ground floor, and the upper floor housed the Jerby, Tabaji, and other families. To that end, several changes were made to the internal divisions. In the mid-1960s, an improvised synagogue operated in the building's central space. In 1986 the Shikmona company succeeded in evacuating the tenants and sealed the structure. Only Yosef Tabaji insisted on remaining in a single room on the ground floor where he lives to this day. The structure's roof along with the wood ceiling has recently been destroyed by fire. All that is left of the wood ceiling and the cornice is the documentation, but here we are getting ahead of ourselves.[89]

The Year of Distribution

> *How they vaunted their "Abbas" carpets, named after the exclusive street in Haifa, just as their peers in Jerusalem took pride in their "Qatamun" carpets, named after the quarter in Jerusalem.*[90]

The Arab tenants housed in the House of Arches in Wadi Salib are, incidentally, exceptions to the rule. The majority of Haifa's Arabs were, as mentioned, accommodated in Wadi Nisnas by the Committee for Arab Affairs in Haifa. The committee's work ended with the completion of the forced housing at the end of July 1948, when, as it observed, "the life of the Arabs had [returned] to normal" and there was no longer any need for it. From this moment onward, the lives of Haifa's Arabs were placed in the hands of the branch of the Minorities Ministry that opened in the city.[91] Bekhor Shitrit was appointed to head the Minorities Ministry. A few months previously he had opposed the destruction of Haifa's old town and warned against linking Israel's attitude toward the Arabs of Palestine to the status of the Jews in

Arab countries. From the outset he showed unusual sensitivity toward the needs of the Arabs remaining in the city in handling their housing problems, upholding civilian considerations against the interests of the military. During the ensuing months the adherence to principles on the part of Shitrit and Moshe Yitah, who headed the Haifa office of the Minorities Ministry, was put to a stern test, since the Haifa Arabs' housing problems did not end with the cessation of the activities of the Committee for Arab Affairs. The Arabs of Haifa were forced to continue to struggle for their right to a roof over their heads over the following months. The military authorities favored complete geographical concentration of all Haifa's Arabs, whereas the civilian arms of government were prepared to make concessions and to consider each case according to its individual merits.[92] Thus, for example, did the Minorities Ministry protest to the commander of the Haifa district about a list of addresses submitted to it with an accompanying demand to concentrate the Arab families appearing on the list, who were living outside Wadi Nisnas.[93] Examination of the list revealed that eight of the thirty-one families were living in Wadi Salib, "which had been designated as a place in which to house Arabs in the order regarding concentration of Arabs issued at the beginning of July." Among the residents ordered to vacate Wadi Salib were Ali Hassan, a Circassian, who lived in a two-room apartment on Wadi Salib Street, of whom it was written that "it is uncertain whether or not he is a Circassian." Most of another apartment on the same street was occupied by a Moroccan Jew, while "only one apartment with one room [was occupied] by Mahmud Alhassan Aljuri (five members) who have lived there for a long while."[94] Upon conclusion of the process of Arab resettling only some ten Arab families remained in Wadi Salib in 1948, but their number had swelled to several hundred Arab residents by 1950.[95]

The rapid concentration of Haifa's Arabs did not allow for an equitable distribution. In the following months, the Minorities Ministry sought to redress the injustice, which left some families living in conditions of excessive overcrowding.[96] There was, however, also a structural injustice produced by the trespassing of Jewish institutions on the confined area that had previously been proclaimed an area of Arab residence, alongside invasions on the part of individuals. Yitah chose two cases in protesting to the commander of Haifa about the injustice and pointlessness of moving the Arabs from one place to another. One of these concerned the building on 59 Abbas Street, which its Arab and Armenian tenants were ordered to vacate within twenty-four hours at the end of August 1948. Yitah noted that "the Arab families were relocated to this building from their spacious homes in the German Colony."[97] Once their residence on Abbas Street had been finally authorized, noted Yitah, aware of their distress, "they went to considerable expense in renovating their apartments, in which they regarded themselves as being accommodated for an extended period with the blessing of the military command." Yitah found it particularly difficult to understand why such measures were being taken against the Armenians. "I find it astounding," he wrote, "that precisely now you have found it necessary to deviate from the guideline regarding the Armenians established when concentrating Haifa's Arabs, according to which they were to be regarded as friendly foreigners and allowed to reside wherever they were living." Yitah's investigation revealed that the building was needed to accommodate the families of employees of the Palestine Electric Company currently held prisoner by the enemy, and he wrote thus: "I am not envious of them, and it is superfluous to stress my sympathy toward them, but it would have been possible to find appropriate accommodation for them elsewhere in the city and even on Abbas Street, in buildings which are being "invaded" despite the confiscation orders issued by the command, which hang from the entrances to many of them. In my opinion the housing planners should find appropriate ways of solving their problems rather than taking the easy and routine option of transferring non-Jewish families from their places of residence." Beyond the isolated instance of injustice, Yitah cautioned that moving the Arabs out of the apartments assigned them by the command as well as the authorized expropriations within the area officially designated for Arab residence in the city "lead the Arabs and other minorities to lose respect for our institutions and trust in their word." But the course of events, as we have seen, had left a bad impression also on Ben-Harush, even though he was by no means an Arab.

Yitah's civilian outlook was foreign to the perspective of the military. The commander of the Haifa region was unimpressed by the severe shortage of housing among the city's Arabs. Reports of black market dealing in apartments in Wadi Nisnas reached his ears. As long as some of the apartments in Wadi Nisnas assigned to Arabs remained unoccupied, he was of the opinion that "there is no point in retaining empty apartments in this area when there is great difficulty in finding appropriate housing for Jews, be they soldiers or civilians."[98] This disparity between the civilian and the military standpoints prompted invasions by individuals. The Provisional

Arab Committee complained of individual and organized invasions of the areas of Wadi Nisnas set aside for Arabs.[99] Some of those seizing property were demobilized soldiers.[100] Civilian bodies such as the Minorities Ministry had only limited power to prevent invasions undertaken with the direct or indirect approval of the military. A letter sent from the Haifa region military police office to the Minorities Ministry in the city demonstrates the Sisyphean nature of the attempt to prevent invasions by soldiers. The lieutenant sent to investigate the complaint regarding invasion reported that "I found a number of soldiers standing in front of the house." His investigation revealed that "the soldiers present had not invaded nor caused any damage to the apartments in this building. Any damage done to the doors of one or more of the apartments in that building had been caused by other people who are not soldiers."[101] The lieutenant concluded, "I warned the soldiers present not to enter and not to touch any part of the apartment without a legal confiscation order from the district director."

We may well wonder whether the soldiers' commitment to abide by the order reassured the tenants in the building on 40 Abbas Street. Ever since the concentration of the Arabs in July 1948 and during the ensuing months, the orderly institutional program of expropriation of Arab apartments had been complemented by clearly criminal acts of theft. Yitah complained to the commander of Haifa:

> In recent weeks the Wadi has served as a field of activity for those in search of apartments who . . . invade the houses of Arabs after "softening up" their occupants by means of various forms of harassment, generally performed by people in uniform who on occasion also carry Stens. A favorable outcome of an attempted invasion is considered to be one whereby the injured Arab is forced to repair the doors and locks following the visits of the invaders, but in many cases he is forced to relinquish part of his apartment "as a compromise" and even to flee from it, something that confines even further the residential space permitted for settlement by the Arab population.[102]

The criminal version of such an event appears in a somewhat different light:

> Jewish youngsters of a certain type, under cover of khaki dress, force their way into family apartments alleging that they have information that the

place serves as a brothel. The Arab citizens stand dumbfounded at the spectacle unfolding around them and the insults to their families. Any attempt on their part to resist is met with a stage-managed Arab-Jewish incident directed by the shameless youngsters, who in their trickery succeed in enlisting to their cause passing soldiers who are lured into "saving" Jews from Arab attack.[103]

The incursions reached their peak in April 1949. Some two hundred soldiers armed with guns arrived in military vehicles and invaded twelve large apartments on Abbas Street and five regular apartments in Wadi Nisnas.[104] Among the invaders were officers who had removed the markings of their ranks so as to avoid identification. When the police refused to handle the evacuation of the invaders, the army took over the task. Even once the invaders had been removed from the apartments—in fact, only in part, since the war invalids among them were permitted to remain for the time being—it proved difficult to arrive at an agreement on the matter. The complaint lodged by the representative of the Provisional Arab Committee, Elias Khousa, that "the situation resembles that in the days of the Turks, who used to attack the houses of the Jews and the Christians,"[105] failed to elicit a clear-cut answer. Polchak, a representative of the Ministry of Defense's rehabilitation department, suggested to Khousa that "the Arabs take up less space and leave some room."[106] Selinger, the police representative, asserted metaphorically: "There are physical laws that state that one cannot preserve an empty space when it is subject to tremendous pressure."[107] Whether out of naïveté or blindness to the logic of nationalism, Vashitz proposed in this instance to establish a joint committee comprising Jews and Arabs to find solutions for the rehabilitation of the war invalids "in order to investigate the housing situation among the Arabs in comparison to the Jews. Among the Jews there are also spacious apartments occupied by only a few."[108]

Alongside the invading soldiers the Jewish Agency began to direct immigrants to the areas assigned to house Haifa's Arabs.[109] The immigrants and the shunted Arabs—"present Arabs" in the language of the documents— were placed opposite each other, ranged against each other. Shihadeh Salah, the deputy mayor, complained that "Mrs. Anna Hoffman and Mrs. Barina Rosner are refusing to vacate his apartment at 120 Jaffa Street in which his sister Hind Shelah and her family of fourteen members had previously resided.[110] While the sister was away, the occupants invaded the apartment, and now that Salah had obtained permission for his sister and her family to return to Israel by means of a special dispensation he was obliged to accommodate them in his home because of the women's refusal to vacate.[111] In light of the principle of equal rights for all citizens of the state irrespective of religion and race as well as promotion of "the general good" by preventing "unbridled lawlessness of this kind," Salah hoped that his matter would be speedily addressed. The extent to which nerve touched nerve and the pain of one was felt alongside that of the other can be ascertained from an application by the Jewish Agency submitted to the Minorities Ministry for assistance in finding accommodation for the Bernstein family, "old and very ill people," whose son had fallen at the front some days previously.[112] To that end, the Jewish Agency informed the Minorities Ministry that "in the courtyard of 97 Jaffe Street an Arab woman is living in a two-room apartment." "According to our employees on the spot," the agency reports, "she has no special license to live there. The Jewish residents in the building (new immigrants that I have housed in these apartments) are full of complaints regarding her presence in this apartment." Because of that, the agency applied to the Minorities Ministry with the request "to remove the Arab woman" from her apartment.

"Did You Enter Without Permission?"

Fierce tenants elbow their way through history.[113]

As Ben-Harush had discerned, 1948 was the year in which the dwellings were handed out. In this respect Israel was no different to many of the nations whose borders and population had undergone drastic changes in the wake of the processes occurring in Europe following the Second World War and their continuation in the decolonization that took place outside Europe.[114] Processes of expulsion and immigrant absorption leading to tension between veterans and new settlers were taking place over the entire Central European space within the short period spanning the second half of the 1940s. The authorities in all these Central and East European lands were engaged in the distribution of abandoned property while committed to a socialist ideology. However, there, as here, a disparity emerged between commitment to principles of equality and practical decision making. "We do not know," writes Ivan Szelenyi,[115] a sociologist specializing in the issue of social inequalities from a comparative and historical perspective, "how egalitarian this reallocation of old bourgeois housing was, who were the primary beneficiaries." Szelenyi is convinced that the transition from suppression of the old inegalitarian capitalist system to the revival of inequality in housing under the new socialist system in the East European socialist nations was precipitous and direct. According to him, "Some, and in fact the best old bourgeois housing, went to the new cadre of the intelligentsia, to the top party and state bureaucrats, high ranking officers in the army and security forces."[116]

Israel resembled the socialist equivalents of its period. The confiscation of buildings, apartments, and factories by the various authorities on the strength of orders issued by military commanders and on security grounds was initially anchored in Emergency Regulations Regarding the Seizure of Property in 1948, and a year later within the framework of the Seizure of Land in State of Emergency Law.[117] This enabled the ordained authority to issue certificates that retroactively legalized the seizure of property during time of war. The occupants in whose favor this order was issued became, in fact, protected tenants. In some instances this law sanctioned acts of appropriation and plunder performed purely for personal gain, utterly unrelated to any other security or public interest: it enabled the exercise of authority in order to undermine a court order issued against the eviction of a tenant and provided an opening for the use of trickery and deceit to delay an eviction order by means of a confiscation order. The well-connected were awarded possession of apartments that they had previously ascertained to be suitable for residence. These irregularities did not go unnoticed by the Supreme Court, which warned: "Apartments are confiscated not for the official, but in order to maintain the essential services of the state, and it is unacceptable to leave the impression that matters concerning confiscation of apartments are decided so lightly, as if it were sufficient for an official to discover an apartment and then approach the relevant authority so as to immediately obtain a confiscation order in his favor."[118]

Just as they had not gone unnoticed by the Supreme Court, these irregularities, which persisted into the mid-fifties, did not escape Ben-Harush's notice. He soon became aware of the vicious circle that took off from a weak starting point, which he attributed partly to those decisive days at the end of the war. Upon his release from army service, in November 1949, he had sought to make a home for himself. This is how he summarized his situation for the committee: "I came home. I had no furniture whatsoever. The family into which I married was also without means, but I nevertheless wanted to build a home, but when I returned home there already were no houses: since I had been a soldier, there was nobody to lay hands on a house for me. I occupied this room that had remained vacant and settled there with my wife. Here began the struggle to make a living and to start a family."[119] Having no alternative, he occupied a room at 12 Eglon Steps, "a small, low room with one window, without electricity," on the margins of Wadi Salib. This was an extremely modest starting point. At a later stage, and after two hunger strikes, he succeeded in obtaining a loan from the Defense Ministry, sold his apartment, and, in return for "key money," obtained an apartment belonging to the Development Authority on al-Morina Street, in the vicinity of Ha-maronitim Street, "a more or less human apartment," in his words, "of a room and a half."[120] At this point, too, it transpired incidentally that the status of the property was not at all clear and that the Development Authority refused to sign a contract with him. "Did you enter without the agreement of the Development Authority?" asked Judge Etzioni. "I don't think that agreement is necessary," replied Ben-Harush. The judge began to lose patience: "I'm not asking whether one needs it or not," he stated. "Did you enter without agreement?" "Without," replied Ben-Harush.[121] He now urgently needed money to open the café, which he hoped would release him from constant economic distress. "I sold the apartment," as he explained to the commission of inquiry, "I bought a small room for eight hundred liras and entered the café. The room had neither a toilet nor a communal toilet; it was in a building that had perhaps been a hotel; each family lived in a room; if it wants to, it puts in some kind of cooking facility, and that's all."[122]

From the discussions of the public commission of inquiry, it emerged that Ben-Harush was not alone among the residents of Wadi Salib in failing to reach agreement with the Development Authority.[123] Heinrich First, owner of the café at 7 Wadi Salib Street, likewise testified that he had had a "run-in" with the custodian. Before taking the store in his father's name he had lived "in Hallisa on the hill, then in Beersheba, then father said come to the store in Wadi Salib." At first he had lived in the storeroom, now he lived in one room of the store."[124] Jacob Friedler, a journalist on the *Jerusalem Post*, had lived for some six years in a room near Wadi Salib after immigrating with his father from England in 1949.[125] His father had been housed in the room by the Haganah. Now Friedler had come to cover the events in Wadi Salib and heard from the residents that "there are many people who wish to leave, but it happens that the apartments they paid for are no longer worth the money they invested two or three years ago." On this matter, so it became clear, there were ethnic differences: many of the Romanian immigrants had left,[126] as had Jews from other European countries, "because they argued with one another." Those of Moroccan origin, on the other hand, found it difficult to ameliorate their living conditions. "Many of them, when they moved apartments or were given apartments," the journalist told the commission of inquiry, "did not inform the authorities, and they are without contracts and have not paid the housing fee, there are people who have been without a contract for many years." "And is this still so?" asked the commission chairman in surprise. "On more than one occasion they issued an eviction order but did not implement it," explained the journalist.

"He who wishes to comprehend how . . . the land laws in Israel came into being," writes Menahem Hoffnung, "must go back and examine the situation created during the fighting and thereafter."[127] This general assertion certainly applies to the residents of Wadi Salib, who all lived in abandoned Palestinian property. The precarious legal basis on which their relations with the Development Authority rested had its origins in the property arrangements created by Israel in the wake of the 1948 war. The political aim of these arrangements was to facilitate exploitation of Arab property for purposes of Jewish settlement by placing the buildings at the disposal of immigrants while at the same time precluding the return of the Palestinian refugees.[128] Emergency regulations, already issued on June 23, 1948, obligated anyone in possession of an abandoned property to register it with the police.[129] These regulations were replaced in December of that year by Emergency Regulations Regarding the Seizure of Property, signed into law by the finance minister at the time, Eliezer Kaplan.[130] This new definition — "absentees' property" — had greater validity than the previous definition — abandoned property. On the initiative of Zalman Lifshitz (also known as Zalman Lif), a cartographic engineer who worked as chief land valuator for the JNF and served as the prime minister's adviser on border demarcation, the provisional regulations became permanent when Israel passed the Absentees' Property Law in March 1950 as well as a law enabling transfer of such property to the Development Authority in July of the same year.

The Israeli legislation somewhat resembles laws enacted in Turkey, Greece, Bulgaria, and Czechoslovakia, and, as far as the Development Authority is concerned, it is closest to the Pakistani model. It facilitated seizure of abandoned property and its utilization for the benefit of the state and the refugees who took sanctuary in it.[131] In passing, we may note that one of the first to find particular interest in the Indo-Pakistani precedent was our acquaintance Schechtman (see chapter 1). In the summer of 1950 he approached the Israeli Foreign Ministry with a request for financial assistance to travel to India for research. Despite the considerable interest shown by the Foreign Ministry "in this issue of exchange of populations" and its belief that Schechtman's study "is likely to benefit not only scientific research—no small matter in itself—but also the affairs of state," his application for funding was turned down.[132] Interest in the Indo-Pakistani precedent grew over time, and the matter of Schechtman's trip gained impetus following intervention on the part of Foreign Minister Moshe Sharett.[133] One small issue still needed to be resolved: Schechtman was a member of the Revisionist movement, which had been expelled from the Jewish Agency. At this point, Nahum Goldmann, the founder and longtime president of the World Jewish Congress as well as, since 1951, the chairman of the Executive Committee of the Jewish Agency, intervened, proposing that Schechtman be allowed to continue his research on the Palestinian refugee matter and issues of population exchange.[134] He would have done so in any event, but as a private individual he needed financial support. It appears that the trip was arranged during the spring of 1951. Abba Eban, Israel's ambassador to the United Nations at the time, was most impressed by the results of Schechtman's research and realized its importance in providing a precedent: "It throws new light on our own problem with regard to treatment of refugee property. It is amusing to rely on the Pakistan proposal for a custodian of Arab refugee property in Israel," he wrote.[135]

To return to our topic: unlike the emergency regulations, the new law required the approval of the Knesset. An attempt was still made at the time to disguise the fact that the law would facilitate the sale of the properties. Eliezer Kaplan, who represented the law under discussion in his capacity as finance minister, claimed that its primary purpose was to create a custodianship for the properties, while the justice minister, Pinhas Rozen, likewise noted the obligation of trusteeship toward the absentees.[136] The fact that the mission of the Development Authority was to transfer abandoned Arab property to Jewish ownership was likewise disguised, and the impression was created that the authority would be responsible for the general development of the country.

An "absentee" is, according to the law, any owner of property who was, after November 29, 1947, a citizen of one of the seven Arab states that fought against Israel, who resided in one of these countries, or who left his regular place of residence in Israel to travel abroad or to any other place that was at the time held by hostile forces. The formulation of the law in general terms while avoiding the use of religious or national categories served to disguise its discriminatory nature. The law empowered the "Custodian of Absentees' Property" to safeguard and administer the property and to evict illegal tenants who had occupied it. A stringent clause transferred the onus of proof from the custodian to the absentee, who was required to provide evidence if he wished to appeal against his categorization as such.[137] Since the definitions of the law declared all the Arab refugees who had left their places of residence during the war to be absentees, the law sent a clear signal and contained an unequivocal political declaration aimed at the refugees to the effect that their property would not be automatically returned to them even if they found a way of returning to Israel. A variety of those in liberal circles, among them the above-mentioned General Zionist Knesset member Jaacov Klebanoff, expressed their reservations about the new regulations. Klebanoff noted, critically: "We are not dealing with enemy property, but with the property of a substantial part of the population of our country, who have and must have very important rights—people who can come to us with very serious claims, financial and moral. We can not treat their property as enemy property."[138] These voices proved unable to prevent the passing of the legislation.

The absentees' property law prohibited its sale, but this stipulation contained a crucial exception: it was permissible to transfer the absentees' property to a "development authority," which, the law stipulated, would be established by a law of the Knesset. In 1950 the Development Authority (Transfer of Property) Law was promulgated, and in September 1953 an agreement was concluded whereby the property was transferred from the custodian of absentees' property to the Development Authority.[139] A total of sixty-nine thousand apartments, houses, and businesses were transferred under this agreement.[140] From this moment onward, owners of properties were given no opportunity to reclaim them, but only to negotiate their worth.[141] This process of negotiation applied only to a small proportion of all the "absentees," those known as "present absentees," namely, absentees according to the legal definition who had legally returned to live in the State of Israel.[142] A law passed in 1973 replaced the principle of negotiated calculation with the principle of compensation, which was restricted to Israeli citizens only and given in the form of government bonds with a fifteen-year maturation date linked to the cost of living index. Geremy Forman and Sandy Kedar note that since Arab Israeli citizens—like the Israeli authorities—regarded compensation as a legal and moral recognition on their part of their disinheritance, many of them refused to apply for it.[143] As this stance was modified over the years, the number of applications for compensation rose.

Examining the way in which Israeli legislation navigates between the rule of law and state security, Hoffnung notes in his book: "The seizure of land in the fifties performed in the name of protection of the State of Israel's external security contributed to the creation of internal security problems in the seventies. Disregard for the basic principles of the rule of law created a feeling that the law was not an instrument for the regulation of property relations in an egalitarian society but rather an instrument for achieving political-national objectives within a struggle between communities."[144] Hoffnung refers here to the events of the Land Day Protest of 1976 and the escalation of Jewish-Palestinian tension in Israel regarding the policy of land expropriation. His words, however, have a validity that transcends the issue of the Jewish-Palestinian dispute and touch on intra-Jewish relationships. The Jewish residents of Wadi Salib likewise sensed that they had suffered an injustice in the matter of regulation of property relations and that this had been done under cover of the law. This feeling was exacerbated by their ongoing relations with the Development Authority.

Virtually all the dwellings in Wadi Salib were administered by the Development Authority.[145] In the Wadi, it registered 394 buildings containing 1,754 apartments that accommodated 2,864 families. The overcrowding in some cases was very severe, and, before the commission of inquiry, the director of the Development Authority's housing department noted that in Wadi Salib "six people and more were living in a single room—6–7 people in two rooms," and even 21 people in one room or 33 people in two rooms; 1,216 of the apartments contained tenants who had "entered OK, pay OK," while those in the remaining 538 apartments had entered and were residing there without a contract. Among the invaders, that is to say, occupants without a contract, were 110 of European origin and some 428 from other countries. The Development Authority claimed that it lacked an effective mechanism of law enforcement in dealing with the "invaders"—those who refused to pay rent or "key money." "So what do we see," complained the director of the Development Authority's housing department before the commission, "the person invaded, we take him to court and are given an order and then we invite the person once, twice, and three times, and when he fails to turn up we invite him for a fourth time and thus in the meantime one year passes, a year and a half . . ." In the case of tenants suffering particular deprivation, he asserted, there had not been one instance in eleven years in which the eviction order had been carried out. The chairman of the commission of inquiry was apparently impressed by the description and his healthy logic prompted an ingenuous question: "You have 500 invaders, according to our definition, and they have lived here for years already; has the time not come to give de jure recognition to a de facto situation since this is known to be a social welfare issue?" His question remained unanswered.

The contradiction between issues of social welfare and the efficient administration of abandoned property was inherent in the transition from an immigrant absorption economy to an orderly economy. This situation, explained the director of the Development Authority's housing department, "requires income, necessitates repairs, and there are repairs for which the law requires them and us to be partners, 45 to 50 percent." The Development Authority did not always honor its commitments. Not only "invaders" but also law-abiding tenants failed to receive adequate maintenance of the property. The Development Authority claimed in its defense that one-third of the families living in Wadi Salib had entered illegally and did not pay rent as required, thereby indirectly explaining the maintenance difficulties. But, in fact, the whole of Wadi Salib suffered from inadequate maintenance, including those tenants who regularly paid their rent to the authority. The issue of poor maintenance of abandoned property had already arisen in the early 1950s. As a result of the hasty population of the apartments in 1948 the properties were totally incompatible with the needs of the new residents. The office for the preparation of an urban master plan reported thus: "On each floor of the large Arab building characteristic of this area, in each building surrounded by a typical large Arab courtyard, in virtually every room a family containing two to eight members was accommodated, although there was only one toilet unit that had to suffice."[146] The town planner attempted to draw the mayor's attention to the tenants' terrible distress: "While the most primitive immigrants empty their bedpans directly onto the street or courtyard and go without a shower, other immigrants suffer badly subjectively from the lack of sanitation." While the legal adviser to the Health Ministry did indeed believe that the custodian of absentees' property could be criminally indicted in this matter,[147] the law stipulated that the custodian was permitted—in other words, not obliged—to go to the necessary expense of guarding, maintaining, and repairing the property it held. When the municipality took measures to preserve the properties, the custodian was obliged to reimburse its expenses only if the assets of the absentee held by the custodian were sufficient for this purpose. This was difficult if not impossible to prove. However this may be, the municipality's sanitation department complained of having to install toilets in apartments unfit for habitation, for which no contracts were drawn up and that yielded no income.[148]

Throughout the discussion held by the Public Commission of Inquiry Into the Events of Wadi Salib, no mention was made of the simple fact that the State of Israel and, for our purposes, the Development Authority had in a way gained an undeserved windfall upon receiving the abandoned Arab property for its use. The Development Authority's formalistic argument regarding the link between the neglect of properties and the nonregulation of ownership relations contained an internal contradiction. The formal contention regarding property presented by the Development Authority to the commission of inquiry did not accord with the precarious legal situation pertaining to the regulation of absentee property. Amid the general silence, a lone voice to raise the matter was that of Deputy Mayor Zvi Barzilay, who complained to the commission's members: "The Development Authority, the institution acting as the custodian of absentee property on behalf of the state, is accumulating rent for housing to be paid to the absentees when peace arrives. Since the establishment of the state, the Development Authority has collected some 10 million liras in rent in Haifa. . . . The institution must invest this sum in renewing the downtown area. The institution should not invoke the name of development in vain."[149]

Selectivity

The Development Authority, and the discriminatory principles it applied to the distribution of abandoned property, was but one of the factors that marked Ben-Harush's inferior starting point in the housing market. His grievances did not end there, and he raised others that proved yet more painful: "I propose checking also the immigration cards, what the Moroccan immigrant received and what the European immigrant received, and they, after all, are supported by all kinds of organizations in America and others, and some are also assisted by the reparations from Germany, and we have no source of help whatsoever. I too wish to move to a project; if I have a good apartment I can pass it on for key money, but if I live in a hovel I cannot pass it on."[150] Ben-Harush's grievance regarding preferential treatment of those of European origin in the matter of housing was not without grounds and was in any case echoed by Ben-Gurion, who did not reject the notion that "there was one instance of discrimination, which may or may not have been justified."[151] He was referring here directly to Israel's special effort to bring to the country the remnants of Polish Jewry by exploiting the window of opportunity afforded by Stalin's death and the assumption of power by Wladyslaw Gomulka in Poland. "It is possible that things were indeed done then that cannot be justified," admitted Ben-Gurion. "There were Jews who had remained in transit camps for as long as three to four years and who deserved a home; they were not given a home, and homes were given to Poles who had arrived a month or two previously. This action aroused great bitterness among the transit camp residents; and this bitterness is justified." Given the inability to resolve the dilemma of whether to grant precedence in order to save the remnants of Poland's Jews or to care for the transit camp residents, Ben-Gurion did not deny the fact that "generally there is no justification for such a thing, giving a home to a Pole who arrived a month ago and not giving a home to the immigrant who came from Egypt or from Turkey four years ago. This has no justification at all." The solution he proposed at that moment, as he forcibly asserted that "we must make an effort so that the transit camp residents will also receive homes and we shall be able to absorb the Jews arriving from communist lands, not at the expense of the transit camps," was altogether too simplistic. Given the limited means available, this was, of course, pure rhetoric, particularly since, throughout the 1950s, Israel granted European immigrants preferential conditions in comparison to those from Morocco.[152]

The negative collective images associated with the Moroccan immigrants were in fact formed already during the first wave of illegal immigration in 1947 owing to the impression made by the poor families with multiple children, most of whom hailed from the margins of the mellahs in the large cities,[153] and by the immigrants who came from the seam between the "native sector" and those undergoing Westernization.[154] The negative stereotype of this group of immigrants that evolved was strengthened in the illegal immigrant camps in Cyprus against a background of alienation and friction, as emerged from the evidence given by Ben-Harush, who had been interned there, before the commission of inquiry. In the face of these impressions, voices were already heard in 1948 calling for a reconsideration of the perception that anyone wishing to immigrate should be accepted. This approach very soon became obsolete and was replaced by another that favored the establishment of a queue for immigration.[155] From here it was but a short step to placing the Western Jews at the head of the queue as well as enforcing a careful and rigid policy of selection on the candidates for immigration from Morocco, one that had not been applied to Jewish immigrants from Europe.[156] Israel began delaying the immigration of Moroccan Jews at a very early stage. In November 1951 thirty-five thousand candidates for immigration remained in Casablanca alone, of whom fifteen thousand had already received exit visas from the authorities. When the Immigration Institution was closed down and its functions transferred to the Jewish Agency's immigration department, there remained sixty-two thousand registered applicants awaiting immigration.[157] With this, Israel began to depart from the exceptional migration policy that had characterized its early years, with no immigration quotas and virtually no restrictions.[158] The national interest, writes Yaron Tsur, was beset by an internal contradiction between the wish to rein in the less than desirable immigration in the short term and the aspiration to continue imbuing people with the Zionist spirit so as to preserve the reservoir of potential migration for a later stage.

From the outset, the migration of the Jews from Morocco took place under the shadow of the apprehension that Morocco would, upon gaining independence, join the Arab League—which it did in 1958—and then adopt a position hostile to Jewish emigration. Over the ensuing years, the Jews living in Morocco found themselves trapped in an intermediate position between nationalist Arab aspirations for independence and French colonial interests in maintaining the current order in Morocco.[159] While the elderly and the more established among them tended toward French rule, there were indications of support among the young generation for the Arabs' aspirations to independence. But both these groups were well aware of the restrictions and risks lying in wait for the Jewish side in any step taken toward overt political involvement. From 1955, amid indications that independence would be achieved in the foreseeable future, the Jews of Morocco concentrated their effort on attempting to forge links with the leading forces in the Moroccan national struggle to safeguard their liberty and security in the future sovereign Morocco.[160] In continuing these efforts, the official representatives of Moroccan Jewry began officially and openly to support the cause of Moroccan independence. They very likely had no alternative, but derived little benefit from these inevitable processes.

As the date of Morocco's independence drew nearer, an increasing number of Jews both there and in Tunisia applied for migration, with the number reaching seventy thousand in 1955.[161] International bodies began to show some interest in the issue. The chairman of the United States congressional subcommittee on migration, Francis Walter, approached Secretary of State John Foster Dulles in September 1955 to suggest that the U.S. delegation try to convince the Intergovernmental Committee for European Migration (ICEM) to provide financial support for the absorption of Moroccan Jews in Israel.[162] Walter justified his initiative by claiming that the Jews of French Morocco were entitled to the status of refugees. Since they were fleeing out of fear of persecution on racial and religious grounds, these migrants were no different than refugees fleeing from communist persecution and were thus deserving of international support and aid, he maintained. Official Israeli historiography asserts that Israel made great efforts to bring its sons back home,[163] but it appears that this version of events has no solid basis in fact. Israel rejected and ignored the fears expressed by official representatives of Moroccan Jewry that Morocco's independence was likely to herald a change in its policy toward migration and to lead to a "closing of the gates." For this reason, migration from Morocco was not recognized as "salvation migration," and its scope was subordinated to external considerations, such as Israel's economic capacity to absorb it. In addition to the limited interest shown by the Knesset in the fate of Morocco's Jews, the state and the Jewish Agency put into practice a highly selective migration policy for these candidates for migration, placed many obstacles in their path, subjected them to criteria that were not applied in other countries, and delayed their exit.[164]

One may well imagine the frustration felt by the Moroccan immigrants in Israel in the face of the delay in the immigration of their relatives.[165] They began to demonstrate in a number of cities in an attempt to bring the plight of their relatives to public attention. In August 1955, nine hundred North

African Jews marched in Jerusalem from Hanevi'im Street, along King George Street, to the Jewish Agency building. Their representatives—the Emergency Council for the Salvation of North African Jewry—met with the agency's leadership and submitted to the Zionist executive a demand for the unification of families in the coming months, abolition of the selection applied to immigration, as well as initiation of a salvation immigration by sea and air in the immediate future. They proposed to finance this immigration by means of an emergency appeal in Israel and the Diaspora and through a special salvation tax to be levied in Israel, which would be rescinded once the North African Diaspora had been eliminated.[166] A demonstration was also held in Haifa, albeit on a smaller scale than the one in Jerusalem. The demonstrators broke into the Jewish Agency's offices in the city and smashed windows.[167] While Morocco did not officially rescind the theoretical right to migration upon gaining independence, it evicted the Zionist bodies handling immigration from its territory and began rejecting applications for migration by bureaucratic means.[168] The number of migration visas issued to Jews dropped from 36,301 in 1956 to 8,758 in 1957 and to 1,803 in 1958.[169] Tens of thousands of Morocco's Jews were no longer able to migrate legally, with some attempting to do so covertly.[170] In the background, their relatives in Israel remained powerless, unable to afford them any assistance.

"Imagine That Some Among Those of European Origin Lived in Luxurious Apartments"

When Ben-Harush raised the issue of the preferential economic status enjoyed by those of European origin, he did so against the backdrop of the cumulative frustration felt by Moroccan immigrants toward Israel's selective migration policy. But, at the same time, his remark touched a particularly raw nerve in Israeli society that went far beyond the question of housing and social conditions. Ben-Harush was treading here on a taboo, judging by the sharp and immediate reaction his words drew from Klebanoff as a member of the commission of inquiry. From aggressive questioning, the latter proceeded to a cross-examination. Ben-Harush managed to assert: "Now there came new immigrants from Europe, and they were all accommodated in more humane housing projects or buildings." One may wonder why this assertion should have aroused Klebanoff's anger, but he in fact lost his self-control. "Where did you live in Morocco?" he asked Ben-Harush. "In Casablanca," he replied. "In what type of building?" "In a fairly decent building." "How many rooms?" continued Klebanoff. "The four of us, father, mother, my sister, and I lived in one and a half rooms. But a room there is a room. I didn't say that I was a rich man in Morocco." At this point Klebanoff chose to put matters straight, commenting: "Imagine that some among those of European origin lived in luxurious apartments."

Klebanoff's annoying and abrupt comment presented a hierarchy of rights and entitlements as if this were a matter of natural justice that required no proof. It was not Ben-Harush the individual, but those of Asian and African origin in general—in short, those who were not of European origin—who were required to recognize and accept this hierarchy without dissent. Klebanoff's statement reverberated through the room without provoking any discussion, as if it were an axiom. Under these circumstances, any counterargument would have been interpreted as blasphemy. The overt text indicated that those of European origin deserved more because they had had more. The latent text suggested something else: not only because they had had more, but because they had been deprived of more. Klebanoff was comparing not merely the Europeans' superior material past with that of those hailing from Asia and Africa but also their superior moral position derived from their status as victims of Nazism.

And indeed to this day, sixty-five years after the Holocaust, this is still perceived as the absolute standard by which the severity of historical injustices is to be assessed.[171] The Holocaust of European Jews is not perceived as a local occurrence, having only limited relevance to the European-Atlantic axis, but as a cornerstone of global "catastrophe awareness," a standard by which those living in the present are required to think of the past.[172] The ongoing international discussion on issues of compensation for historical injustices over the past two decades, that is, since the end of the cold war in 1989 and the creation of a new context for the airing of historical claims for restitution that were neutralized throughout that period, has acquired an additional aspect that could not have existed in the 1950s. Just as the Holocaust has become the yardstick for dealing with past crimes, the compensation granted to the victims of the Holocaust is becoming a model of precedent for claims to compensation for all historic injustices. Reparations and compensation that Germany has paid and continues to pay the victims of the Holocaust since 1952 through international Jewish organizations and the State of Israel are perceived as the event that inaugurated a paradigm that has general validity for processes of recognition of historical responsibility, compensation, and reconciliation wherever they may occur.[173]

The paradigmatic significance assumed by the reparations and compensation is viewed with dismay by some historians. They fail to discern any element of historic greatness in this cold, calculating, bureaucratic act of bargaining.[174] And it is indeed difficult to regard their net worth, seen through the lens of their pedantic, bureaucratic, and punctilious implementation, as a shining example of humanity. It is for this reason that the intellectual discussion is beset by the constant tension between two fundamental approaches: a skeptical approach, expressed by historians whose expertise lies in the minute reconstruction of the fiscal aspects of the reparation agreements, as opposed to the approach taken by those focusing on the wider significance, who stress mainly the unintended, indirect, and generally positive consequences of these same processes. Among the latter one finds, for example, Elazar Barkan, who developed the concept of "neo-Enlightenment,"[175] and others such as the historian Charles Maier, who has noted that "reaching agreement must in effect desacralize the loss no matter what the protest of the victims or survivors. That is precisely the point of the exercise: to remove the losses from the realm of the sacred, the never to be forgiven, into the realm of the politically negotiated. . . . The hitherto opposed parties—perpetrators and victims—are reaching across the gulf of historical hatred to resume a dialogue that will allow them to live together under some overarching rules of comity and coexistence."[176] Before linking these theoretical approaches to Ben-Harush's assertions, let us return for a moment to the events of Wadi Salib. The Wadi Salib demonstrators did not stop at expressing their grievance against a police force that shoots an unarmed drunkard. Among the various slogans aired during the first demonstration, held soon after the shots, was one whose connection to the event was altogether unclear. "They're selling arms to the Germans!" shouted the demonstrators. And indeed, from 1957 to 1959, as an offshoot of the cooperation on security matters between Israel and Germany, arms deals were concluded between the two countries that included the purchase of German submarines by Israel and the purchase of artillery shells by Germany. A superficial interpretation may see the demonstrators' slogans as additional evidence that the Herut movement was behind the riots in Wadi

Salib and had inflamed passions. This political party was well known for its absolute rejection of the reparation agreement with Germany. Precisely toward the late 1950s, however, against the backdrop of the arms deals, it transpired that Herut was beginning to lose interest in the Israeli-German issue and had removed it from its public agenda. As Shimshon Unichman, a Herut member of Knesset, wrote: "In its time the war against Germany was sacred. However, once the Knesset endorsed reparations, and there was no longer any hope that the Germans would not pay up, the war became superfluous. Even were we to achieve a great victory in the next Knesset, we would not be able to form a coalition if we wanted to give up reparations since public opinion is against this. And every prime minister, including Menahem [Begin], will be obliged to receive special armaments from Germany as well, if others do not want to give them."[177]

Feelings of resentment are not updated from day to day, and the Wadi Salib demonstrators probably had little reason to monitor Herut's position regarding Germany on an ongoing basis. It is indeed quite possible that they continued to adhere to attitudes to which they had been exposed for many years. But their position on this matter may well have been motivated by different factors unrelated to the platform of any political party.

Had Ben-Harush been able to peruse the data accumulated by the Bank of Israel, these would have revealed to him facts to which he had reacted intuitively. The bank's data showed that in 1959 one in ten of all urban Jewish families had received a one-off individual compensation payment from Germany.[178] In addition, approximately 1 percent of families received recurring compensation in the form of a pension or *rente* in 1958. Up to the beginning of 1959, one-off compensation had reached some fifty-one thousand families. One in every six families of European origin living in Israel received some kind of compensation from Germany. In the mid-1960s, only a few years after the events of Wadi Salib, compensation payments swelled the annual disposable income of its recipients by over 40 percent. These were large sums by any standard, and they initially flowed into the savings of the Holocaust survivors. Shortly afterward, some two years after receipt of the individual compensation, to be precise, only one-third remained as liquid savings, and in the long term only one-fifth of the sum, linked to foreign currency, remained in this form. The bulk of the money went toward consumption. A survey conducted by the Bank of Israel on the effect of individual compensation payments on consumption and savings in Israel revealed that "some two to three years after receipt of the compensation over sixty percent of it is invested in real estate and virtually none remains in the form of liquid assets."[179] Ben-Harush did not err in identifying the compensation from Germany as a decisive point on the way to accumulating real estate in Israel. Research conducted within the framework of the Bank of Israel in the late 1960s revealed that in the first decade of the flow of individual compensation payments they led to a growth of 25 percent in the physical property of the recipient families, that is, apartments, home appliances, and motor vehicles, and to a trebling of the financial assets of these families.

Ownership of assets—first and foremost, ownership of real estate—is a key to socioeconomic status in many places, and particularly in Israel, where real estate prices soared in the 1950s. Apart from the psychological significance and emotional security afforded by property, real estate has obvious economic worth that turns its ownership into a clear sign of social stratification.[180] We should note here the ostensibly self-evident fact that an apartment is a sustainable asset. Furthermore, wealth accumulated in housing is the main if not exclusive component of family property among most families. Housing is likewise a major component of the total intergenerational transfer of family wealth and as such is a decisive factor in the prospects for well-being and success of the next generation. Regarding the Israeli case, Ben-Harush pointed out two elements, seniority of residence and ethnic origin, as factors that have shaped the Israeli housing market. Nowadays there is general consensus as to the existence of an ethnic disparity in this market as well as to the weight of seniority in the housing market, although the issue of relations between all the components that have created this disparity in Israel remains a contentious topic.[181] At the end of the 1950s, Israel was experiencing a housing boom. Those who succeeded in acquiring quality real estate in the urban centers thereby ensured the economic future of the succeeding generations. Individual compensation, without doubt, served to widen the ethnic divide in Israel by enabling Jews of European origin to purchase high-quality property during the decisive years. This conclusion does not, of course, apply to those who refused on principle to accept compensation payments, those whose application for compensation was incorrectly processed for technical reasons, and those who were ineligible on grounds of mental health.

Ben-Harush's assertion that the compensation paid by Germany constituted a component in the disparity between Ashkenazim and Mizrahim was certainly true at the material level. But his argument was also valid at the symbolic level, and it was perhaps just this that aroused Klebanoff's ire. The commission of inquiry, so it sometimes seems, refused to recognize that the social and economic status of a certain number of the North African immigrants had declined following their immigration. The notion that they too, just like some of the Western Jewish immigrants, had not only immigrated—"ascended," according to the Zionist vocabulary—but had also descended, that is, had lost property and seen their professional status decline upon being uprooted from their homes in Morocco, was at the time rejected out of hand. When another witness told the commission that prior to immigration he had been "a jeweler to the sultan of Morocco in his palace," and added that "I can tell you that the amount of silver and gold that we handled was greater than the number of potatoes in the Talpiot market," Judge Etzioni hastened to correct him, saying, "but the only thing is that these did not belong to you."[182] Those of Moroccan origin, to use a concept developed by Elazar Barkan in a comparative discussion on compensation, reconciliation, and return, were perceived as "unworthy victims," a category he uses to describe groups whose victimization is not at issue, but who for various reasons are not found worthy of recognition and empathy. Barkan was speaking of victims who were found to be unworthy because they are regarded as bearing some responsibility for the events that turned them into victims.[183] The Jews of Morocco, I shall contend, were found in these historical circumstances to be "less deserving" than those who, because of the terrible suffering they had endured, were more deserving.

The discussions of the past two decades have refined our analytic tools, and through them we are able to discern the material and symbolic significance of compensatory processes within the fabric of Israeli life. They allow us, as well, to appreciate the way in which the reparation agreement and bilateral Israeli-German relations nourished the sentiment of discrimination among the residents of Wadi Salib. And indeed, in retrospect—and without detracting in the slightest from the recognition of the pain and suffering experienced by the Holocaust survivors—one may contend that the return of property and the partial compensation that some of them received in Israel encompassed a dual rehabilitation: within the context of the relation between victim and perpetrator, return of the property signified retroactive recognition of their identity and rights. Every process of compensation is founded upon an account of history. Even though the perpetrator and his victim may not necessarily agree upon the overall version of history, compensation is conditional upon the perpetrator's willingness to accept his responsibility. This retroactive recognition has a dual effect: it restores to the victim his status among his erstwhile torturers, while at the same time establishing his status in the country of refuge. Material compensation endows the victim with a kind of "dual citizenship": it restores to him his civil membership in the country of the perpetrators and reflects on the status of the migrant as a refugee in his new land.

The refugee who receives compensation does not represent the common historical case. The twentieth century has accustomed us to viewing the plight of the refugee as a static situation or, as Liisa Malkki puts it in her research, to seeing the refugee as someone who exists outside the cosmological order of things.[184] People of European origin have to some extent enjoyed a special status within the state of Israel, even before the Eichmann trial shook Israeli consciousness, since the compensatory processes afforded them a symbolic rehabilitation.[185] "Imagine that some among those of European origin lived in luxurious apartments," was how Klebanoff confronted Ben-Harush. And it was indeed easy to imagine this. It was these compensatory processes that retroactively certified the world of yesteryear. This did not happen in the case of the Jews who came from Arab countries. Their bygone world remained shrouded in doubt. One doubts that Klebanoff was able to envision Ben-Harush's large room in Casablanca. At this stage Ben-Harush could provide no evidence of this. And thus, without accreditation, Ben-Harush was nothing but a resident of the Wadi Salib neighborhood of Haifa, an abandoned Muslim quarter lying at the foot of Mount Carmel, downtown near the port.

3. Evacuation

City Lights

THE MOROCCAN IMMIGRANTS SETTLED IN THE ABANDONED ARAB properties of Wadi Salib in two waves. The first reached the neighborhood directly from the immigrant camps toward the end of 1948. This was in part a spontaneous initiative by the immigrants themselves. Reacting to the severe hardships in the immigrant camps, they went in search of improvised housing solutions with the support of the authorities. Neighborhoods similar to Wadi Salib were settled at the time, such as the "large area" in Jaffa, the Sahneh in Lod, and the Salameh neighborhood near Tel Aviv.[1] The second wave arrived in a roundabout manner when the immigrants chose to abandon the settlements to which they had been directed through Israel's population dispersal plan of the early 1950s. The later arrivals were obliged to make do with lower-quality accommodation, generally in dilapidated structures and cellars, since the better dwellings had already been occupied or settled in 1948. This later population in abandoned property was not the result of prior planning. Whereas in 1948 it had taken place through the immigrants' own initiative, to which settlement authorities lent their support, in the early 1950s this activity did not accord with the authorities' intentions and, indeed, subverted them. "The place attracted [them]," is how an early apologetic version described this chapter of history in a book published in honor of Abba Khoushy, Haifa's mayor. The book's authors attributed the late influx to Wadi Salib to its convenient geographic location, only a few minutes from Herzl Street, close to the downtown commercial centers and the port. But it was also the properties' ambivalent legal status that initially had its advantages. Dwellings could be passed from one person to another without having to obtain the authorization of the Development Authority, which refused to take rent from the new residents so as to deny them any rights as tenants so long as it had not received its part of the "key money." Property tax was also not paid in full, particularly in the case of welfare-supported families.[2]

The influx of Moroccan immigrants from the rural immigrant settlements to the "abandoned property," from village to city, was, in a way, a rehearsal, a second round, a repeat broadcast. The migration of Morocco's Jews involved several processes unnoticed by the later view that concentrated solely on the transition from Morocco to Israel. In reality, for many of the migrants, the transition to Israel was preceded by an internal migration in their country of origin, a process that would repeat itself as they settled down in the new country. The process of internal migration from village to city was a sign of the times in post–World War II Morocco. The population of Casablanca, for example, grew from fifty thousand in 1912 to one million individuals in the early 1950s.[3] An identical phenomenon was reflected in the life of the city's Jewish community: in 1945 close to fifty-two thousand Jews resided in Casablanca, and a mere four years later, in 1949, their number had risen to sixty-three thousand.[4] Only one-third of the increase represented natural growth, while the remaining two-thirds stemmed from internal migration. A similar trend, albeit involving smaller numbers, was apparent in Marrakech, Rabat, Fez, and Meknes, and in a number of small communities in country towns and villages.[5] The Jews were an integral part of the rapid process of urbanization undergone by Morocco, with some 60 percent of them concentrated in the five largest cities: 25 percent of Moroccan Jews resided in around twenty medium-sized and other towns, and only 10 percent lived in rural areas.[6] The Jews comprised approximately 9 percent of Morocco's urban population, a figure almost four times greater than their proportion among the general population.[7] "Here too the large city attracts those living in the villages who come in search of an imaginary paradise and find only withering penury," wrote Feuerstein and Rishel,[8] a pair of Israeli scholars who traveled to the mellah in search of an explanation for the educational backwardness among the children of Moroccan immigrants in Israel. While the rapid process of urbanization in the mid-twentieth century was accompanied by a gradual exodus from the traditional Jewish quarters, around half of Moroccan Jews still lived in them. In Casablanca the number of Jewish residents of the mellah reached some twenty-five thousand.[9]

The size of the mellah was similar to that of an average Muslim neighborhood in a Moroccan city, but its population density was in some cases threefold and even fourfold that of the Moroccan lower-class quarters. The mellah functioned as an independent urban autarchic unit that supplied the residents' needs through markets and commerce. Small businesses were generally located on the street leading to the heart of the mellah and adjacent to it, while the residential alleys branched off further along. Some of the dwellings contained no more than one room; most lacked running water and were unconnected to the sewage system. Cooking was done outside the living room in the inner courtyard shared by several families.[10] There were those who found considerable charm in this way of life. Elias Canetti, the Jewish author of Bulgarian descent and refugee from Vienna living in London, wandered around the Marrakech mellah in 1954 in the company of English colleagues and could barely contain his excitement: "I had the feeling that I was really somewhere else now, that I had reached the goal of my journey. I did not want to leave; I had been here hundreds of years ago but I had forgotten and now it was all coming back to me. I found exhibited the same density and warmth of life as I feel in myself. I *was* the square as I stood in it. I believe I am it always."[11] Canetti's perspective was very different from that of others who were generally alarmed by what they saw. "The stench there will never leave my nostrils," recalled Myrtle Karp, an American active in the United Jewish Appeal, who paid a visit there, "children with shorn heads, and the trachoma illness in their eyes; to grasp that people were living thus, this was something that none of us had seen even in the slums of our cities," she recounted.[12] Seeking the roots of the distress experienced by Moroccan immigrants in Israel in the land of their origin, Feuerstein and Rishel naturally likewise surveyed the mellah from a viewpoint different than Canetti's and found there severe neglect.[13] They described their experience thus:

Eighty percent of the families live in a single room. . . . The illumination in the rooms is inadequate and they are without running water . . . a single toilet serves many families . . . the habits of modern hygiene are nonexistent here: they seldom wash—only so far as to comply with religious duty; kitchen utensils are kept in a dubious condition, and foodstuffs remain uncovered in the alleys covered in flies, including meat, the smell emanating from it providing reliable evidence as to its lack of freshness.

Bereft of any romantic notions of poverty, the two scholars asserted unequivocally: "Anyone who tours the mellah of the large cities will state unhesitatingly that there is only one means by which to correct this abject condition, namely, their complete demolition and the construction of new cities or new neighborhoods in their place."[14]

Such a proposal, however, took no account of the economic conditions prevailing in the country, which would have hampered any attempt to deal with the severe housing shortage.[15] Throughout the Second World War and the years thereafter, no building activity whatsoever had been undertaken in Morocco. Exacerbated by the high birthrate and internal migration, the shortage of housing and overcrowding remained unaddressed for many years. The condition of the Jewish residents of the mellah was one of the side effects of the colonial policy of urbanization. French settlements in the French colonial areas of control, in general, and the cities of northern Morocco, in particular, served as fertile ground for innovative modernist experiments in town planning.[16] These initiatives were directed primarily at serving the convenience of the French settlers, ignoring the local non-French population over a prolonged period. The slum areas on the margins of the European settlement went unnoticed by colonial urban planning. In the mid-1950s the Moroccan government did indeed decide to allocate budgets to public construction needs and to encourage private construction for the benefit of the mellah's residents. This initiative, however, was but a drop in the ocean: its restricted scope could not meet the growing needs, while its high cost dictated exorbitant rents. This program therefore provided a solution of sorts to the upper middle class and perpetuated the helplessness of the lower class.[17] Since there was no indication of any reform of Morocco's urbanization policy, which, in any case, went beyond the authors' brief, Feuerstein and Rishel vigorously asserted that "the only realistic solution is thus to empty the *mellah* through immigration to Israel."[18]

Did this assessment stem from naïveté? Was it just baseless rhetoric or did it merely betray ignorance? By that time the various arms of Israel's absorption establishment had unanimously formed a negative assessment of Morocco's Jewish city dwellers. This had begun to evolve against the backdrop of the smarting failure of the "youth immigration" operation of 1952.

When the young people mobilized by Yanni Avidov, the Jewish Agency emissary in Casablanca, went on the rampage in the intermediate staging post in Marseilles, Avidov was obliged to explain their behavior:

> Paris, France, these are magical words for all Moroccan youngsters; France stands at the pinnacle of all the aspirations of every Moroccan. Year after year every young person there dreams of the free life and happiness in this land. And perhaps their enthusiastic ambition to immigrate to Israel was in some way fired by the knowledge that on the way they would see France and stay over there, and upon arriving there they therefore suddenly unwound and it was difficult to restrain them and set them back on the right track.[19]

Yitshak Raphael, head of the Jewish Agency's immigration department, was likewise compelled to admit that "these are young people who have come here without parents and without relatives. They are without supervision. These youths are thrown on to the street. . . . They provide reinforcement to the youngsters roaming the markets, deal in theft and contribute to the underworld in the alleys of Jaffa and Haifa."[20] Those harboring general reservations about the immigration of Moroccan Jews were even more disturbed by what they saw in the mellah. Dr. Eliezer Matan, confidant of Dr. Haim Sheba, director general of the Health Ministry, and his representative in Casablanca, rejected plans to treat individual neighborhoods in the city for trachoma since he considered it to be a social disease, akin to alcoholism, which could not be cured under the present circumstances. For this reason he was in favor of concentrating solely on the villages and recommended delaying immigration from urban areas.[21] There were many who supported the position then gaining ground that explicitly favored the immigration of rural residents over that of the city dwellers.[22] In a letter to Ben-Gurion in March 1953, Ze'ev Haklai, director of the Jewish Agency's Casablanca office, noted that "the general condition of health [of the villagers] apart from trachoma and scalp ringworm, which are curable, is better than that of those living in the cities and ghettos."[23] Avidov made a similar assessment: "Those from the cities are ostensibly people of European culture in every respect, while those from the villages are virtually illiterate. . . . When you get to know them better you come to realize that those who appear to have absorbed culture superficially are no more than Levantine weaklings . . . bereft of any higher aspirations."[24] In the spirit of these assessments and observations, particularly stringent regulations were applied to city residents who showed interest in immigrating to Israel.[25] Nobody now had any intention of "emptying the mellah through immigration to Israel." Rural Jews lay at the heart of the immigration effort, and, if at all possible, the authorities preferred to relocate them as entire villages.

Population Distribution

The disaffection evinced by the Israeli establishment toward urban Moroccan Jews was in some respects a manifestation of its inherent antiurban sentiments. Pioneering Eastern European Zionism regarded the city as something inferior.[26] With the village at the center of their vision, the pioneers tended to regard urban Jewish existence as a cause of "Jewish pathology" and invested considerable effort in curbing the Jews' natural tendency toward the city.[27] Arthur Ruppin, for many years head of the Palestine Office of the Jewish National Fund, clearly expressed the deep duality that characterized the position of socialist Zionism toward urban life.[28] He regarded the influx of the Jews to the large cities of the Diaspora as the source of all the evils that had beset the Jewish people.[29] The transition to the large city had, in his opinion, enabled the Jew to cast off all restraint, indulge his desires, and free himself from the authority of the Jewish community. In direct contrast to the conservatism of the village and the town, urban permissiveness had, according to these viewpoints, paved the way to religious conversion and mixed marriages.[30] This ambivalence found particularly extreme expression within the social democracy taking shape in Haifa, a city with a strong Jewish working class and a well-developed socialist ethos. Abba Khoushy, who more than anyone else shaped the character of the city, first as leader of the Haifa Workers' Council and later as mayor, expressed his suspicions succinctly: "The Levantine Palestinian city," he wrote in 1925, "has begun to take over the burgeoning society, our soft public body is being eroded from within. The city sucks from us most of our strength so as to subdue it, to destroy it." He was particularly dismayed at the pioneers, who "dash our hopes, they prefer the city to the village, upon disembarking from the ship they remain in the city. It is more comfortable in the city, a high salary, many pleasures, cinema, opera, good clothes, the life of Europe, the city attracts. . . . They began to build a pyramid here, and instead of placing it on the foundation they place it on its head."[31]

In the prestate period, however, this antiurban ideology had failed to stem the influx of Jewish migrants to the city. In the years 1932–1935 the proportion of urban residents among the general population of Palestinian Jews reached around two-thirds. As in other colonial societies, the Jewish population of mandatory Palestine was mainly concentrated in the large cities. This concentration had begun under Ottoman rule and continued apace under the policy of the British Mandate.[32] Of the 650,000 Jews living in Israel in 1948, some 400,000, or 62 percent, resided in the three main urban centers: 225,000 in Tel Aviv and Jaffa, approximately 100,000 in Jerusalem, and around 75,000 in Haifa. The settlement institutions viewed this development with disfavor during the Mandate period, but they could do nothing to change it.[33] It was only the demographic and geopolitical consequences of the 1948 war that created new opportunities for regional planning.[34]

The planners and architects who worked under the auspices of the various government ministries were deeply influenced by the concepts of urban planning prevalent among their postwar European colleagues. Aspiring to a new spatial arrangement, underpinned by the idea of urban decentralization through the establishment of new small towns on the periphery, the adherents of these modernist European concepts sought to provide a solution to the severe shortage of residential space.[35] Despite grandiose plans for the establishment of seventy-two new towns, only thirty such towns were built during the State of Israel's first decade. In most cases, owing to economic and planning constraints they failed to achieve their principal purpose of serving as the basis for a social reordering within the framework of the Zionist productivization project.[36] Of the thirty towns, eleven were established around the core of a former Arab town while seven others were built in the vicinity of destroyed centers in the heart of the erstwhile Arab rural area. Only some ten towns were built from scratch. The constraints of location reflected in these numbers were compounded by a lack of planning. Owing to financial difficulties, no industrial centers were constructed alongside these new towns. As a result, their residents became a source of cheap urban labor, in places located close to established urban centers, or, under other circumstances, part of an unskilled, casual agricultural workforce.

The objective of decentralization likewise underpinned the idea of establishing the immigrant settlements. The legal apparatus for directing the settler-migrants to border areas followed the principles of population dispersal as laid out in the document titled *Physical Planning in Israel*.[37] By dividing the country into planning districts, the program drawn up by Arieh Sharon, head of the government's planning department in the years 1948–1952, sought to disperse the population and the immigrants throughout the land, "according to its economic, security and social needs," thereby reducing concentration of the population in the three large cities that had resulted from political and economic constraints during the Mandate period.[38] "Without such a policy," the document warned, "inevitable natural forces would, along the line of least resistance, lead the masses to the existing large centers and leave the [other] regions of the land without people and initiative."[39] A study of patterns of settlement and residence in other countries of migration in the "new world" indicated that migrants tend to gravitate to coastal cities. The Israeli planners were determined to counter this trend at all costs, even by resorting to coercion. The principles of the program devised by Arieh Sharon and his colleagues, as Zvi Efrat notes in documenting the influence of modernity on Israeli architecture, were applied with considerable tenacity, "even if at times they were inconsistent with professional discretion, even if they entirely failed the test of economic logic, even if they turned the 'melting pot' rhetoric against itself and created, in effect, severe geographic and social segregation between veteran residents and new immigrants."[40]

The document setting out the physical plan for Israel was in fact composed between the two immigration waves emanating from Morocco—the first between 1948 and 1951 and the second arriving mainly between 1954 and 1956 and directed for the most part toward agricultural settlement. The implementation of the program of population dispersal bore little resemblance to Sharon's proposal for a national plan.[41] The disparity between the program and its implementation stemmed from a variety of constraints as well as from the ambivalent attitude of the political leadership toward urban settlement. The aim of Israel's first government was to link the absorption of immigrants to the rapid and widespread distribution of settlements in sparsely populated areas, thereby preventing, as noted, an unwanted concentration of the population in the large cities. While the planners envisaged a regional plan and the establishment of urban settlements that would serve as the basis for the preparation of a national development program, the political leadership's vision was fixed, first and foremost, on rural settlement. Inspired by the European experience, the planners sought to establish a series of small towns, but these proposals deterred those attached to the governing pioneering ideology since they appeared to signal a return to the despised Eastern European Jewish town. The planners and the political echelon were likewise divided by their views regarding agricultural settlement. The former envisaged an integrated regional economic and social system based on a mixed agricultural and industrial economy. They presumed that this system would prove itself to be flexible, enabling town dwellers to be absorbed in the countryside at times of industrial crisis and, conversely, to allow villagers to find jobs in the towns during recessions in agriculture. This planning, however, disregarded the ideological predominance of the communal agricultural settlement and the importance attributed to self-reliant labor. The worldview of socialist Zionism rejected the notion of mobility between village and town and was even more opposed to hired labor in agriculture. For these reasons the principle of settlement dispersal as contained in the proposed plan was adopted in isolation from the plan's other principles, which were simply ignored.

Alongside the founding of the immigrant *moshavim* (*moshav* = semicollective agricultural settlement) in the spirit of the dispersal program, the Jewish Agency and the moshav movement hastily decided to settle some of the immigrants in abandoned Arab villages. This move was a bone of contention between the moshav movement and the kibbutz movement. Whereas the former encouraged and supported it, the kibbutzim regarded the phenomenon with a mixture of ideological misgiving and pure self-interest.[42] While coveting the lands of the abandoned villages, they claimed that "the way of life that has evolved in the abandoned villages lacks a healthy and constructive economic foundation, with the shop and the kiosk providing the sole panorama. . . . This is the way of life of the small Diaspora town (*shtetl*), without the charm of the Polish and Lithuanian town." "Before our eyes," they asserted, "the well-known *Katrielibka* materializes."[43] The image of the immigrants in the eyes of the settlement department of the Jewish Agency and the people of the kibbutz movement was probably not very different. It was the interests, the ideology, and the general perception of the situation that distinguished them. As head of the agency's settlement department, Ra'anan Weitz regarded the immigrants as potential settlers of the Galilee hill area and the Jerusalem corridor. Originating from countries with a backward economy and low standard of living, they would, he believed, become accustomed to the harsh living conditions in these areas. While this policy may have represented a hasty, albeit nonspontaneous effort to solve the pressing problems of the time, its guiding principles had been part of the arsenal of the settlement establishment for many years. It was Arthur Ruppin who had proposed an identical settlement formula on the eve of the First Word War when head of the Palestine office in Jaffa, some forty years before the migration from North Africa. Distinguishing between the needs of the Eastern European Jewish immigrant and those of his Oriental counterpart, he asserted unequivocally that the latter required different solutions since he was accustomed to a lower standard of living and to the climate and way of life of the Orient and because he married at a young age and would arrive in Palestine with a family. According to Ruppin, "The Oriental Jewish laborer is satisfied with a low wage, which he earns as a laborer . . . but he longs for the life of the city, where he can live among hundreds and thousands like him. For this reason, in the case of the Oriental Jew . . . we need to settle him immediately upon immigrating and to implant him in his place of work. This can be done most successfully by simply placing at his disposal a modest house with a garden plot, initially as rented accommodation and later against long-term payments."[44] The kibbutz representatives expressed reservations about such programs, attacking them on moral and social grounds. They regarded the program as an attempt to create "a class of farmers resembling the Arab *fellahs*, which will in the end lead the impoverished villagers to abandon their homes and gravitate to the margins of the large cities." One may cast doubt upon the purity of the motives behind these assertions. The kibbutz people had their eyes on part of the land and, in any case, were not overly concerned with the absorption effort. But the scenario of abandonment they portrayed did come to pass, to a degree, and when it occurred the settlement department proceeded to wage all-out war against it.

"Have You Any Idea of How We Jews Have Lived Here in the Land of Israel?"

"A most baffling saga," was how Ra'anan Weitz, director general of the Jewish Agency's Settlement Department, defined the North African immigrants' exodus from the settlements.[45] In the years between 1948 and 1958, he told the Public Commission of Inquiry Into the Events of Wadi Salib, the settlement department had founded 251 agricultural settlements for immigrants. These were intended to serve a triple function: the settling of Jews throughout the land and particularly in the border areas in which Israel's sovereignty was still disputed; absorption of immigrants; and the supply of agricultural produce to the local market.[46] It was thus not only part of the state's territorial and economic planning that was at stake but also "a process of socialization with a disciplinary dimension of the first magnitude."[47] Eighty-two, or one-third, of the total number of immigrant moshavim were entirely settled by North African immigrants.[48] "The mass immigration," notes Efrat, "was both the problem and the solution."[49] Directing them to the countryside was a preventive step, precisely because the political leadership assumed that they would be attracted to the city. As they were being directed to the countryside, some decided to abandon it in favor of the city.

The immigrants' internal migration and the decision on the part of hundreds of immigrant families to take their fate into their own hands, abandon the inadequate solutions provided by the state institutions, and seek their fortune in more promising parts encompassed all forms of settlement, both the improvised ones and the permanent solutions. In the autumn of 1951 hundreds of immigrants began to abandon the transit camps and, seeking accommodation in the vicinity of their places of work, to invade residential areas and crowd into other transit camps in the center of the country. Here they were joined by those who had chosen to abandon the immigrant settlements. The turning point occurred in the early 1950s not because of the numbers of those leaving the immigrant settlements, which were smaller than in previous periods, but because of the stand taken by the institutions regarding this phenomenon from this time onward.[50] Immigrants had already been designated for pioneering rural settlement in the years preceding the establishment of the state. Those reaching the city were people who had failed to adapt to the demands of the pioneering life, often in its socialist version.[51] But now the settlement institutions laid a heavier hand on them. From the early 1950s onward, the state settlement institutions looked askance at any attempt by the immigrants to free themselves from the pioneering mission assigned to them.[52] Their position on those infiltrating from the country to the city became firmer and on occasion vengeful. The importance of Israel's border region transcended its strategic-security advantages and touched the central nerve of the socialist Zionist vision. According to this Zionist doctrine, the "new man" was supposed to turn his back on the city. The refusal on the part of the migrant-settlers to accept the ruling of the settlement institutions thus challenged the entire antiurban Zionist perception. "The only thing they understand is to provide for their families; like the primitive city denizens they do all they can to achieve this," proclaimed a report by the Jewish Agency's Settlement Department critical of the settlers.[53] The settlement bodies showed little understanding of the migrants' tendency to prefer the exciting commotion of city life to life on the border. "The yearning for a worthless life and for conditions in which to put the women and children to work in service jobs or as hawkers," said Levi Eshkol in a Knesset debate on the desertion of immigrant settlements, "sometimes blinds the eyes of too many heads of family. I know that the lights of Tel-Aviv's suburbs lead astray and attract."[54]

Desertion of the countryside was perceived as a rebellion and as a phenomenon that threatened to thwart the population dispersal program. The Jewish Agency's response to the immigrants' initiative was therefore speedy and determined. In conjunction with the Interior Ministry, it decided to exert an "iron rule;" namely, to deprive those immigrants leaving the places of residence assigned to them in transit camps, labor villages, and immigrant settlements of housing, employment, and essential services.[55] In cooperation with the police, local authorities, and employment bureaus, the agency exerted social control over those leaving and meted out punishment to them, thereby creating moral panic around the issue. At first sanctions were applied against settlers who preferred "outside jobs" to agricultural work. There were, in fact, clear reasons for this preference. Many of the settlers had no agricultural background and in many cases were sent to settlements lacking an adequate basic infrastructure for making a living. Finding themselves chained to an agricultural smallholding that failed to provide a decent living, the settlers sought a way out of their financial hardship. They chose to make the relief works provided by the state their main source of income and complemented their livelihood with outside jobs on neighboring kibbutzim and in established villages and, in the mean time, neglecting their agricultural holdings. While these jobs did indeed improve their immediately parlous financial situation, they simultaneously turned them into a cheap source of unprotected labor. The state viewed this step as an act of heresy. In turning the border settlements into no more than a place of residence, the settlers were rejecting the settlement establishment's "productivization" framework, and it responded by initiating legislation designed to eradicate the phenomenon.

The Law of Candidates for Agricultural Settlement was passed by the Knesset on July 28, 1953.[56] The law's misleading title concealed the simple fact that its true function was to facilitate the evacuation of unsuitable settlers. It was intended to protect the settlement endeavor from the new settlers and assisted the state in protecting its property by failing to provide for any contractual obligation between the state and the settlers. The law enabled the state to evict from their home settlers who failed to meet any one of five conditions defining their commitment to an agricultural way of life. The law's draconian nature prompted considerable criticism, although it resulted in less than fifty prosecutions. More important than the actual sanction was the general threat of reprisals against any deviance from the agricultural way of life. The sanctions, however, did not end here, and those actually meted out to the settlers who decided to leave the settlements to which they had been sent were even more severe.[57] The repertoire included various practices ranging from the placing of impediments to outright punishment: coordination with transportation and haulage cooperatives that were required not to transport immigrant families without a special license issued by the Jewish Agency; withdrawal of or delay in transferring food coupons during the regime of austerity upon a change of address; active intervention on the part of the police in stopping the internal migration by setting up roadblocks; the requirement to hand over immigrant cards to agency counselors in the border settlements; collection of rental for the property and charging for use of agency property in cash for the entire period spanning the day of entry to the settlement and the day of departure; refusal to grant alternative public housing, and refusal to refer the migrants to places of employment through the labor bureaus.

The Public Commission of Inquiry Into the events of Wadi Salib was given a rather detailed description of the agency's absorption process. The "surprising" change in the methods of absorption, Kalman Levy, director of the Absorption Department of the Jewish Agency's Haifa and Northern District Office, told the commission, occurred at the onset of the large influx of immigration from North Africa.[58] "From ship to settlement," or "from ship to the development areas," the process was called, the practical expression of which was "from ship to waiting house, from ship to an admittedly temporary home, but a ready-made and orderly one."[59] The houses prepared in advance, "asbestos houses," or "tin structures attached to a house," but in all cases prefabricated houses, in some cases turned out to be "unsuited to certain families arriving with the North African immigration." "Possibly the immigrants didn't feel comfortable in them," noted Levy. "We took the approach," he explained to the commission, "that there is no longer a need to absorb like the large cities Haifa and Tel-Aviv." For this reason it was decided to send them "directly to the housing projects and jobs prepared in advance by the government." Explanations were provided already on the ship, where the classification was conducted. "There was full cooperation," he noted, "possibly in some cases due to a lack of knowledge." Now, as they underwent classification, they were registered with the health funds, and the dues for the first three months were paid for them. Dry provisions for eight days were also given to the new immigrant, "and with his luggage he boards the bus that transports him to his absorption location, and there a team of Jewish Agency employees awaits him and hands him the key to a dwelling." "Some rather meager furniture, a few kitchen utensils, a kerosene burner, cutlery," are provided with the house, "since we want the housewife to commence the housework immediately."

But not everything turned out as they had wished. "To our regret," related Mr. Levy, "some of the families . . . began infiltrating, leaving their homes and migrating to the large centers, where the cafes and cinemas enchant them and on the other hand also the livelihood and employment opportunities, and in this respect we are in a weak position" No great disparity was in fact found between the extent of the exodus among settlers in general and that among the North African settlers.[60] Overall, 31 percent of the immigrants failed to be absorbed in the immigrant settlements compared to 34 percent among the North African immigrants. "The difference is that in order to settle down elsewhere the North African immigrants require the assistance of the authorities," explained Ra'anan Weitz. He attributed the tendency to leave not to the economic conditions but rather to the local leadership in the settlements. He divided the North African settlers into three groups: those originating from villages, educated city dwellers, and uneducated city dwellers. The last of these, he asserted, were the most problematic, since "they have no leadership and come fragmented, and not always does a leadership emerge among them that leads them to lay down roots in the place." While he was not inclined to single out the North Africans in this respect, noting that the exodus had no particular ethnic characteristics, he did indicate one distinctive factor which he termed "educational," namely, the ingrained negative attitude toward agriculture as something inferior "that has taken root over generations."

In fact, it was impossible to gather from Weitz's well-ordered lecture before the commission whether or not the Jewish Agency's settlement policy was tainted with ethnic prejudice. Weitz did not deny the relative advantages conferred by length of residence in the country. Those who had arrived in 1949 from the transit camps in Cyprus were settled in the center of the country, while later arrivals were settled in the Negev or the hill regions, in harsher and more isolated areas, that is. Those who had arrived earlier enjoyed not only geographical advantages but also received a more generous financial allowance. Regarding outright ethnic discrimination, however, Weitz claimed that "there are but a few formal complaints." He concluded by relating that "the best way is to be quite open and not to conceal anything. In conversation with them I even use terminology that has emerged from these problems. Someone comes to me and says I am discriminated against and he, Feldman or Rosenberg for example, is not. I then ask him, do you think that because he is a 'vuzvuz' (a derogatory term for Ashkenazi in Israeli slang) or in the opposite case I ask, because he is black? I use their own terms and these terms exist and one should see things as they really are." It was, nevertheless, difficult to ascertain anything from this coarse explanation, and Judge Etzioni appeared to lose patience, not overly impressed by this informal style of management. "What do you mean by 'because of being "vuzvuz"' or because of being black?' That there are no direct complaints but merely indirect ones?" he pressed Weitz. Now he was given a more technical and detailed explanation of the manner in which the settlement department resolved assertions of discrimination. "If anything happens we ask the nearest sociologist to investigate and to propose to the settlement department how to resolve the question and handle the matter," Weitz explained to the commission, and the discussion resumed its formal course.

Kalman Levy told the commission of inquiry that the Jewish Agency's absorption department had shown no interest in settling these immigrants in the abandoned Arab property.[61] "The main cohort of the incessant influx into the abandoned area," arrived in the first three years, up to 1951. These were in the main people from the displaced persons camps in Germany, immigrants from Hungary and Romania, a small number of immigrants from Iraq, and a few Moroccan and other North African Jews. In the latter half of the 1950s the policy was to direct the immigrants to the border regions. If there were immigrants who flowed from the border areas to the abandoned Arab property in the cities, they did so against the will of the settlement institutions.[62] For migrants to Wadi Salib, aspirations to reunite the family, dispersed throughout the land, and the desire to provide their children with a better education than that available in the border area perhaps combined with a longing for city life and the opportunity to recreate the life of the mellah in Morocco, with its communal character including synagogues, ritual baths, and so forth. If the Jewish Agency assisted immigrants to settle in abandoned urban Arab property, it was out of necessity, only once the immigrants had, of their own initiative, occupied the dwellings and presented the agency with a fait accompli. It was the abandoned Arab land on the border rather than the abandoned Arab property in the cities that caught the planners' attention.

The information that Kalman Levy shared with the commission of inquiry regarding the settlement of immigrants in the abandoned urban property was, however, partial and misleading. It was true, but was not the whole truth. The settlement department had, in fact, approached the custodian of absentees' property in 1953, requesting him to prevent the transfer of dwellings in his possession to those who had left immigrant settlements. Public housing companies such as Amidar likewise received clear instructions not to offer alternative housing to those leaving an agricultural settlement until they had settled their debts to the Jewish Agency. Given the meager means of the majority of those seeking to leave and their dependence on public resources, these measures, as Adriana Kemp correctly notes, were liable "to prove disastrous to them."[63]

It would appear that the interrogation of the representatives of the settlement institutions did not entirely satisfy the members of the commission of inquiry. It seems as though the evidence given by Kalman Levy led the chairman of the session to the conclusion that the population dispersal mechanism was rather unprofessional. Levy, in fact, was unable to provide any clear answer regarding the professional qualifications of those in charge of the vocational and geographic classification of the immigrants. Answers such as "We have three serious employees at three meetings on the journey" or, alternatively, "three senior officials who have working experience," and "they are social workers" led to further questions. In concluding his answers, Levy was forced to admit that "we have no professional counselors." It was perhaps this simple admission that led the session chairman to cast doubt on the overall validity of the evidence. "When you spoke of dropping out of the development areas," he probed, "you concluded by complaining that in addition to the matter of employment there is a further reason for their leaving, the enchanting cafés and cinemas in the city. I don't see anything wrong in this; I also like to sit in a café and I ask why is it that in the towns of the development areas no one thought of opening various forms of entertainment that would suit the way of life and needs of these people." The answer was somewhat laconic. "As best we could," replied the head of department.

Erasure

The report of the commission of inquiry concluded as follows:

> The neighborhood of Wadi Salib in Haifa is a poor neighborhood, overcrowded, built on the slopes of gulleys, its buildings pushed and squeezed together with some of them built one on top of the other; its alleys are winding and most are a series of steep stairs, in the best tradition of a crowded residential quarter in an old Arab city. In compressed and dingy structures, among which are hovels unfit for human habitation, families with many children live in crowded conditions while not every such "dwelling" has minimal sanitary arrangements. . . . The conditions of life in it are extremely harsh, despite the efforts of the municipality to maintain the cleanliness of the neighborhood's streets and alleyways.[64]

Wadi Salib had, incidentally, already in the past been accorded considerable attention by public committees. In 1937 the future of the Wadi had occupied the Haifa Committee, a body set up by the Jewish Agency with the aim of dissuading the British from implementing the Peel Commission's recommendations whereby Haifa was to attain the status of an international city and would not be included within the territory of the future Jewish state. A section of the report prepared by the Haifa Committee prior to the visit of the Woodhead Commission addressed the issues of the purchase of buildings and land. It focused on an account of the advantage gained by the Jewish community in this sphere over the Arab population in the city of Haifa and the greater Haifa area. The Haifa Committee's report placed particular emphasis on future trends. The program of prospective purchases created the outlines of the future urban planning of the Jewish city. The report charted the city's non-Jewish neighborhoods, mapping them according to religious and ethnic affiliation as Christian, German (the German colony), and Muslim. Most attention and the major part of the future development plan were devoted to the last category, which included the old town, Wadi Salib, Nazareth Way, and Arab Hallisa. Development in the context of the Haifa Committee's report meant turning Haifa into a Jewish city.[65]

According to the understanding of the Jewish Agency and the city leadership as formulated in the Haifa Committee's report, the Jewish element was to play a decisive role in the city's development and as such should supplant the Arab elements at key points of the city. Aware that the intention of compelling the occupants of the Muslim neighborhoods to leave their place of residence could be interpreted as a breach of their natural rights, the report's authors chose to invoke the social welfare argument. "The predominantly Arab quarters of the city are in most part outright slum areas and are filthy by nature," they wrote. "The worst of these are the Muslim quarters of Wadi Salib and the old town, which constitute a conglomeration of crowded buildings housing people in overcrowded conditions and rickety structures, all infested with pests, with sewage flowing along the narrow alleys that serve the neglected tenants. If we add to this the fact that these quarters, inaccessible as they are, serve as sanctuaries for criminals and miscreants, the picture is complete."[66] In light of the situation, noted the report's authors, Jewish purchase of the Eastern neighborhoods would constitute a generous step toward the original residents, who would be moved to a healthier environment in the vicinity of Haifa, with accessibility to places of employment in the city ensured by means of construction of the requisite roads.

It appears as though the report's authors realized that someone was liable to find fault with their intention to transfer the original Muslim population from its place of residence. They were therefore quick to present arguments directed at "the abstract moralist," as they referred to this position, who may ask a naive question regarding the possibility of returning the original population to the neighborhoods following their renewal:

> The answer to this question lies in the fact that in light of the location of these areas they are destined for rapid urban development, which the backward Arab population cannot endure. On behalf of the general inter-

est and progress in general, these sites should fall into the hands of those willing and able to develop them to the greatest extent, namely, into the hands of the Jews. The evacuated Arabs, who will establish themselves through the sale of their property, would do well to settle in areas suited to a semirural suburban population in the vicinity of Haifa that meet their special needs and habits, and they will be able to begin a clean life in a preferable environment.[67]

The year 1948 did indeed appear to present the opportunity of carrying out a sweeping program of renewal when the Muslim population abandoned the city. The general conditions, however, and in particular the vast number of immigrants and the problem of housing them, precluded implementation of the radical changes envisioned by the Haifa Committee in 1937. As we have seen, the neighborhood was very soon populated by new and equally destitute tenants. Leaving Wadi Salib's architectural foundations untouched, and neglecting to renovate its infrastructure, owing, in part, to the ambiguous legal status of much of the property, the Haifa Municipality commenced in the early 1950s to undertake a cosmetic erasure of Wadi Salib's Arab past. The insignificant presence of a few Arabs in the neighborhood did nothing to arrest this process. The municipality did not, however, invest much effort in concealing Wadi Salib's Arab character and made do with changing names.[68]

The Committee on General Affairs and Street Names that convened in March 1951 addressed the issue of principle of some one hundred streets with a non-Hebrew name.[69] Unsurprisingly, the issue of the Arab names was raised during the committee's first meeting. The deputy city engineer began by venting his "private opinion," according to which it would be difficult to change names "familiar to the masses," and counseled "care in this sphere and not to indulge in a wholesale change of Arab names."[70] While no proper argument ensued, it is evident that the committee members held divergent views. One of them insisted that it was necessary "to take a critical look at all the Arabic and English names and do this quickly." Another committee member even thought that "the matter of changing the Arabic names is most urgent." One of them proposed as a general rule "that a name related to the history of Haifa be retained even if it is an Arabic one," while another member proclaimed that "the non-Jewish names should be reconsidered," since he doubted that "these names now suit our city." The assertion by the head of committee, a Mr. Malley, that 80 to 90 percent of the "non-Jewish" names were Arabic and would need to be changed indicates that even at this stage a sweeping move was contemplated. The meeting decided that there was no point in changing the Arabic names of streets inhabited by Arabs.

The committee concerned itself with changing the street signs as well. While the Arabic script would indeed be retained, it would appear below the Hebrew script. The English script could not be dispensed with because of the tourists. Maintaining the multilingual nature of the signs is less surprising that the continuation of the bilingual—Hebrew-Arabic—documentation of the minutes of municipal meetings up to 1951, even though this no longer had any practical grounds given the changed circumstances. These remnants of the binational past, however, would disappear when Abba Khoushy replaced Shabtai Levy as mayor. Whereas Levy, born in Istanbul and a graduate of the Constantinople faculty of law and a fluent Arabic speaker, had maintained the tradition of equality throughout the years of his incumbency, which spanned the Mandate and Israeli epochs, Khoushy represented different traditions. Upon acceding to his position, he was quick to approach the Haganah Members Organization in the city requesting the submission of a comprehensive list of all the sites that had witnessed decisive battles for the city,[71] likewise requesting a list that would serve to perpetuate the names of Haganah members who had fallen in the city.[72] The list submitted by the Haganah veterans included forty-one names, among them names for the perpetuation of service units and concepts of the Haganah, names of operations and events, and various other names, such as "Sappers Alley," "Signalers Alley," "Slick Alley," "Roadblock Defenders," "The Jewish Mother" and so forth. Of the names on the list the following were immediately accepted: "Haganah Square," "Liberation Rise," "Independence," and "The Heroes." The remaining names were submitted for discussion by the committee.[73]

The Names Committee was quick to discuss the proposals submitted by the Haganah veterans.[74] After coming to decisions regarding streets in other quarters of the city, such as changing the name Salah al-Din to "The Heroes Street," it decided on two changes within the area of Wadi Salib. The name of The Bourge Street, which leads to the Wadi and, according to one of the preliminary proposals, was due to be named "Maoz" (stronghold) Street,[75] was now changed to "Ma'aleh ha-shihrur" (Liberation Rise) Street, despite the protest of committee member Shoval, who preferred the literal trans-lation in the form of the name "Ha-metsuda" (the fortress) Street. Shoval took a consistent position; even at the first session he stated his opinion that one should not take into consideration the sound of the Arab names but rather their content.[76] The committee proposed changing the name of Iraq Street, named after the "Iraq Petroleum Company" (IPC), which had been instrumental in founding the Haifa refinery, to "Olei Bavel" (Babylonian im-migrants) Street. In the end it was named "Kibbutz Galuyot" (ingathering of the exiles) Street. In the south of the neighborhood, Stanton Street, named after the city's first British governor, was changed to "Shivat Zion" (return to Zion) Street. The continuation of this street, Iraq Street, was, as men-tioned, named Kibbutz Galuyot Street. The names of other transportation axes bordering on Wadi Salib were also changed. Hajj Way near the railway became "Golani Brigade" Street, even though this brigade had played no part in the fighting in the city.

The trend toward a unified language led to discussion regarding the term *wadi* itself. The Haifa Municipality secretary referred the matter of *wadi* to the Language Council in Jerusalem, along with various other issues regard-ing the difficulty of defining terms and nicknames within the city's public sphere.[77] The questions were phrased in a general manner: "What denotes an alley? What is the difference between 'rise' and 'steps'? The meeting point of four streets with a small island in the middle—is this a 'plaza' or simply a crossroad; what is the size of the area to be named a 'square'? and so forth."[78] In the same context, the Language Council was asked for the correct translation of the term *wadi,* and whether this could be replaced with the term *gorge?* In the end it was decided to translate the term *wadi* as *gai* (valley or ravine) and to change all the Arabic names of wadis in the city and its environs as soon as possible.[79] The committee decided to visit the wadis and to find them names suited to their distinctive forms.

Wadi Salib, however, was not merely a geographic route but also a neighborhood and a street. A "toponomic contradiction" was revealed in the word *salib,* which is Arabic for cross.[80] No true explanation of the name is available, and we have only a popular account provided by the British mis-sionary Frances Newton, who founded a school under the auspices of the ecclesiastical mission in Wadi Salib at the beginning of the previous century. The origin of the name, she related, was to be found in a large cross en-graved by anonymous pilgrims on a huge rock resting on the upper part of the wadi that could be seen from a distance at a time when the wadi was still far from the settled area of Haifa. The cross, if it ever existed, disappeared during construction activity toward the end of the days of the Turks. Now, in the time of the Jews, the neighborhood began to appear on the lists of neighborhoods and streets to be renamed, alongside others such as Ard al-yahud, the German colony, and, surprisingly, also Wadi Nisnas.[81] Opinions were divided as to the advisability of changing the name of the last of these.[82] Some indeed proposed calling Wadi Nisnas the "Shem neighborhood" or the "Shem and Japheth neighborhood," while others opined that the existing name be retained since the population was Arab and the name had no political or nationalist connotation. As to Wadi Salib the neighborhood, the committee members unanimously favored changing its name to "Ha-portzim" (the breachers) neighborhood in memory of the battles that took place there.[83] Two months later new initiatives popped up. A unanimous decision was now made "to annul the name 'Wadi Salib' and to name the place '*hagai*' (the valley), without indicating that it was a riverbed or ravine."[84] This decision was made together with another unanimous decision to change the name of "the German Colony" to "Bnei ha-heikhal" (Sons of the Temple), thereby referring to its Christian religious association while ridding it of the disturbing German context.[85]

The efforts at finding Hebrew names for Haifa's streets continued throughout 1953. In Wadi Salib and in other neighborhoods of the city there still remained many streets with Arabic names. Al-Afghani Street, Irbid Street, Ha-wadi Street, Tariq Street, Khatib Street, and 'Umar ibn al-Khattāb Street were mentioned by name in a direct application by Abba Khoushy to the Names Committee with the request "to devote sufficient time as soon as possible in order to propose to us original Hebrew names for all these streets." "We must once and for all rid ourselves of this curse," wrote Khoushy.[86] And the longed-for changes were indeed to be made over a prolonged period.[87] While the streets on Wadi Salib's perimeter, mainly large thoroughfares and major transportation routes, were given names with clear nationalist connotations, the quarter's narrow alleys and some of its stairways underwent only minor changes. Only the pronunciation of the names of streets denoting places was adjusted to accord with the Hebrew. Amman Street became Amon Street, Bisan became Beit She'an, Ekron and Aqaba retained their original names as did Irbid Steps, whose name remained unchanged and Yaman Steps, which became Teiman (Yemen)

Steps. Ben-Harush, as we recall, in 1949 laid hands on a room in Eglon Steps. These had previously been named Ajlun after a city in the ancient Emorite kingdom, while the previous tenants had referred to them informally as the Mufti Steps. A very small number of streets named after an Arab figure likewise retained their names. Examples include 'Umar ibn al-Khattāb Street, named after the second Muslim caliph, and Tariq Street, named after Tariq ibn Ziyad, the Arab warrior who in AD 711 captured Spain from the Christian Visigoths. The steps named after the former mayor Hassan Shukri retained their original name.

Other Arabic names were changed over the following years.[88] Al-Afghani Street became Barukh Marcus Street, named after Haifa's rabbi, born in Lithuania. Khaled bin Walid Street, named after the Muslim warrior who led the Muslim army into the battle for the Yarmukh, changed its name to Yehiel Street, after Yehiel Chelnov, among the founders of Hovevei Zion and a central figure in the war of languages at the Haifa Technion. The steps named after Walid were renamed Miller Steps after a local industrialist born in Lithuania who had done metalwork for the Turkish government at the time of the establishment of the Hejaz railway. Nuzha Street was changed to Rabbi Ohanna after Rabbi Binyamin Nissim Ohanna, a native of Algiers and rabbi of Haifa and the Haifa district toward the end of his life. 'Umar Mukhtar Street, named after a Libyan freedom fighter who fought the Italians and was hanged in 1931, likewise had to make way for the lyricist of the national anthem, Naftali Hertz-Imber. These changes continued into the 1960s, even as the Wadi was evacuated. One of Wadi Salib's streets, we should mention in passing, was some years ago named after Ben-Harush.

"They Merge and Forget Their Origin"

And how short was the way from Abbas Street to the seashore. And how wide the world was in those days. The entire Carmel was ours, as was the sea. Even Janinat Abbas, as we called the Bahai Gardens, was open to us. Our whole world was open to us, the valley and the mountain, the sea and the land, and between them Muaras, namely the open spaces, that have since become Kiryat Eliezer.[89]

Despite the twenty-two years that elapsed between the Haifa Committee and the Public Commission of Inquiry Into the Events of Wadi Salib, and even though the city's ethnic and national components had changed beyond recognition, it appears that the guiding principles of the city's Jewish urban planning, which had never looked kindly upon the Arab town, remained steadfast. The conclusions of the commission of inquiry in 1959 blended with the trends toward modernization that had preceded it. The commission plainly believed in sweeping action designed to eradicate the Oriental way of life. The report sealed the fate of Wadi Salib in asserting that "overall, a neighborhood such as this has no right to exist in a modern city such as Haifa, and in any event, if it does exist it requires a good measure of upkeep, maintenance and care."[90] It was but a short step from this conclusion to the elimination of the neighborhood and the move to a public housing estate.

The housing estate, or project, is not an Israeli invention. A *shikun* (estate), according to the Even Shoshan Hebrew dictionary, comprises "residential buildings constructed according to a uniform plan or for a certain population of tenants."[91] It had its equivalents, both in social-democratic Western Europe and in socialist or communist Eastern Europe. Unrelated to the nature of the regime, public housing had its heyday in postwar circumstances, when, against the background of the destruction, the authorities were required to provide rapid solutions for residents deprived of accommodation by the war. In England, for example, public housing developed directly after the First World War, driven by Prime Minister David Lloyd-George's desire to provide adequate housing "for the heroes who won the war." The English Housing and Town Planning Act of 1919 established the legal foundation for this development. Public construction, maintains Cliff Hague, was the outcome of agreements and direct contacts between the state and the market and prevented the emergence of a civil society.[92] National and international construction companies built for the middle and upper middle classes, which were able to afford the price, while the state, through the mediation of the local authorities and utilization of companies dealing in the construction of uniform housing blocks, built for those of lesser means. In passing we may note that this type of division of labor created different standards of building and housing, which would later give rise to resentment and feelings of deprivation, as evinced by the Israeli case. In England a perception developed among local councilors and municipal departments, particularly those controlled by the Labour party, that public housing was a way of "providing for the needy" and should be organized along rational lines by laying down objective criteria. This gave rise to the expectation that the recipients should be thankful and would take good care of the property. "Paternalism," asserted Hague, "was a key element in the mental model associated with council housing, and the role of civil society was to stand patiently as a member of a waiting list, until such time as sufficient 'points' were accumulated to merit the offer of a tenancy."[93]

While the nature of public construction in the Eastern bloc was indeed different,[94] here too it was the aftermath of war—the Second World War—that created an urgent need for rapid and low-cost building.[95] Surprisingly, the socialist states likewise failed to maintain equality in public housing and merely created and recycled segregation. Ivan Szelenyi maintains that "an ideologically egalitarian housing policy and urban planning produced an inegalitarian system of housing allocation, and produced, and keeps reproducing, the residential segregation of occupational groups."[96] What ostensibly appears to be a contradiction is revealed to be quite simple: while socialism and capitalism turn out to be rather insignificant in the context of the reproduction of inequality, it becomes evident that urban planning, namely, city engineers, local politicians, low-level government officials and bureaucrats, in effect fill a role identical to that of investors, investment banks, and real estate companies in the capitalist economy. In reality it is the actions of those involved in socialist urban planning rather than their intentions that count. As Szelenyi puts it: "They create inegalitarian cities not because they wish to do so, but because they operate as key agents in a new social structure, which is shaped by a new type of class antagonism, thus they cannot do anything else but reproduce the system of social privilege and the asymmetrical distribution of power in this structure."[97] These internal contradictions between socialist rhetoric and ideology, on the one hand, and the reproduction of inequality, on the other, characterized not only the communist bloc countries but also 1960s Israel.

The evacuation of Wadi Salib was undertaken in light of a worldwide tradition of public housing. Those in charge of slum clearance in Israel were aware of the international precedents in the U.S., Belgium, Denmark, West Germany, Italy, Holland, and England. From these countries the formulators of the Slums Clearance Act learned that "a partial attack upon the slums will be of no benefit and the clearance of one slum will only lead to a worsening of the already rundown conditions in another slum."[98] For this reason they sought a sweeping and coordinated solution that would synchronize the act of dismantling with the process of building. In one decisive aspect, however, the Israeli context in general and that of Wadi Salib in particular differed from social-democratic Western Europe and socialist Eastern Europe. The public housing complex served in Israel as an instrument of social ethnic engineering and transcended its accepted role in other places as an instrument for the creation of social class justice. "Ethnic density perpetuates the way of life of the countries of origin regarding the family milieu and education of the children," asserted Zvi Barzilay, the deputy mayor, in his evidence before the commission of inquiry. "They transfer an analogy from the Diaspora, from their environment abroad, that which enveloped the Jewish ghetto in Marrakech and in Casablanca with a sense of scorn, discrimination and deprivation."[99] His argument thus reflected the accepted opinions of the time, particularly the suspicion toward residential environments with clear ethnic characteristics. According to these widely held views, the demand for housing estates should be linked to the condition that they "must be based on a mixed population, without ethnic density." Equally forceful and of practical significance was the position of Mayor Abba Khoushy, as expressed before the commission:

> As to the very existence of Wadi Salib, already at the time of the War of Independence I came up with a plan to blow up Wadi Salib and I submitted a plan for renewal of the place, but it could be done only once all the residents had been removed (and, in order to remove the 3,144 households now, we need 32 million liras, and I would suggest that we doubt anyone who promises to do this in a matter of days). The population can be removed over five to six years—most of the population and without allowing others to enter, and then one could bring in bulldozers and flatten the ground and build other structures. The municipality has a plan for housing for everyone—and we wish to do this—but we proposed a method of population distribution rather than building special projects for members of one ethnic group—this is a wonderful instrument for merging the exiles. They merge and forget their origin.[100]

As an example, Khoushy mentioned a housing project built in the Kiryat Eliezer neighborhood in the city, "in which people of all ethnic groups reside, and as time passes they will forget and recognize that whoever lives here is a Jew." The transition to a housing project, however, was a complex matter. The devil, as we know, is in the details, and those details dictated the overall course of events. When the authorities in Haifa began planning the evacuation of Wadi Salib, the city had already endured the prolonged and arduous precedent of the evacuation of another neighborhood, Ard Ramel, or the Shemen neighborhood, as it was called in Hebrew, located close to Haifa Bay and the Kishon River.[101] The episode of Ard Ramel was the consequence of a mistake. When the Jewish Agency housed immigrants in the neighborhood in 1948, as it did in the other abandoned neighborhoods, it was unaware that part of the neighborhood's property was owned by Jews.[102] It was only when the Jewish owners claimed their property that the authorities were forced to address the matter. True, the agency expressed its willingness to assist in the transfer of tenants who could produce documents proving that they had been directed there by the authorities, but many of them, even if they had in the past possessed such documentation, had lost it in the meantime. The legal issue was compounded by a serious sanitation problem. Ever since the floods that Haifa experienced in 1955, the neighborhood was regarded as "a serious sanitary hazard and a grave social and welfare problem for the city."[103] The various authorities found it difficult to coax the tenants into vacating the place voluntarily and tended to employ extreme methods of persuasion. The representative of the northern district health bureau, for example, proposed that "an army unit hold maneuvers in the place and create the impression that it presented a security threat and then a large part of the residents would flee." The director of the settlement department of the Jewish Agency suggested a plan "to annoy the residents of places of dubious reputation in the neighborhood and establish a police station in the place." Irrespective of these creative solutions, it was decided to try to mobilize a number of bodies including the owners of the land, namely, the Development Authority, the State Tax Office, the Palestine Land Development Company, and private owners, to participate in a concerted financial effort to enroll the residents in a housing savings plan with the cooperation of the Jewish Agency, the Housing Wing of the Labor Ministry, and the evacuees themselves. It was further decided to direct "the youth and those capable of working" to work in the countryside within the framework of the "From City to Village" movement. The municipality derived inspiration for the evacuation plan in Haifa from the experience of Tel Aviv Municipality in Jaffa.[104]

As a basis for the evacuation of the neighborhood—a step later to be replicated in the evacuation of Wadi Salib—it was decided to conduct a survey, which revealed that the majority of residents had arrived in the country between the years 1948 and 1952. Their economic status varied considerably and was defined according to the surveyors' impression as "good," "orderly, "with furniture," "modern furniture," or "primitively arranged" and "neglected."[105] Most residents were, incidentally, gainfully employed. The negotiations with the residents over the conditions of their evacuation, however, apparently reached an impasse, and they refused to accept the proposals put forward by the authorities. As the matter was being discussed and the attempts at persuasion continued, the neighborhood's residents became hostages to their refusal when the municipality chose to exert pressure by adamantly refusing to handle their ongoing complaints regarding sanitary conditions that endangered their lives. It saw no "moral-public justification" in the requests for ongoing handling of sanitation problems considering that all the neighborhood's buildings had been decreed to be "illegal and unsanitary" and "slated for demolition."[106] One can but imagine the bitter suffering endured by the residents as the neighborhood's evacuation was postponed for years. It was only in the spring of 1959 that a final announcement of the neighborhood's evacuation was made and the residents were called upon to register for a housing project.[107] The precedent of Ard Ramel provided an inkling of what was in store.

A day prior to the first incidents in Wadi Salib, the director of the Housing Projects Department submitted a request to the mayor to appoint a representative of the municipality who, together with him, would be authorized to conduct a final examination of the list of candidates drawn from those who had registered for evacuation of Ard Ramel.[108] In the meantime, the matter had become a clear political issue. Rumors circulated among the neighborhood's residents that only Mapai members and sympathizers would be eligible to move to the housing projects. The two deputy mayors, Zvi Barzilay and Yosef Nussboim, attempted to calm the residents of the Shemen neighborhood. "You should know," they both announced, "that every citizen and neighborhood resident can register and his right to a housing project will be preserved. As members of the committee chosen to handle this issue, we shall be on our guard to make sure that no resident is discriminated against or deprived. Party affiliation will not determine one's position in the queue for the project, but only seniority, family status, and welfare status."[109] The residents' dependence on an administrative machinery whose deliberations were not transparent, but whose motives were often blatantly clear, would not cease upon evacuation from the abandoned property and, in certain respects, would become more entrenched.[110] There were, incidentally, always those whose fate and dependence were even more bitter: the last "illegal" residents of Ard Ramel, Arabs, were evacuated on Thursday, June 7, 1967, when, in the midst of war and on the pretext of security considerations, they were removed from their shacks, which were destroyed together with their possessions. The municipality refused to address the claims for compensation submitted by the destitute residents since the shacks had stood on land owned by the Israel Lands Administration.[111]

"I Came to Live in a Grave While We Were Still Alive"

The evacuation of Wadi Salib was one stage of an overall operation aimed at eliminating Israel's slums. It was among those neighborhoods of "abandoned property" diagnosed as having "primitive and even rickety structures."[112] Its status was identical to that of other neighborhoods slated for evacuation: neighborhoods in Jaffa, Kfar Shalem, and al-Shaykh Muwannis. The general decision to evacuate Haifa's slums was made by the Housing Ministry together with the municipality in the early 1960s.[113] The order of priority regarding "evacuation and demolition of the underprivileged areas" was headed by the Shemen area, followed by Wadi Salib up to and including Hamagenim Street and, lastly, Ard Yahud.[114] The population destined for evacuation in Haifa differed in certain respects from that in other cities. Its proportion among the general population (22 percent) was lower than that in Jerusalem (28.1 percent) or in Tel Aviv (36.5 percent).[115] The proportion of those of European origin among those destined for evacuation was considerably greater in Haifa, standing at 57 percent as against 38.6 percent in Tel Aviv and 22.1 percent in Jerusalem. The proportion of those of Asian origin among the future evacuees in Haifa was especially low, while the proportion of those of African origin was particularly high, at 29.1 percent. The overcrowded living conditions of the residents in the neighborhoods slated for evacuation in Haifa was no different to those in the other big city slums. These measures were primarily intended "to eliminate and renew" the neighborhoods of abandoned property that extended along the length of the bay in downtown Haifa. Their buildings were characterized "by the format of the neglected neighborhoods of typical middle-eastern cities with high density building, most without sanitation in the buildings and some without sewage in the neighborhood."[116] And indeed, the gross density of the resident families varied between 17.4 families per dunam (1,000 square meters) in Shikmona and 8.8 families per dunam in Wadi Nisnas. In Wadi Salib the density at this time reached 11.8 families per dunam, a high level by any standards and in relation to an overall average of 5 families per dunam in the slum neighborhoods and 1.1 families per dunam in Haifa's entire urban area of jurisdiction. A truly essential difference between Haifa and the two other large cities was the high concentration of slums within the territory of the "abandoned property." The Israel Lands Administration, a public body set up and run jointly by the Israeli state and the Jewish National Fund, was estimated as owning 85 percent of this territory. Given these conditions, the evacuators in Haifa were spared the confrontation with private elements. Relying on the little experience that had accumulated, mainly on the experience of other countries, the drafters of the Slums Clearance Act proposed a desirable mode of evacuation and formulated it as a golden rule:

> It should be clearly spelled out: a slum cannot be eliminated bit by bit. As long as a part of the neighborhood remains, the resident is disinclined to move out and postpones his exit. The neighborhood as such remains, although its dimension diminishes. To this we must add that people are always added to the neighborhood through natural birth or by transferring their residence to it. For this reason it is imperative to deal with the entire neighborhood, to eliminate it as a slum and establish a modern neighborhood in its place.[117]

All activity regarding sale or transfer of land owned by the Haifa Region office was consequently put on hold. The freeze was accompanied by close inspection aimed at preventing the residents from exploiting the temporary situation by subdividing their dwellings and adding structures or introducing new tenants in the area.[118] When the general intention to evacuate residents to the projects was revealed, the number of applications for assistance and rapid transition began to grow. In their personal letters to the mayor, the applicants revealed unbearable living conditions. Hannah Naim of Shemesh Street in Wadi Salib applied to the mayor on behalf of her asthma-suffering children, asking that "you transfer me from this place to a different place in order to save me and my family."[119] Mr. Simmel Brish of Shivat

Zion Street likewise applied directly, relating that "since I had no financial means I was not in a position to purchase a suitable dwelling, I moved into one room without checking it out and I subsequently saw that I came to live in a grave while we were still alive. The walls are wet, there is no light whatsoever, a moldy room with a bad odor of mold that has brought upon us rheumatism, asthma, as we breathe the contaminated air in which we have lived all the time, apart from the unpleasant odor emanating from all the surrounding toilets."[120]

Mrs. Cohen of Ha-eglon Street complained that her application to move to a housing project had been rejected without "any fatherly feeling," even though she had furnished the authorities with letters of recommendation from the hospital, the regional governmental health bureau, and the rabbinate, which supported the request on the part of "a Jewish mother who is obliged to raise six children in such awful housing conditions."[121] Mrs. Mazal Cohen of Nuzhah Street likewise hoped for redress in applying in person to the mayor and explaining that "we are six people crowding into one very small room located opposite a slaughterhouse from which the odor reaches our small room and prevents the children from eating." Owing to neglect of the sewage problem, she was furthermore obliged to place a bucket below the kitchen sink, "which adds further pollution to the children, who go to drink from it when I let my guard down for a moment."[122] Her neighbor, Mrs. Rachel Yosefson of Nuzhah Street, a widow who worked as a cleaner at the Haifa Employment Bureau, wrote that she was living "in a dingy basement lacking air . . . and although I supposedly have a dwelling I sleep outdoors since it is impossible to sleep in my basement."[123]

All these applicants, however, were initially rejected irrespective of their personal distress, since their cases were not found to be of supreme urgency. While the room occupied by David Alkarif on 11 Umayya Alley was evacuated,[124] the handling of the case of our acquaintance Heinrich First of 14 Wadi Salib Street dragged on. He asked to be evacuated "since I am the head of a family of five souls—and my wife is pregnant, living in one room with no means at all with which to purchase a project dwelling."[125] The Governmental-Municipal Haifa Slum Renewal Company harbored doubts as to his eligibility. It preferred to destroy part of the dwelling of First's neighbors and to give him one of its rooms.[126] It later transpired that "Mr. Heinrich First handed part of his dwelling to a subtenant against key money and sent his wife to the USA." His reliability as an eligible candidate was eroded by this new information, but it remained unclear as to how one could resolve the contradiction between the decision to destroy part of the adjacent dwelling and the announcement handed to First, according to which his apartment was located in a stable building built of stone that was not labeled for demolition just yet. The numerous requests submitted by David Ben-Harush, if indeed this was the same man, to exchange the grocery store on 18 Amman Street were likewise consistently rejected.[127]

The delay in evacuation, grave as it was, was not due to the individual circumstances of the residents of Wadi Salib but to the fact that their dwellings, as luck would have it, were located in areas that could not be evacuated and eliminated en bloc. Despite the residents' distress, the directorate of the Governmental-Municipal Haifa Slum Renewal Company decided not to raise the quota of project apartments earmarked for the Wadi Salib evacuees and to allocate such apartments only in cases where it was possible to evacuate an entire building.[128] This obstinacy led to an absurd situation in which the company continued to refuse applications submitted by the residents of Wadi Salib, even though it had apartments available in the new projects and construction work was ongoing.[129] It was only due to the mounting pressure that the company decided to purchase the land from the Israel Lands Administration and extend the right to housing to the residents of the entire area.[130]

Urban renewal turned out to be a coordinated activity that left no room for hesitant residents to consider and plan their actions with care and that allowed them no leeway for a change of mind. The plan called for rapid clearance of the site and the demolition of the buildings thereon. Differences of opinion between the Haifa Municipality and Amidar, Israel's national immigrant housing company, soon emerged on this issue, since the latter enabled some of the evacuees to transfer their dwellings to new tenants against payment of key money, thereby making it impossible to destroy the vacated dwellings.[131] It was only once Amidar had promised to demolish the buildings that the Haifa Municipality agreed to contribute to the cost of clearance.[132] Partial demolition posed a danger, since it created hazardous sites or allowed squatters to infiltrate the empty buildings.[133] Life in the neighborhood during the prolonged demolition process was by all accounts unbearable. Parts of buildings, unstable walls remaining after partial demolition, damaged roofs, broken windows, dangerous electrical connections, and partially sealed spaces endangered the residents and, worst of all, the lives of the children.[134]

It was thus important that each step be seen as irreversible. The residents were trapped in the gap between the authorities' desire to create an incentive to move, at times even in the faint hope of making a profit, and their attempt to minimize the public outlay on their account as far as possible. The hope of a profit was fueled by the neighborhood's location and, more precisely, by the high value of land in the city centers in which the slums were located, and the possibility of constructing multistory buildings on the area in the future, once it had been cleared. The possibility of uniform construction and development of tall, multistory buildings raised hopes that "the considerable expenditure and effort involved in clearing the area for renewal, the resettlement of the residents there and the award of appropriate compensation to them and the owners of the land and buildings on the renewal site will be covered by the value of the extensive and free tract of land that will remain available for building and usage."[135]

For a moment it appeared that Wadi Salib had a future. Its land belonged, as mentioned, to the Israel Lands Administration, which agreed to sell it all or, to be precise, almost all of it to the Slum Renewal Company.[136] The sale agreement was signed between the Governmental-Municipal Haifa Slum Renewal Company and the Israel Lands Administration's director, Yosef Weitz, on April 1, 1963.[137] In this area and on the Shikmona strip—the remains of the old town that were joined to Wadi Salib according to the urban plan—there remained only a few properties that were privately owned or owned by the *waqf*.[138] These were expropriated at this time, their value to be determined by the government assessor. Two Christian churches still stood in the way of creating a continuous strip under public ownership. The Israel Lands Administration had already expropriated all the private properties apart from the churches and was now engaged in parallel negotiations with the owners over their purchase. Meanwhile, the architect Gideon Kaminka drew up a general plan for the area. He proposed a grandiose program that included multistory commercial structures and high-rise residential buildings, entailing exploitation of high building percentages of some 200 percent of the gross area. The program further included extensive built-up areas on two levels, a public garden as an extension of the existing garden in the Shikmona area, green areas, and a site for a public building. Kaminka went as far as dreaming of a plot for an elementary school and a kindergarten. On the "site," he proposed, "the two Christian churches would remain as well as one or two of the old houses that were of architectural value as a 'memento.'"[139] Mr. Yosef Cohen, the city engineer, announced that the program had yet to be studied and examined. This did not augur well for the future. The obstacle of the churches and the waqf property was, incidentally, due to be resolved shortly in the best possible manner: Yehuda Baharav, director of the Haifa Slum Renewal Company, was happy to announce that the expropriation of the waqf property had "at last been implemented in a decisive manner."[140] "We have of course yet to hold negotiations with the owners over compensation, but as far as ownership is concerned the properties are being transferred to the company and we can already clear and demolish them." Fate, however, smiled upon the two churches. They remained standing.[141]

An even more complex issue was that of individual compensation to the residents of Wadi Salib. This was set at the sum of the deposit required to purchase alternative accommodation, that is, approximately one-quarter of the value of the purchased property. The remaining cost of the apartment was due to be paid by the evacuees by means of loans and mortgages. A solution of this kind could have seemed attractive only to those who held positions and were currently employed, whose relative financial security enabled them to take on long-term commitments. Yet the majority of Wadi Salib's residents had no basis on which to make such a commitment. Under these circumstances, the clearance program turned out to be a protracted one, and those engaged in formulating the law began to consider raising the ceiling of the government's compensation to the evacuees. Company officials devised a particularly creative solution with regard to those residents without means and also to welfare cases: they chose to give grants to evacuees who lacked any resources whatsoever at the expense of the evacuees with meager means.[142] The grants were funded by raising the price of apartments in the new housing projects by one hundred liras for a regular apartment and fifty liras for the small apartments. This was a progressive solution based on the best tradition of social democracy: the poor financed the welfare of the poorest.

"Truly Human Trash"

The Shikmona Company was given responsibility for implementing the Wadi Salib clearance project. Beginning its operation in 1962, over the ensuing ten years it evacuated 3,001 families in the city, including 1,878 from Wadi Salib.[143] Yehuda Baharav, a senior engineer with Haifa Municipality, was appointed to the post of general director of the company or, as this role was termed, "Director of the Slum Elimination Company." He had to acquaint himself with the material very quickly. "The population was truly human trash concentrated in one place," he reminisced in an interview at the end of the 1980s.[144] To implement the program, Baharav appointed a Mizrahi Jewish official "whose mentality would be close to that of the evacuees."[145] The official's mission was to visit the houses and persuade the local population to embrace the idea of clearance. An office that opened in the neighborhood during the afternoon hours provided information and enabled discussion among the residents. The municipality, incidentally, took no chances and placed a policeman and municipal inspector at the entrance to protect the official.[146] The "Working Mothers Organization" likewise took up the cause of persuasion, employing an "individual and direct approach," by which an established family adopted another family in dire socioeconomic circumstances.[147] Members of the organization were asked to "go together on visits to an entire street," "at a time when the family, or at least the wife, is at home," and "to free sufficient time for a quiet and detailed conversation." The aim of the visit was to discuss an exchange of dwellings with the family and discover the true reasons for its refusal to exchange their present accommodation. "The second step" was to "invite the family or parts thereof to a cup of tea in the adopters' home" and, following "a strengthening of the ties, to try to persuade the family to move to a better dwelling." The organization equipped its employees with instructions pertaining to the accompaniment of the families due to move to the new projects. Thus, for example, "[to make] an attempt to counsel [them] on maintenance of the cleanliness of the apartments, use of the sanitary appliances, the cleanliness of the stairways and the yard."

The municipality offered the residents of Wadi Salib several alternatives. They could choose to purchase an apartment, pay "key money," or rent a condominium or an apartment in the housing estates, either on their own initiative or through the mediation of Shikmona. "The entire process of evacuation, payment of compensation, and offer of alternative accommodation to the same family," Baharav remembered, "was prolonged and difficult and problematical, mainly because we adhered to the principle that the process should be a voluntary one. No law relating to this matter was promulgated, as was done in the USA for example—an evacuation law."[148] "We proceeded," the Shikmona report concludes, "to construct the housing projects for the evacuees not on the clearance and renewal site where they had lived but in the city suburbs, in the older neighborhoods, in neighborhoods with an established population and immigrants of different social strata."[149] The projects designed to absorb the evacuees were erected in seven neighborhoods throughout Haifa, in Kiryat Shprinzak, Ein Hayam, Allenby, Gesher Paz, Neveh Yosef, Maimon-Gedalyahu, and in Ramot Remez. The new occupants were obliged to purchase the dwellings. Applications for rented housing were flatly rejected.[150] Lacking previous experience, the authorities conducted the clearance process by trial and error. In two of the first projects to be built, Shikmona was ordered to erect large buildings of thirty-six and even forty-eight apartments. These small apartments—fifty-six square meters divided into three rooms—and adjacent to a "small and socially weak" neighborhood, proved to be a failure.[151] Seeking to integrate their clients rapidly into their new environment, the planners avoided building large estates. They believed that planning of this type would facilitate the "distribution" of the evacuees and their intermingling with the established population. To succeed, however, such a move required additional steps in areas other than real estate. A resident of the middle-class Neveh Sha'anan neighborhood, for example, sought to prevent the "assignment" of "the new occupants" to the homes of the veterans; in other words, the employment of the Wadi Salib evacuee women in the households of their established veteran neighbors, and contacted Ruth Dayan, the well-known director of Maskit, a state-run Oriental craft enterprise. The objective was to train these women in handicraft by means of a course run by the Labor Ministry and to enable them to produce ornaments in their homes and sell them to Maskit.[152]

A more heterogeneous population with respect to their origin, in the dry language of social research, moved to the housing projects,[153] namely, not only those of North African origin. It also included those born in the country, in Europe, and in Mediterranean countries. Evacuation to a housing project, in fact, suited only the relatively well established among those living in Wadi Salib, since they were required to take out loans and indebt themselves, something that only those who believed they would be able to comply with the loan conditions over a prolonged period were prepared to do.[154] The living conditions of the evacuees over the ensuing years were severely affected by cutbacks in public expenditure. The city engineers, for example, sagely determined that there was no medical proof that climbing stairs could be detrimental to the health of elderly people. To cut costs, some of the buildings in the housing projects rose to a height of five stories without an elevator, in utter disregard for the elementary needs of elderly residents and mothers of small children.[155] In the Kiryat Eliyahu–Allenby project the apartments were not equipped with a water boiler but merely with preparatory piping.[156] "We have noticed," Baharav told the meeting, "that a large group of the occupants install a solar water heater, break down the walls and also damage the buildings aesthetically." In order to prevent this, Baharav proposed that electrical boilers be provided with the apartments. His suggestion was accepted with a slight modification: it was decided to include a boiler with a slightly smaller capacity than usual, of around eighty liters.

A general lack of clarity as to which of the authorities and various bodies bore financial responsibility for the evacuation process clouded the transition. Tenants were moved into the Neveh Yosef neighborhood before the infrastructure was completed. The representative of the Housing Ministry in Haifa remained unperturbed by the conditions. "A little building waste remains, which can be removed within a day or two. And the development of the courtyards is almost complete. Only the gardening is yet to be done and the municipality is now paving the roads and sidewalks."[157] These were routine occurrences. "When needs be, and we have no choice, we move people, mainly new immigrants, also into apartments where not only the exterior development is incomplete, but also without floor tiles, glazing, exterior plaster, and so forth," he noted. There was still no clinic in Neveh Yosef, and the Housing Ministry proposed "erecting a prefabricated asbestos structure as a temporary clinic," if the health fund would agree. A kindergarten and club had yet to be built, and likewise a playground.

As people began moving in, there were still no stores. The only five stores constructed in Neveh Yosef were sold by the Housing Ministry to South American investors who had not yet opened them. This was an unreasonable decision in view of the growing distress of the Wadi Salib merchants who were asking for assistance as they saw their livelihoods dwindle in the evacuated neighborhood.[158] But the Housing Ministry had considerations of its own, promoting "a policy encouraging immigration from prosperous countries that are in need of a livelihood here." The issue of the livelihood of the evacuees was obviously not a major consideration in the evacuation process. Albert Algrisy, a shopkeeper on Shivat Zion Street and head of a family of nine, dared to apply to the mayor in writing and inform him that his livelihood had been compromised once his street had "emptied completely by your order."[159] "As you transferred the entire neighborhood for various reasons, thereby destroying our livelihood," he felt, "you are also obliged to make a store available to me in an appropriate location, in place of my current store." "I hope that you will address this problem in the correct manner so as to prevent me from seeking other ways that will surely be unpleasant." The deputy mayor chose to regard the application as a veiled threat and responded accordingly. "Since when does the municipality exchange stores for citizens when business in the existing store is not to the owner's liking? From your letter one may gather that we should not have moved families out of slums so as not to harm your livelihood, heaven forbid. This is a mistake, sir, and you are likewise mistaken in your threat, which frightens no one." He continued by advising Algrisy "to desist from wistful thoughts" and to take a practical approach.[160]

Shikmona's primary concern was to provide the evacuating families with dwellings that would ease the overcrowding they had experienced in Wadi Salib. The guideline was to provide a room for every two family members.[161] While this measure was indeed maintained as a statistical average, close to 40 percent of the evacuees in fact lived almost three to a room, with 4 percent above this.[162] If one takes into account the small size of the apartments and the fact that some one-third of the evacuated families had four to six children, and a fifth had more than seven children, this datum is not surprising.[163] Statistics show, incidentally, that in some 40 percent of Wadi Salib households three to four people shared a room.[164] On the face of it, the evacuees who moved to the project should have experienced some relief from the overcrowding, but interviews and surveys conducted with the project residents in the mid-1970s showed that the subjective perception of overcrowding had not dissipated. Many of them complained that "the overcrowding disturbs [us] often or almost always at work, at rest, when doing homework," "that there are too few rooms, or that [the rooms] are too small."[165] The conductor of the survey failed to find a satisfactory explanation for this and offered a variety of conjectures: the people had not, he suggested, freely chosen to move to the project, and this perhaps accounted for some of the criticism. Comparisons with neighbors with few children enjoying greater prosperity perhaps sharpened the awareness of discomfort.[166]

The good of the children and the wish to enhance their opportunities figured prominently in the official rhetoric, in urban planning, and certainly in the families' set of considerations. "In all the social settlements in Israel the first generation bears the yoke and the suffering, but for the children — this is a redemption," participants in the meetings of the Governmental-Municipal Haifa Slum Renewal Company maintained. In this respect, local policy merely reflected national policy. Ben-Gurion represented a conventional social-democratic outlook at the time regarding this matter, which put its faith in the omnipotence of social engineering performed through deliberate social-democratic policy. In this spirit, from the early 1960s onward, he rejected all initiatives aimed at establishing a government ministry that would concentrate on the problems of the Mizrahi community in Israel. "I do not believe that a special ministry will solve the problem," was how he rejected applications on this matter, arguing that "this is not a 'professional' problem that can be addressed by a special ministry, it is primarily an educational problem, and education is at the center of the problem. This is a problem of learning a trade and a problem of housing."[167] Ben-Gurion flatly rejected demands to establish a government ministry that would handle the "merging of the exiles" and diverted the discussion to "constructive" channels. He sought to locate the social distress within the four walls of the home as he set out clear social goals:

> Closing the educational gap between the children of the poor, mostly members of large families, and well-off children. The latter come home from school to an attractive and spacious dwelling to do the homework, and most of the parents are qualified to help their children with their assignments, while the children of the poor have no dwelling, and when they come home from school they spend the entire day in the street and their parents are incapable of assisting them with the assignments, and in their small, cramped apartment there is no room to do the homework.[168]

The educational distress, incidentally, could perhaps have been solved even prior to the events that placed Wadi Salib at the forefront of public attention. The *Haaretz* correspondent who extensively covered the issue of welfare in Haifa noted that the Alliance Israélite Universelle institutions in Teheran and Baghdad, as in other cities in the Middle East, had succeeded in conditions worse that those pertaining in Wadi Salib, as had the mission staff, by employing the simple solution of an extended study day. Such an expedient had never been introduced to the neighborhood; moreover, many of the children had been obliged to study in two shifts.[169] Some of the parents preferred to register their children with the independent religious schools, which failed to exercise close supervision of their attendance, and many children were found wandering the streets and engaging in street crime.

The educational achievements of the evacuee children, once they had moved to the housing estate, did little, incidentally, to support the conviction that the slum clearance would close the educational gap. One may cast doubt upon the extent to which the children's special needs were addressed. In the Kiryat Shprinzak housing project for evacuees, the municipality was obliged to purchase two apartments on the ground floor from the slum renewal company in order to adapt them by means of a separate entrance to serve as temporary classrooms for children with learning disabilities until a permanent institution was built for this purpose.[170] Examination of the educational achievements of the evacuee children in the new housing projects indicated that "not only did the largest group of children remain unchanged, but the trend is downward rather than showing improvement."[171] Judging by the surveys, many of those evacuated to the new projects likewise failed to sense a real improvement in other areas of life. While garbage collection from the homes as well as street cleaning and illumination had indeed improved, in other no less elementary areas they reported a decline in the quality of life. The residents expressed marked dissatisfaction with the children's playgrounds and sports facilities for the youngsters. This was a population with a high proportion of children.

Semi-City

Zionism was a project of replication, drawing its inspiration from existing models. The early Israeli concept of social democracy likewise oscillated between different European urban planning concepts. One of the models, from which the Israeli public housing project developed, was the Viennese one.[172] Since the early 1920s, "Red Vienna" had been built as a model of municipal socialism and the core of a socialist state in the heart of a hostile conservative environment.[173] Between 1923 and 1934, the Vienna Municipality built sixty-four thousand dwellings for some two hundred thousand people. Housing was perceived as a process of reshaping. The Viennese social-democratic movement sought to transform the popular culture of the working class into an aware and mobilized worker culture by means of housing, supported by additional institutions in the fields of education, health, and infant care. Thus, although the Viennese public housing project apartments were small and modestly equipped—albeit including running water, toilets, gas, and electricity—they were accompanied by extensive community services, laundries with the best technology of the period, showers, kindergartens and crèches, clinics, libraries, grocery stores, halls, theaters, and even cinemas. As the new structures became an amalgam of residential and public buildings, the tremendous public construction project carried out throughout Vienna became a clear expression of the development of a socialist urban culture. The residential units were let at affordable rents, while the buildings and their occupants were satisfactorily integrated into the urban transportation fabric.

The Viennese model developed in the face of and in opposition to the *Siedlung*, the public housing system that crystallized in Germany following the severe housing shortage after the First World War, when there was a shortfall of some two million housing units.[174] The German social-democratic Siedlung had a clearly suburban character, with the small, relatively low-cost and rent-controlled residential units built expressly on the outskirts of the cities and, in fact, beyond them. Vienna did not have the land reserves that were available to Berlin and Frankfurt when they built the Siedlung. Since Vienna was a city-state, any attempt at purchasing or acquiring land beyond the municipal boundaries would have involved a complex constitutional procedure.[175] But, beyond this constraint, in the early 1920s the Viennese social democrats preferred the urban "courtyard" model to the suburban Siedlung on ideological grounds. Since they wished to bring about overall social change, including a change in the gender-based division of roles and in the status of women, they regarded the establishment of the accompanying community services as essential, and these could by no means have been provided within the sparse housing structure of the Siedlung model, but only within the concentrated urban density.[176]

In the 1920s and 1930s both these models found their way into the arsenal of the local public housing developing in Palestine. This was a time of fierce competition between the various sectors, which were constantly seeking to mobilize supporters as an inseparable link was formed between the clientele and the political parties that backed the settlement bodies. The Israeli social-democratic concept, as we have seen, vacillated between the Viennese urban model and the suburban model.[177] The Viennese model found a partial equivalent in the shape of the *Me'onot Ovdim* (workers' dwellings) established by the Histadrut thanks to its economic and organizational power. The labor federation purchased blocks of large plots and combined the open areas of the plots that generally surrounded the local apartment building into a "large, communal public space, both protected and affording protection."[178]

In a late critique of this concept, Zvi Efrat notes that "the workers' dwellings sought to take from the city more than they contributed to it; and, rather than bolstering the street, their continuous walls created a screen that concealed it and defined an introvert, exclusive, parasitic existence that could not make do without the city and its urbanism and yet was unwilling to accept its logic and the bourgeois-liberal source of its vitality."[179] There is certainly some truth in his assertion, as the Viennese precedent likewise incorporated a defensive element that protected it against foreign external influences, namely, capitalism and the hostile bourgeoisie. The workers' dwellings were erected mainly in Jerusalem and in Tel Aviv, always with considerable financial difficulty owing to the high cost of urban land in Palestine.[180]

The other model, very different and suburban in nature, was that of the *Krayot Amal* (working boroughs). Zvi Efrat describes it as "retiring, minor, modular, quasi-rural, ex-urban from the outset,"[181] adding, "compared to the European source of garden cities and garden suburbs, the *Krayot Amal* were less nostalgic and artistic than class conscious; less romantic than productivist; less 'return to nature' than 'settlement' and 'working the land'; less lawns and ornamental gardens than auxiliary economies and vegetable patches; less tranquillity and security than transition stage and training for the only worthy path: from the consumer city to the productive village."[182] The Krayot Amal had a clear advantage from the Zionist perspective, since, extending over large tracts of land, they played a spatial role similar to that of the agricultural settlement.[183] The Krayot Amal model developed primarily in the vicinity of Haifa, such as that in Kiryat Haim, and was a hybrid that combined the romantic spirit of the European garden city with the agricultural soul of the Israeli social-democratic concept.[184] Haifa, claims the geographer Elisha Efrat, is the only city in Israel whose leadership adhered to pioneering and socialist values in the context of an urban framework by turning the city into a semi-kibbutz or into a "semi-city by focusing on neighborhood units."[185] It was this semi-city model, rather than the Viennese model, that exerted the decisive influence on Israeli housing concepts when the transition was made in the early 1950s onward from an essentially circumscribed project—the Histadrut built only 6,150 units up until 1947—to the huge program of immigrant absorption and settlement.[186]

This, then, is the background to the slum renewal program in Haifa, during the course of which the lower class was dispatched to the suburbs. The city centers were supposed to be inherited by the middle class, but this scenario, namely, the renewal of Wadi Salib, did not come about. Consignment of the lower urban class to the suburbs fitted in with other contemporary trends, primarily with the spirit of the persistent Israeli effort toward population dispersal. It seems unlikely that anyone at the time recognized that urban centralization could be a key to quality of life.[187] Zvi Efrat ironically describes the Israeli model as a new paradigm, an amalgam of "a suburban garden-city in a Western welfare state and a peripheral industrial town on the outskirts of the Bolshevik Empire."[188] The suburbanization of Haifa, the removal of the people of Wadi Salib from the heart of the city, a minute's walk from the center, to far-flung neighborhoods was but one of the many manifestations of Zionist ambivalence toward the city.[189] At first the authorities tried to delay the immigration of the city dwellers among the Jews of Morocco, but once they had actually arrived additional measures were called for. Whereas the initial attempt to force the immigrants to live in agricultural settlements along the border failed when many immigrants took matters into their own hands and moved to the city, the second attempt to push the North African immigrants out of the city center to its outskirts succeeded. What the Israeli social-democratic approach failed to achieve at the national level was implemented at the local level in Haifa, its bastion. The fundamental contradiction-riddled attitude toward urbanism as a necessary evil to be grudgingly accepted found its expression here.

The marginality of Wadi Salib's residents was topographically manifested in this sweeping move. As long as they lived in Wadi Salib, in the heart of the city at walking distance from the commercial center, they had not sensed this. Now that they had been shunted to the suburbs, these urbanites began to feel ill at ease. Thus, for example, they became aware of the lack of public transportation that should have connected them to their lives, their work, their friends, and their family.[190] They appeared, in fact, to be rather lonely. A preliminary report by the "Community Work Bureau" within the Haifa Municipality, which proposed that the immigrants be transferred to the housing projects in groups so they would be able to preserve their existing social networks in the downtown, was apparently not taken into account.[191] A collective transition, the report believed, "will not lead to the cessation of contact and to the severing of ties with relatives, family members, or citizens of the same [Moroccan] city." The dry statistical data on the Wadi Salib evacuees, who were destined to be exhaustively surveyed over the following years, indicate a decline in the proportion of families most of whose friends were living in the neighborhood and a rise in the proportion of families alleging that they had no friends at all. In parallel, the proportion of families seeking entertainment in the city in the evenings was considerably higher.[192] "The question," wrote the author of the survey, "as to whether we should regard the severance of the ties of friendship in the Wadi and the increase in time spent outside the home in the evenings as a positive or negative phenomenon is one of values, which we, the sociologists, had better not attempt to answer, but rather make do with trying to understand the wishes of the relevant population."[193]

Understanding, however, was by no means a simple matter. "Even if the respondent understood the significance of the question put to him, and even if he was able to answer it, we should still be skeptical with regard to the reliability of his response," complained two researchers sent out to conduct a field study among the evacuees living in the housing estates. With an equal measure of consternation and irritation, they wrote:

> We very often presented a certain question to some person, evidently intelligent, but he contradicted himself! There were even amusing cases in which the interviewee said something and its opposite in the very same sentence: "It's a pity that they didn't disperse us all among other ethnic groups so that they wouldn't all remain together like in Wadi Salib, but the Ashkenazim in the block beside us, we don't get on with them. With us in the block there are no problems, thank God, they're all our people."

Go try to understand from such a sentence whether this is a case of self-repellence or self-attraction; or perhaps the disclosure of an ambivalent position? Or maybe a mixture of Israeli values and Moroccan values?[194]

The researchers offered, in this context, a fairly convincing explanation of the inconsistency that their Moroccans revealed during the course of their participant observation. Incidentally, the expression "our Moroccans" by which the researchers chose to refer to the group of interviewees during their work, so as to distinguish them from other Moroccans and refrain from applying their conclusions to the entire Moroccan community in Israel, "should not be regarded as having any dismissive connotation. The respondents themselves used it in conversation with us, exhibiting a distinct sense of humor and complete lack of a sense of inferiority as to their ethnic origin."[195] Let us return, however, to the phenomenon of inconsistency, which the researchers explained as a duality of value systems. "What was characteristic of the group that we studied," they interpreted, "is that the Moroccan values in Israel are gradually incorporated into their explicit value system, whereas the unfathomable value system remains essentially 'Moroccan.'"[196]

"I Asked If There Was a Synagogue There, They Said There Was"

Understanding a people's culture exposes their normalness without reducing their particularity. (The more I manage to follow what the Moroccans are up to, the more logical, and the more singular, they seem.)[197]

Apart from this minor stumble—"our Moroccans"—Moshe Hazani and Yeshayahu Ilan succeeded in composing a delicate and moving ethnography. Under the dry and palpably unpromising title *Social Consequences of Urban Renewal: The Ethnic Synagogues in Wadi Salib and Their Social Role,* they touch upon the deepest essence of the clearance of Wadi Salib. Some forty synagogues known to the Religious Council of Haifa, and in all probability some twenty more private and small ones, appeared to have operated in the neighborhood. Most had been established through the initiative of the residents themselves. "The neighbors would get together and say why should we go far, we'll make a synagogue of our own. They would lay hands on a room or something unimportant and do what was necessary to it. And if later there were too many they would say let's make another so they went and made another one next to it."[198] Apart from the coffee bars, which so appalled the police and the commission of inquiry, it was the synagogues around which Wadi Salib's social life was woven. These remained completely invisible to the secular eyes of the urban planner.

As long as they lived in Wadi Salib, the synagogue was an integral part of the Moroccan residents' everyday lives. "I would return from work," one of the residents related, "pop into the house and go off to the synagogue. We would pray *Minha* (afternoon prayers) and not return. No. The friends would talk there. One says this, the other says that. And we would stay on or go. After *Ma'ariv* (evening prayers), yes" (Hazani and Ilan, p. 52). Within the routine of hard work shared by many of the residents, the certainty of this undemanding daily get-together was a ray of light. "In Morocco," one of the residents recalled, "there were no laborers [among us] at all, and we were happier with the way we made a living. Here we rise early for our hard work, the bus has already left, and he is agitated. But there [in the synagogue] it's different. There everything is freer. As you sit with them it is more like [being with] brothers" (p. 58). The synagogue was a ray of light not merely because of the sense of security it imparted to those who came there, but also because it modified social differences. The key to social prestige within the synagogue's walls was essentially different to the social stratification outside and was totally unrelated to occupational prestige and economic class. Heredity, origin, administrative duties performed within the synagogue, and, above all, erudition, these were the valued qualities within the synagogue, and, therefore, so the researchers discerned, "a cleaner may enjoy greater prestige than a merchant or a skilled worker" (p. 58).

The change of occupation forced on many of Wadi Salib's residents by their immigration to Israel, or at least on those for whom work had been found as opposed to those who had become unemployed, placed a heavy burden on many of them. "Throughout the week we work hard and are agitated. On Sabbath eve we meet one another and shed the nervousness," one of them told the researchers (p. 58). They found comfort in the afternoons and evenings and most of all on the Sabbath. "They used to meet with one another, on Shabbat, this one was family, that one a friend of his, talking, recounting, they were happy then. They went to synagogue A to meet one another, and each would tell about his situation, and one would encourage the other and say things will be OK, and the other would ask how he was, and he would tell him, and then one would help the other" (p. 58). "I sit there contented always; that's my life—don't want to be anywhere else," reminisced one of the interviewees (p. 57).

The synagogues, however, were not high on the city builders' list of priorities, in fact they took no notice of them whatsoever. "They told me go to the project, I asked if there was a synagogue there, they said there was, only three hundred meters to walk" (p. 31), one of the Wadi Salib evacuees told the researchers. This information, however, was very sketchy. They were not lying when they told the evacuees that there was a synagogue in the new neighborhood, but this was not the whole truth. Those evacuated from Wadi Salib to Kiryat Shprinzak were told that there was a synagogue on Eli ha-Cohen Street. It subsequently turned out that for some "this was too far . . . one must walk four bus stops. Up to Ein Ha-yam . . . you go uphill and downhill and it is hard to get there" (p. 81). Further yet than the geographic location was the cultural remoteness of the religious style of worship. The planners assigned the Salonikan synagogue in Kiryat Eliezer to those evacuated to Kiryat Eliyahu. "I came there then, I didn't know it was a synagogue of Greeks. Now I'm not happy about sitting at home on my own, and if they ask me I tell my friends not to come" (p. 31). And his family reinforces the interviewee's words: "He didn't want to live here . . . we had difficulty in persuading him; we told him there is a synagogue there, since, after all, there are Jews there, and how can there be Jews without a synagogue? Now the poor man sits alone all day at home, doesn't go out, doesn't see nothing, because he's a pensioner and like he's on his own always" (p. 31).

It would be no exaggeration to maintain that the old people's world collapsed following the move to the housing estate. "For my dad," one of the interviewees explained, "this is almost his entire world. He knows nothing but the synagogue. Goes to pray, doesn't know anything else. . . . There are old people here who don't work and have nowhere to go. So why shouldn't they sit in a synagogue?" (p. 82), asked another respondent. A different interviewee added: "If there is no synagogue, he sits at home arguing with his wife about what to do. Apart from that, he deteriorates, sits at home all day long, what should he do at home, can't be at home all day. Half a day is enough. I have a sick father too, so if there is a synagogue, he's fed up at home, goes to the synagogue, fed up with synagogue, comes back home, goes for a walk, goes to synagogue. He has a place to go. Sits with them together and he has someone to talk to" (p. 82).

They would sit during the day and read verses from the psalms and from the *Zohar*. When one of the congregation held a celebratory feast, they would bring up their chairs and gladly participate. From time to time, they would attend a lesson and some of them studied. Tea, coffee, biscuits, and an immersion heater were provided by the community. Each worshipper was asked to contribute a lira or two for this purpose during the Sabbath service. Women volunteered to take care of the arrangements. When they moved to the housing estate, all this came to an end. "How come they didn't build even one synagogue [on the project]. How come they provided for the children, built them a club and a kindergarten, and they didn't take care of us that we should have something of our own?" (p. 94).

It is doubtful whether the town planners took note of the simple fact that the synagogues of Wadi Salib served an ethnically homogeneous congregation. The reference group was in fact smaller still: each of the small synagogues catered to those who had come from a particular city in Morocco. If they were particularly few in number, they joined a synagogue of those originating in a different city, and when their numbers swelled they would establish a separate synagogue (p. 101). In itself, this fact is not in the least singular. "Were we to exchange the words 'Meknes,' 'Casablanca,' 'Marrakech,' with the words 'Lithuania,' 'Galicia,' 'Romania,' and so forth," the researchers correctly asserted, it would all sound "natural," and in this context also familiar (p. 102). "They pray one word this way and the next that way. They turn words upside down. We take the book and pray like the book, you understand, but they do something else, this is a habit so to say from abroad, they are used to this and pray like this and we do the same also from abroad, we pray like this" (p. 99). This should surely be obvious to anyone, "someone who is attracted precisely to his accentuation and inflection and tradition, then here it doesn't attract him this synagogue [the Salonikan]" (p. 99). "The Salonikan synagogue is large and splendid," and even though "the Salonikans are very good people," and even though "they make us welcome," and they "respect each and every one" (p. 94), the new residents of Kiryat Shprinzak did not feel at home there. "In Stanton," one of the evacuees relates:

They allowed a young boy to progress to be a prayer leader or reader.

A boy with a good voice they gave a chance to sing. Here it's impossible since this is a place not ours and there are many people and we have no right to demand this and there we could do everything. There were child prayer leaders or they sang sections, like with the Ashkenazim. At the Salonikan there is a regular cantor, and they don't allow anyone to go up to pray, and this also hurts sometimes, but we can't say a word.   (p. 95)

To the differences in the style of religious worship was added the unease of social class distinction. Because he was unable to take an active role in the religious ceremony the worshipper could not compensate for the ongoing class-based frustration in the secular world by acquiring religious stature. This was compounded by the clear economic disparity between the Saloni-kans and those of Moroccan origin. While the Salonikans did not expect the Moroccan worshippers to make a contribution, the latter found themselves embarrassed at their limited financial means. Since they felt ashamed in face of the Salonikans—"contractors and owners of businesses"—they made contributions of over ten liras when called up to the reading of the Torah, which was beyond their financial means and far more than the one or two liras that had been the norm in Wadi Salib (p. 95).

This was in all probability not merely a matter of blindness on the part of the planners, but also a manifestation of general insensitivity. Follow-ing prolonged pressure, the municipality agreed to allow the residents of Kiryat Eliyahu to use the neighborhood kindergarten for prayer over the high holidays. The joy and relief were boundless. "We organized the com-mittee and the neighborhood, we took this club, and they brought a torah scroll from our synagogue where we used to worship in Stanton, and we brought everything here . . . everyone was content a hundred percent and everyone was happy" (p. 110). The high holidays, however, came to an end, and with them, apparently, the happiness. The municipality had no inten-tion of turning this temporary measure into a permanent arrangement. The neighborhood committee's entreaties were to no avail. When they refused to leave—"we couldn't leave since we had been so content one Sabbath, two Sabbaths"—the municipality resorted to extreme measures. "They took this kindergarten and they brought a vehicle and inspectors, and we paid a fine for the removal, that they impounded the torah scrolls with them and now took the torah scrolls back to our synagogue in Wadi Salib" (p. 110). All the submissions, requests, and urging were fruitless, and the response of the authorities was clear: "Then they said, we have built you a synagogue that can take from five hundred, six hundred people, the Ministry of Religion said, the Salonikan one, they said we have built it for the whole Allenby neighborhood" (p. 111).

Similarly arbitrary measures were taken in Kiryat Shprinzak. Once the residents had grown tired of the three- to four-kilometer walk to the synagogue on Eli Cohen Street in Ein Ha-yam, they began to improvise. At first they obtained a school classroom, then a small prayer room in the gymnasium. "The room is large enough," one of the interviewees related, "but it is unbecoming for a synagogue. Boys and girls exercise there and ropes on the ceiling—it's not pleasant at all. Torah scrolls in a side room. There's a Holy Ark in the hall. Permanent. And all week long they do xercise (sic). The Holy Ark here and xercise (sic) here. Have you seen anything like it? And big girls in shorts" (p. 111). Formal applications submitted by the evacuees to the slum renewal company to allocate an apartment in the Haviva Reich project and a request for assistance in establishing a synagogue for Oriental Jews in Ramot Remez were rejected. Since the minutes contain no reference to any discussion on the issue, we may assume that the rejection decision was unanimous.[199]

Abba Khoushy presented "a method of population dispersal" to the commission of inquiry, as in the Kiryat Eliezer project, "in which people of all ethnic groups live, and over time they will forget from where they have come and recognize that anyone who lives here is a Jew."[200] And the clearance project was indeed Jewish, exclusively Jewish. The application submitted by a Christian Arab family evacuated from a slum neighborhood in the city requesting the assistance of the Defense Ministry's Rehabilitation Bureau in allocating it an apartment in an evacuee housing project was unanimously rejected on the strength of the assertion that "it is not in the best interest of this family, as a lone minority family, to be housed in the company of those living in this evacuee housing project."[201] "Jew," however, according to Abba Khoushy, referred only to a national category, in the sense of descent, whereas the Jew residing in Wadi Salib was someone entirely different, devoid of any existence beyond his communal religious context. As one of the residents complained: "Much is missing without the sage. Here we don't have. We have no one. No one. There is no one to give a sermon, teach *Zohar*. There is no one for the people to turn to who will be their leader. The Moroccans greatly respect the sages. And they are left alone and even forget that they are Jews, so it is with the children."[202]

Purity and Danger

The climate of the Mediterranean countries determines the external features of life: in the north the closed house is the centre of life—not only of family life, but also of social, cultural, and economic relations. Men leave their houses only for special reasons which bring them into the street or the open air. It is different in the Mediterranean region. There the center of personal and social life is the open place, the Forum or the Aguora, the cafés with their seats on the pavement, the open shops and booths. The reliability and mildness of the weather permit the great open-air theaters. This life in the open air brings more intimate comradeship than does the seclusion of the northern houses. Speech flows more easily, men are not so cut off from one another, they meet everywhere, and this intermingling produces a natural, unconstrained, hearty democracy: Intercourse is not so stiff, men are more impulsive, voices are louder.[203]

Many of Wadi Salib's residents, the majority in fact, opposed the public housing solution suggested by the Governmental-Municipal Haifa Slum Renewal Company. As the years passed, the housing projects lost much of their attraction for future evacuees,[204] who began to prefer alternative housing in the vicinity of Wadi Salib, in the downtown, and in Hadar's older quarters. The alternative housing survey conducted in the late 1960s by the Governmental-Municipal Haifa Slum Renewal Company indicated that 70 percent of the evacuees in Haifa preferred "replacement dwellings" to the housing projects.[205] Approximately one-quarter of them chose dwellings in Hadar ha-Carmel and some 42 percent chose to live in the downtown.[206] Most of those choosing alternative housing were older than those moving to the new estates. One of the surveys characterized them as people "whose life patterns are more traditional."[207] Their preference for the replacement dwellings, "whose architectural style also tends toward the middle-eastern tradition,"[208] was attributed by the author to their traditionalism: "The fact that in a considerable number of these apartments the hygienic appliances are not up to the accepted standard in a modern apartment did not, apparently, disturb these evacuees to such an extent that they are forced to change their accustomed way of life. When given the choice they preferred the familiar and traditional to the modern and foreign."[209]

The survey author's appraisal reflected the period's modernist ethos. Urban housing and planning policy has been motivated throughout the twentieth century by a desire "to clean up" the physical environment of the lower classes—in many cases the urban working class—thereby modifying social reality.[210] Urban reform programs were created in the spirit of nineteenth-century hygienics and were subsequently streamlined by architects of the modernist movement, housing reformers, and urban planners.[211] These views were founded upon environmental determinism, while their social legitimacy was derived from a rational definition of needs. Yet the preference shown by the majority of Wadi Salib evacuees for alternative dwellings rather than the new housing estates could have turned out to be quite rational.[212] Even though 34 percent of those who chose alternative housing still lived in crowded conditions of over three people to a room,[213] they did not often complain. "It is precisely in places that are objectively more crowded," concluded the survey, "that the occupants complain less of overcrowding."[214] They likewise failed to complain of deterioration in urban services; their condition was, in many respects, probably better than that of the occupants of the new housing projects, many of which were built on the outskirts of existing built-up areas without basic infrastructure installed to meet the needs of the new residents. Within the pro-modernist context of the slum renewal company, the decision of Wadi Salib's residents to forego the supply of housing in the new projects and to prefer old-fashioned apartments was perceived as surprising, even though this choice was far cheaper for both the occupants and the public housing bodies.[215] It appears that only one member of the board of directors representing Haifa Municipality, the architect Kaminka, understood something about the urban setting that was beyond the remaining management team; he regarded the refusal on the part of the residents "to go up to the projects in the hillside neighborhoods," as vindication of his claim that "among us, just as abroad, there is a stratum of residents who prefer to be city dwellers. It is difficult to remove them from their environment, particularly to isolated neighborhoods and slopes so steep that in my opinion, as an architect, they should not be built upon at all."[216]

The partial failure of the Israeli ethos of modernity, as manifested in the evacuation of Wadi Salib's residents to the new housing estates, indicates the disparity between social imagination and spatial imagination characteristic of the city's planners. David Harvey has pointed out that social imagination enables people to comprehend the general picture,[217] both in regard to one's personal life and in relation to a wide range of people, in an attempt to mediate between individual and society through an understanding of the historical role of the individual; geographical imagination, on the other hand, "enables the individual to recognize the role of space and place in his own biography, to relate to the space he sees around him, and to recognize how transactions between individuals and between organizations are affected by the space that separates them."[218] The city planners did not manage to bridge the gap between social and spatial imagination. Their integrative perception, as formulated in Abba Khoushy's saying "they merge and forget their origin," lacked any geographical imagination and could even be said to be oblivious to the spatial aspect.

Modernity and integration, within the context of national projects, are not independent universal values. As in other nation-states, in Israel they too serve national objectives, and in conditions of national conflict their validity varies to an even greater extent, depending on whether they are applied to the classes of the dominant majority or the minority.[219] While the Governmental-Municipal Haifa Slum Renewal Company did indeed deal with Arabs in some of the city's slums within the framework of its renewal programs, this population played a marginal role within the overall clearance project. A survey conducted in 1962, in parallel to the clearance of Wadi Salib, showed that only 67.9 percent of Arab households had running water, only 30.7 percent were connected to power, and 43.3 percent had no toilet.[220] The Zionist concept of modernity, which already in early programs such as those of the Haifa Committee in 1937 was selective and exclusive in nature and referred primarily to Jews, remained thus to a large extent also after the establishment of the state.

Haifa explicitly chose demarcation with regard to its Arab population and after 1948 reproduced the segregation practiced in the city prior to the war. With regard to the Jewish residents, on the other hand, at least at the official level, the trend was toward integration. The Western city, according to Max Weber, is distinguished by its integrative character, which is a consequence and outcome of the city's dependence on the migration of foreigners and outsiders.[221] Every city throughout the world, maintained Weber—one of the first theorists of the city—was established by alien settlers who had no ties to the place prior to settling there. The severing of tribal allegiances and earlier traditions of the city dwellers, as well as their release from former dependent relationships, stemmed, in Weber's view, from a shared economic aspiration for growth and success that determined the integration of the newcomers. Occupational associations and spatial characteristics would, as part of this process, replace previous tribal identities. In the ancient Greek *polis*, asserted Weber, a collective tribal identity had indeed been preserved within the frame of urban citizenship, while in the cities of Northern Europe in the Middle Ages newcomers were accepted into the fold on an individual basis. But in the end, and despite all the differences, the European city succeeded in including the aliens within the civil body. Civil equality naturally became a condition for the development of the city and a necessary outcome of urbanization.[222] It became an integral part of the Western city's character, as an association of citizens subject to the rule of law valid only for them. The Western city, according to this reading, is the source of modern citizenship.[223]

Contemporary writing on urban studies follows the tradition established by Weber, which links urban processes of integration to civil equality. Against the background of ethnic heterogeneity in the large cities over the past decades, and in the light of the multicultural discourse, however, the nature of the questions is changing. What is actually wrong with segregation? Is group closure problematic in itself? Is it necessarily correct to support in every instance a mechanical perception of merging on the basis of the relative proportion of the various groups within the population, asks the researcher Iris Marion Young, as she raises critical thoughts on sweeping integration.[224] Mutual attraction on the part of the members of the same group as manifested in patterns of segregated residence is not inherently problematic, she asserts, and is certainly less problematic than the opposite trend that denies group affiliation.[225] Processes of integration, she argues, are generally directed from the strong to the weak. It is only the weak who are required to change their way of life; an integrative perception of residence ignores the need of members of excluded and marginal groups to live close to one another, and if integration proves a failure the blame is placed on them.[226]

The idea of integration, Young asserts, mistakenly concentrates on patterns of group closure rather than on issues of preferences and deprivation: "The idea of integration tends to focus on the wrong issue. According to this ideal, the problem of segregation is also the problem of separation, and the remedy is mixing in proper proportions. The primary issue becomes mixing as such, rather than the production and maintenance of privilege and deprivation, which is the main harm of segregation."[227] The negative element of ethnic-based segregation, then, is not to be found in the attraction of the excluded in mutual closeness, but in completely different aspects: in the fact, for example, that such segregation undermines the principle of equal opportunities and curtails freedom of choice of residence, in that it creates privileges and advantages for various sectors of the population and its very existence makes it difficult to rectify these wrongs. Young goes on to allege that the process of segregation causes the privileged to lose sight of the advantages they enjoy. Her main cause for concern is the social blindness produced by this situation. Segregation, she maintains, obscures the privileges from those who enjoy them in two ways: in removing the plight of the underprivileged from the range of vision, while at the same time establishing the position of the average person as a privileged one.[228] Segregated living undermines the sense of justice on the part of the privileged: they are likely to fail to discern injustice and also to be unaware of their relative advantages in the given circumstances, since they experience their residential environment as being absolutely ordinary.

Susan Bickford offers a similar argument from a different perspective.[229] Urban segregation generates blindness towards the other, which Bickford sees as a real danger to the development of democratic imagination and participation. The real essence of the public domain is to be found in the multiplicity of its various simultaneous voices. The natural locus of these various voices is the city square. The segregated suburb is the direct antithesis of this polyphony. Bickford's point of departure is American, and it is from here that she derives her insights. The orderly and well-maintained white suburbs and the black ghettos in the large cities, she asserts, are two sides of the same coin: those whom we are accustomed to seeing by chance as we make our daily rounds of the public space influence our image of the citizen and of the person with whom we wish to maintain civil contact.[230] The danger of segregation lies, then, in the loss of the multivocal public democratic sphere and in the curtailment of the democratic imagination.

The assertions put forward by Young and Bickford are of a general nature, and their insights into civil blindness have a universal validity. They examine urban segregation as a microcosm of the general issue of citizenship while linking the social to the political realm and the local to the national, allowing the urban space its due standing within Western democratic discourse. But it is precisely because the writing of Young and Bickford addresses the discourse of urbanism and citizenship that it exposes more than anything else the limits of applying existing theoretical studies of urbanism to Israel in general and to the case of Wadi Salib in particular. The minority in this case does not comprise labor migrants who join the population, but the remnants of a local community, native in part, half of the population of the former city that in an instant was transformed into a small minority. The segregation practiced nowadays in Haifa between Jews and Arabs is not voluntary but was forced on the Arab minority in the city in 1948 and thus constitutes a link in Israel's general policy toward the minority. Despite the apparent chronological continuity, the residential segregation between Jews and Arabs is not a direct extension of the communal segregation that existed in the mandatory city. Wadi Nisnas cannot thus be explained solely by means of a discussion on segregation. The legal status of Israeli Arabs prevents us from discussing them and the Mizrahi Jews in the same breath and draws very clear boundaries for the validity of the equation between them and the Mizrahim regarding issues touching upon the link between urban patterns of residence, identity, and civil equality. Discrimination, we may argue, exists only among equals, that is to say, among Jews. Since we lack other tools, however, we must make the best use of that which is available to us, making the most of it while remaining aware of its limitations. Legal geography may assist in this to some extent, since it examines civil status within a space with direct reference to the legal apparatus.

Like Young and Bickford, the legal geographer Richard Ford regards the big city, the metropolis, as the arena in which the tension between difference and discrimination is to be resolved, and he therefore concentrates on a legal-geographic analysis of urban segregation.[231] The importance of the analysis offered by Ford lies in its exposure of the vitality exhibited by the machinery of segregation and discrimination even after it has lost the legal foundation on which it rested in the past. In the Israeli context, neither in the present nor in the past has there ever been any legal foundation for intra-Jewish ethnic-based discrimination, by contrast to the issue of the status of the Arabs. Furthermore, it is Ford's analysis of the preservation and reproduction of segregation in ostensibly free-market conditions that gives his discussion relevance to our issue. "Residence is more than a personal choice; it is also a prime source of political identity and economic security," Ford stresses, and because of this "residential segregation is more than a matter of social distance; it is a matter of political fragmentation and economic stratification along racial lines, enforced by public policy and the rule of law."[232] A space that is racially signposted, asserts Ford, tends to reproduce and perpetuate racist segregation even after the legal framework that created the segregation no longer exists; a liberal residential policy free of segregation laws operating in a space that was ethnically coded in the past will continue to perpetuate the former patterns of segregation. Even without segregation laws, and even in the absence of prejudice, "whites" will prefer "white" quarters. They will do so because the formerly "white" quarters preserve the advantages they have accumulated from the time when they enjoyed advantages by virtue of legal, structural, institutionalized discrimination and enable the current residents to enhance and preserve their economic advantages. All the more so in the real world, where some measure of racism and prejudice will always endure. Furthermore, in a world of prejudice the racial and in our case the ethnic mark reflects upon the economic and social attributes of certain neighborhoods and determines their public image.

The analysis offered by Ford provides several tools that aid one in understanding the decline of Wadi Salib after 1948. The neighborhood's unfavorable image was associated with the segregation pertaining within the city during the period of the British Mandate. In other words, it was implanted in Wadi Salib's Arab-Muslim era. This image reflected upon the paucity of municipal and state resources invested in development of the neighborhood following the establishment of the state, and this in turn contributed to its deterioration. This process became more acute owing to the legal status of the buildings and dwellings in Wadi Salib, a status of "absentees' property," which is of utmost importance to the plot of the narrative but goes beyond the context of Ford's discussion. The signposting of Wadi Salib as a rundown area was reproduced and perpetuated after the establishment of the state, when the more successful among the new immigrants, Ashkenazim, for the most part, were quick to leave the neighborhood when an opportunity presented itself. Since those remaining in Wadi Salib, mainly Mizrahim, belonged to the lower socioeconomic strata, they confirmed the inferior image of the former neighborhood. The integrative step that the authorities wished to take by vacating the remaining residents to the housing projects was only partially successful. The epithet *evacuees* that stuck to those who chose to move to the projects over the following years became a synonym for poverty and social deprivation and a stigma.[233] Renewal of the city center, a solution to which most of the residents showed an inclination in preferring alternative housing to a project apartment, would perhaps have proved more successful. It may have contributed to the emergence of an urban culture that was weakened during the suburbanization of the residents of the city center.[234] For this, however, a spatial imagination was required as well as a perception different from the integrative one adhered to by Haifa's urban social democracy. Desegregation, for example, a futuristic model proposed by Ford for such dilemmas, which strives toward creating fluidity among groups having well-defined cultural attributes. Not the eradication of the differences, asserts Ford, but rather rendering the boundaries traversable is the solution that accords with the spirit of current trends in multicultural urban planning. No such solutions were available in the 1960s.

4. Khirbeh

Altneuland

Fantastic reports by travelers have touched up the city. In reality it is gray: a gray-red or ocher, a gray-white. And entirely gray against sky and sea. It is this, not least, that disheartens the tourist. For anyone who is blind to form sees little here.

—Walter Benjamin and Asja Lacis, "Naples"

IN THE AUTUMN OF 1895 THE BERLIN ZIONIST WILLY BAMBUS made his way from Zikhron Ya'akov to Haifa by horse-drawn coach. As he surveyed the spectacular vista of Haifa Bay, with Acre emerging in the background, it occurred to him that this exhilarating piece of nature was no less beautiful than the Bay of Naples. But it was just this topographic resemblance that brought into relief the tremendous difference. How could Haifa and Acre compete with Naples and Portici? The natural beauty, he felt, did not find its full expression, since it lacked "the enlivening element of human activity," of the shore and the sea, which "in the past" had bustled with life.[1] Without tourist attractions, uncharacteristically clean for an Oriental town and "healthy," the small town induced in him a certain sense of dreariness.[2] A similar view met First Lieutenant Said Ruete on his journey to Palestine in 1894, accompanying the German consul to Syria and Beirut. He approached the town from the north, likewise traveling by horse and coach, and complaining of the dirt. The horse covered the distance from Acre to Haifa in three-quarters of an hour, with the coachman urging him on unduly—to Ruete's mind. After passing with the speed of lightning through Haifa's eastern parts, which left no particular impression on Ruete, his spirits lifted upon setting eyes on the red roofs of the German colony, on which he reported expansively in the booklet he published under the auspices of the German Colonial Society.[3] He was not the only European traveler to prefer the German colony to the Arab residential areas, since it, unlike the "oriental squalor," left a favorable impression by virtue of its "order and cleanliness" and because "its friendly houses are altogether European."[4] Ruete did not allow the general appearance of neglect to blur his vision. Haifa's chief value, he explained in a lecture to the members of the German Colonial Society in Berlin-Charlottenburg, was to be found in its hinterland, namely, the valley of Jezreel, which, he considered, was potentially no less fertile than the Hawran region of Syria. What was lacking was only the manpower required to cultivate the land in a rational manner. "The moment that these plots of land are settled by planned European migration, the rich harvest will find its way to Haifa and spur its growth." Willy Bambus was likewise not taken aback unduly by what he saw. As the port city of the Galilee, Haifa, he wrote, was of utmost importance to the Jewish colonies in this district as well. The Jews, he thought, should take greater note of this than they had done thus far.[5] Another Central European tourist chose to adapt the impressions of desolation and neglect left upon him on his visit to Palestine in 1898 in a utopian novel rather than in a travel diary. In his book *Altneuland*, published in 1902, Theodor Herzl chose to bring his protagonists, the Viennese Jew Friedrich Löwenberg and the Prussian aristocrat Mr. Kingscourt, back to Palestine after an absence of twenty years.[6] Herzl's utopian Haifa of 1923 bears no resemblance to the "dirty, neglected [alleys], full of vile odors" and "the colorful Oriental poverty" that cries out from every corner,[7] as these had appeared to Löwenberg and Kingscourt on their visit to Jaffa in 1903. This is "a wonderful city," "supremely beautiful." In Herzl's colonial fantasy, Haifa becomes an international transport hub within twenty years: "All lines of the railway network to Asia Minor, the building of which had commenced in the previous century, have been operating now for some time." "Today," proclaims David Litvak, an Eastern European Zionist redeemed from the degenerating Jewish experience in the Diaspora, to the two visitors:

> trains run now to Damascus, Jerusalem and Baghdad. Since the railroad
> bridge over the Bosphorus was finished, it is possible to travel directly,
> without change of cars, from Saint Petersburg or Odessa, from Berlin or
> Vienna, from Amsterdam, Calais, Paris, Madrid or Lisbon to Jerusalem.
> The great European express lines all connect with the Jerusalem line, just
> as the Palestinian railways in turn link up with Egypt and Northern Af-
> rica. The north-to-south African railway (in which the German emperor

was interested as long ago as the 1890's) and the Siberian railway to the Chinese border, complete the railway system of the Old World. We are at an excellent junction in that system.[8]

It was not long before the railway blueprint sketched by Herzl, enchanted as he was by technology, began to take shape. Ten years after the appearance of *Altneuland,* one could already travel by train from Haifa to Damascus and even from Damascus to Haifa, albeit third class but on a daily basis.[9] One had to change trains at Samakh, a three-hour journey, and from there travel a further nine hours to Damascus. A travel guide published that same year reported that a railway line was soon to be built, passing from Afula through Jenin and Nablus on to Jerusalem, and that upon its completion about one year hence it would connect to the Turkish railway network or, more precisely, to the route of the Hejaz railway. In view of these developments, the guide foresaw, Haifa would, upon completion of the transportation network, rapidly develop into one of the country's most important cities.[10]

It was indeed this railway line, on which construction began in 1904 at the point at which Wadi Salib entered the coastal plain, that had aroused the small Mediterranean town from its torpor.[11] A new spirit of entrepreneurship was in the air. For example, the prices of houses and land rose sharply on the eastern slopes of Mount Carmel, which began to develop in the wake of the involvement of Jewish, German, and foreign merchants in the plans for the building of the railway and the expansion of the harbor. The prevailing architectural style likewise underwent modification with the migration of wealthy Muslim and Christian merchants. Spacious two- and three-story houses built with chipped stone and surrounded by gardens began to spring up in various parts of the city. While wealthy Muslims built their homes in the vicinity of the Hallisa neighborhood; wealthy Christians built theirs close to Wadi Nisnas. The construction of the railway also indirectly contributed to the growth of the city's Jewish population.[12] Some of the city's new residents came from Acre when the latter lost its predominance owing to the construction of the railway.[13] These were Mizrahi Jews from Morocco, Syria, Izmir, and Constantinople, who, by the end of the first decade of the twentieth century, would constitute an absolute majority of the city's Jewish population.[14] With the technological developments and growth of urban industry, the number of Ashkenazi Jews in Haifa also began to rise. These groups were portrayed as "the refined Sephardis" and "the coarse Ashkenazis" in a guide published by the Prussian Cartographical Department for the exclusive use of German soldiers during the First World War.[15]

The Hejaz railway was to change Haifa's appearance. It was named after its destination—the Hejaz region in the western Arabian Peninsula—and was planned to reach Mecca. When construction eventually ceased in 1908, it had reached Medina. Thousands of Muslim pilgrims came through Haifa port to flock to the Hejaz railway station on Haifa's eastern outskirts. Their journey to Medina had now been shortened by many weeks and was now comfortable, safe, and economical. The station furthermore served to transport goods: equipment for the construction of the main line on the outward leg and the export of grain from the fertile Hawran region to Europe on the return trip. The British deputy consul was constantly complaining of price rises in the years 1905–1907: everything became dearer, rents doubled, and the price of land increased threefold and more. Construction of a proper harbor was for the time being postponed owing to budgetary constraints. Other initiatives likewise failed to materialize prior to the First World War.[16] This task was left to the British.

Like the other large stations in Damascus, Daraa, Ma'an, and Medina, the Haifa train station was built according to the European model. Palm and orange trees were planted alongside the line.[17] The workshops and management offices were built in close proximity to the station. With the building of the railway and the harbor wharf, thousands of rural workmen from within the country as well as from Lebanon and Syria began to flock to the city. These regions belonged to a single political framework governed by the Ottoman Empire.[18] The railway became the largest employer in the country at the time and, naturally, in the city as well. The harbor was likewise in need of many manual laborers. The railway laborers came from Safed and Aleppo, the railway and port clerks from Acre and Nablus, while others hailed from the vicinity of Haifa, Nazareth, Damascus, and Lebanon, and from Ramleh and Jaffa and their environs.[19] The new labor migrants launched tens of locomotives and passenger cars, most of German manufacture, as well as hundreds of Belgian-made goods wagons. They also gave to Haifa its Arabic name, Umm al-'Amal (Mother of Work). They began to build their homes, initially close to the railway station and continuing from there upward along Wadi Salib and to the various neighborhoods of the city,[20] grouped together according to their identity and place of origin. The migrants from Nablus and its surroundings settled in lower Wadi Salib, Wadi Rushmia, and Ard Ballan around the core settlement formed in the 1880s and early 1890s. Istiqlal, the central mosque of Haifa's Muslim Arabs, was built in the lower part of Wadi Salib. Over time the neighborhood acquired greater social and economic diversity but retained its Muslim religious homogeneity. Some of the more prosperous Muslims chose to move to the city's eastern or southern outskirts to escape the poverty, filth, and degradation.[21] One could well understand the reasons for this. "The old town, with its narrow and winding alleys, makes an unpleasant impression; the modern part to the north-west is prettier," one of the guide books noted.[22]

In the year of *Altneuland's* publication, the Encyclopedia Britannica decided to devote a separate entry to Haifa in its revised edition.[23] While this occupied a meager fourteen rows, it could be seen as a sign of the times. In the previous edition, published twenty-two years earlier, Haifa was not mentioned at all. In 1902, by contrast, following a short description of the location of the coastal city, the encyclopedia informed its readers of the intention to construct the railway line to Damascus and to build a harbor. "Once these projects have been completed," the encyclopedia noted, "Haifa will become the most important port on the Syrian coast." It was clear that a modern harbor was needed to exploit the economic potential of the city afforded by its unique topography and location. Prior to its development, the harbor could handle only a limited amount of passenger traffic. One could sail from Jaffa to Haifa by steamship, a journey of some six hours. Russian, Austrian, and Egyptian steamships called at the port once a week while French ships put in once a fortnight.[24] The bay, which offered shelter from the south and southeasterly winds, allowed ships to anchor and passengers to alight with greater safety than at Jaffa.[25] Its condition, however, was far from adequate. "The harbor, by the way, is not good," the Baedeker travel guide warned, "the steamships are obliged to anchor far beyond it."[26] Indeed, so long as the harbor had not been expanded the ships were unable to unload cargo and offload passengers in bad weather. The unloading machinery and the equipment in general were antiquated, ships had to anchor at some distance from land, and motor and steam launches were employed to bring passengers and goods ashore.[27]

The Turks built the railway line while the British took on the task of constructing the harbor. The initiative of the Turks proceeded from north to south. They built the railway line from Haifa to Medina en route to Mecca. Toward the end of World War I, they even completed the line running from Cairo through Qantarah and Lydda to Haifa, thereby, in effect, connecting Haifa to the Suez Canal.[28] The British, for their part, initially surveyed Haifa from India and later built a pipeline that was to carry petroleum from Mosul to Haifa, from east to west. The Hejaz railroad lent impetus to the British initiative by rocking its government's equanimity. Apprehension grew in the British Ministry of War that the railroad would serve to transport German-Turkish forces for a combined attack on the Sinai Peninsula and the Suez Canal.[29] Haifa Bay was pinpointed in 1907 by the Sub-Committee for Indian Affairs as a suitable site for the landing of the forces required to block such an attack. Various committees set up during World War I to submit recommendations regarding the prospective British area of control in the Middle East in the event of a British victory agreed that this should include the entire system of ports and railroads connecting Haifa to Baghdad and Mosul. The military advantages to be gained by a British landing in Haifa Bay during the course of the war combined with an awareness of the potential benefits of an imperial port of transit in time of peace.[30] When the Sykes-Picot agreement was concluded in 1916, the English chose to ensure their control over Haifa Bay with the intention of establishing a free port there. Whereas the path of the Hejaz railroad had proceeded apace to Mecca in Ottoman times, the British, driven by strategic considerations, invested their efforts in a civilian and military imperial transportation system between Egypt and Iraq and on to India. By the end of the war, Britain had established territorial continuity from the eastern Mediterranean basin to the Persian Gulf. The advantage of Haifa port lay in its capacity to serve the Mesopotamian-Indian hinterland.

Construction of the harbor in Haifa did not stem from local needs.[31] Haifa was far from the centers of production and consumption, most of which were located along the Jerusalem-Jaffa axis, and some distance from the rapidly developing Tel Aviv and the region of citrus orchards in the central coastal area and the southern Sharon. From the local Arab perspective, Haifa had in any case been separated from the "al-Dakhiliyya," the hinterland of Damascus and Hawran, with the division of the Mandate territories. Its geophysical advantage lay in the possibility of building a deep-water harbor, while its geopolitical attraction stemmed from the convenient connection with the other areas of British control in the Middle East. The navy base in Haifa was intended to secure the safe passage of British forces to India, and this advantage was compounded by a further cardinal consideration: it would be convenient to lay the petroleum pipeline to Iraq through Haifa, that is, along a particularly short route that passed through British-controlled territory. The development of Haifa harbor and the consequent development of the city were thus closely linked to the British imperial interest in oil. In 1908 British franchisees discovered large quantities of oil in southwest Persia. In 1911 the home secretary Winston Churchill discontinued the use of coal to power the ships of the Royal Navy in favor of oil. From this point onward British policy was governed by a clear interest in maintaining control of and access to its oil resources. Britain took an important step in this direction when it succeeded, in 1914, in increasing its share in the Anglo-Persian oil company to 51 percent. In 1927 large oil reserves were discovered in Iraq, which soon became the main source of oil in the Middle East after Iran. The oil in Bahrain, Kuwait, and Saudi Arabia, on the other hand, was discovered during the 1930s. The defense of its sources in the Persian Gulf became a major element of British policy in the region. This issue remained of prime importance within Britain's imperialistic framework in the area from World War I up to the end of the British Mandate in Palestine.[32]

From 1919 onward the British Ministry of War began to conduct surveys with a view to establishing a route for laying a railway line and an oil pipeline between Haifa Bay and western Iraq.[33] Further such surveys were conducted on several occasions over the following years. The idea of the railway was eventually abandoned, but the oil pipeline did materialize and tilted the scales in favor of the construction of the harbor in Haifa. The decision to locate a modern harbor in Haifa was made in 1923. In 1926 the British parliament passed a law providing for a loan for Palestine and East Africa, and once the British government had successfully floated a loan of 4,475,000 pounds sterling the initial work of deepening the basin and draining the adjacent area using the sand removed from the sea began in 1929.[34] The pipeline carrying oil from Mosul was laid between 1926 and 1934 and was connected to the refinery built in the Zevulun Valley nearby Haifa when this was opened toward the end of the 1930s. The export of oil from Haifa port had already begun in 1934. In 1937 a separate wharf for the conveyance of oil was built.[35] A British tourist guide asserted in 1934 that "since it became the terminus of the 'Iraq Petroleum Company's' pipe line, and since the construction of the new harbour, Haifa's importance, both as a port and a commercial center, has grown enormously, and it is obviously destined for still greater development."[36]

Initially it was still unclear who would benefit from the momentum of development ushered in by the British Mandate. Among the local Arab intelligentsia, doubts began to grow as to the advantages that these programs promised for the Arabs. An open letter addressed to Winston Churchill in the local Palestinian journal *al-Karmil* as early as 1921 expressed the following:

> Those of us who are thoughtful recognize Britain's purpose in maintaining its influence over the Arab lands. It is to transform Palestine into the port of Iraq, the Arabian Peninsula and India. It is to hold control over this bank of the Suez Canal. It is to exploit Iraqi oil and to establish British factories in Iraq and to create in the whole Arab region and Palestine a market for British goods. Thoughtful Arabs begrudge you only this—that you have delivered the port of the Arab countries into foreign hands so that they can rob us of our economic resources.[37]

Just as the writers in *al-Karmil* had identified the risks inherent in the British initiative, the Jews well understood that the city's economic development, and in this case that of the harbor, would promote Jewish migration and also contribute directly to the Zionist enterprise.[38] From an early stage the imperial interest shown by the British in the region had been linked to the national struggle, and for this reason it was important to verify which of the parties involved would benefit from the economic boom. The Zionists had reasonable grounds to assume that the strengthening economy would better serve the Jewish cause, but this outcome could not be left to fate. Lord Melchett, the English Zionist, who was most impressed by Haifa harbor on a trip to the region in 1927, clarified these matters. In another twenty to twenty-five years, he foresaw, Haifa port would reach the level of the harbors at Genoa or Alexandria. But he issued this warning against undue complacency: "And nevertheless this is not a Jewish thing. It is Haifa's geographical location that makes it the country's exit point. . . . Others have already realized this. They are beginning to purchase land, to seize positions. Should we fail within the next five years to do something together, it may be that the ideal that we have set ourselves in Palestine will never come to fruition. I am not worried by Palestine's future economic development. This is assured. The question is only who will take possession of it."[39]

While Melchett was warning of complacency among the Zionists, others believed that the development of Haifa's harbor was all to the good. The Jewish migrants, unlike their Arab counterparts, would arrive in the Land of Israel from the sea and enter its gates through the port. The scale of the British initiative gave notice that there was no cause to doubt that Britain would maintain its involvement in the region or to fear that British commitment to the establishment of the national home would be compromised.[40] Once Haifa harbor had been expanded, so it appeared, the port would connect Europe to the entire Near Asia area: Syria, Hawran, East Jordan, Egypt, Iraq, and the Hejaz region. Since these were still developing areas, it was as yet difficult to assess the future needs of the economies of the lands bordering mandatory Palestine. The dimensions of future export and import were likewise unforeseeable. But, in light of the new circumstances, the Zionist institutions could be forgiven for tending to assume that Haifa would become "the western gate of the Orient."[41] "Should the Haifa harbour be built one day," the Zionists assumed in 1929, "the city will develop with lightning rapidity, all the imports and exports of the country and gradually of the entire Hinterland, for instance Trans-Jordan and Mesopotamia, will pass through Haifa." Sharing a network with Jordan, Mesopotamia, India, and Iran and connected to Damascus, Cairo, and Beirut, Haifa, was destined to become the largest city in the country.[42]

"Haifa Lacks Any Singular Architectural or Historical Character"

Things, however, turned out differently.[43] "The rapid and pronounced development of Greater Tel Aviv in recent years as compared with the much slower development of Greater Haifa would seem to contradict the geographical factors in the regional environments," the geographers Amiran and Shahar wrote in 1961.[44] "A generation ago," they reminded us, "most planners who gave attention to the development of major towns in Palestine were of the opinion that Haifa would emerge as the country's chief industrial town and its main center of international trade."[45] These expectations, the pair concluded, had been disappointed, even though Haifa had enjoyed a propitious starting point: as the largest port in the country with a natural connection to the heartland and from there to Damascus, Jordan, and as far as Medina; as the Mediterranean port of choice for conveying oil from Kirkuk in Iraq, with the largest oil refineries in the Mediterranean basin from 1939 on, it had been given a most promising start. Tel Aviv, the authors emphasized, lacked such advantages. It could offer only citrus groves against Haifa's oil, and what was the value of rolling oranges compared to the flow of oil? The connection to the country's heartland was likewise tenuous in contrast to that of Haifa. But it was nevertheless Tel Aviv rather than Haifa that doubled its population from 1945 to 1957.

Tel Aviv, so it transpired, possessed other less obvious advantages.[46] Established as a Jewish city—in fact the only large Jewish city prior to 1947—Tel Aviv attracted Jewish migrants who chose to live there rather than in the mixed cities of Haifa and Jerusalem. The migrants brought with them capital and investment, which spurred industrial development even though the basic conditions were not particularly conducive. Tel Aviv strangely turned its back on its primary resource, the sea, but even this mistake failed to hinder its development.[47] The concentration of Jewish population and capital encouraged many organizations to establish their main branches in Tel Aviv, thereby emphasizing its centrality. Once the state of Israel was born and its borders were formed, Tel Aviv's central location came to complement its overall preeminence. In the transition from mandatory territory to nation-state, that is, from an area of British imperial influence to the State of Israel, Tel Aviv's advantages proved decisive.

Haifa, for its part, failed to protect its primacy. Whereas in 1937 the members of the Haifa Committee had been keenly aware of the existential national importance of securing Haifa's status as a Jewish rather than an international city within the framework of the future Jewish state, the city soon lost its supremacy following the transition to statehood. Haifa's status had previously been derived from its location at the major crossroads of an imperial space. This was the source of its economic and political power during the Mandate period. What set the city apart, despite all the difficulties, was its multinational character and its nevertheless fragile existence as a dualistic yet shared civil society. With the ending of the Mandate, and in light of the new geopolitical circumstances, the city lost its clear advantages. The regional conflict and Israel's subsequent complete isolation from its neighbors immediately reduced Haifa's importance on the global commercial and economic map and eliminated the markets and prospects for development that had been pivotal during the time of its rapid growth. The departure and flight of the majority of its Arab residents precipitated the abrupt loss of its multinational character. Within a few short weeks, Haifa became a

Jewish city. Precisely because of its multinational past, Haifa had suddenly lost a singular asset vis-à-vis Tel Aviv, which had been a Jewish city from its inception. The city soon found itself grappling with the integration of Jewish migrants, some of whom came from Arab states. Wadi Salib was one of the arenas in which this process played itself out. It provides living evidence of the failure of social and spatial imagination and demonstrates the inability of urban planning to translate the local modernist-socialist ethos into an overarching urban vision. The elimination of Wadi Salib, its demolition and its preservation as a ruin over a period of several decades, symbolized more than anything the denial of the city's Arab past, whereas the partial and problematic rehabilitation of its residents symbolized the unease felt in the face of the Arab birthplaces of its Oriental residents.

While the fate of Wadi Salib was sealed with the report of the commission of inquiry that investigated the riots, it was primarily urban planning that finally brought about its demise. Fairly simple calculations lay at the bottom of the matter. The *Wadi Salib Survey* (1968) prepared by the Industrial Development Company Ltd. for the Housing Ministry's Department of Physical Planning for submission to the Construction and Clearance of Renewal Areas Authority in early 1968 gives one an inkling of the true motives for the demolition and exposes the short-term considerations that led the town planners to take a dim view of Wadi Salib. On the strength of the accumulated experience of slum clearance gained in the U.S., Britain, and Sweden, the report's authors drew attention to the relation between two major variables in town planning: land and buildings. Rapid growth of the world's urban population, they asserted, leads to increasing demand for these primary resources. This development creates two contradictory phenomena: "The fall in value of the old buildings resulting from overuse and the rise in the value of the land occupied by these buildings resulting from a rise in the demand for urban land without a parallel rise in the supply of such land."[48] The potential exploitation of the land lends it greater value than that of the existing buildings and creates an incentive for demolishing them. For this reason a negative incentive is in fact created for proper maintenance and renovation of the existing structures. "The more the value of the building declines, the greater are the chances of selling the plot and the cheap structure for the sake of demolition and reconstruction," they explained, asserting that "the existing economic-legal system does not sufficiently encourage orderly maintenance of the urban structure. A change in existing taxation will provide an incentive for allocating private funds for maintenance and renovation of the structures, which is a desirable phenomenon, both for the individual and the public."

Maintenance? The survey's data on this matter is self-explanatory. The foundations of Wadi Salib's power grid and public illumination network were laid out in 1927, and most of the existing network was installed between 1933 and 1936. All the power lines in Wadi Salib, apart from those on its boundary, were aboveground. Buildings evacuated in the 1960s were disconnected from the grid, and their occupants were left in a state of permanent darkness. The condition of the sewage and drainage systems was even worse. Part of the neighborhood was served by a section of sewage line built at the time of the Turks. In 1924 a major collection point was installed on Wadi Salib Street, whereas construction of an urban sewage system commenced in 1929 and was completed in 1943. The drainage network covered only the southern and central sections of Wadi Salib, while the north of the Wadi remained unconnected. Virtually no telephone network, incidentally, existed in the surveyed area; there were hardly any private subscribers and not a single public telephone throughout the neighborhood.[49]

Owing to the area's legal status as "absentees' property," virtually no privately owned land existed in Wadi Salib.[50] Of the 145 dunams contained within Wadi Salib, 63.8 percent was owned by the state, while 25.5 percent of the remaining area was made up of roads, alleys, stairways, and paths. Religious institutions owned 2 percent, and only 7.2 percent was in the hands of private individuals, most of whom were Arab residents who had remained in the Wadi following the establishment of the state. The land, then, was owned by the Development Authority and the buildings by Amidar, which levied the monthly rental. The public maintenance body did not evince great interest in its property.

The inner logic of the act of demolition seems at times to have been elliptical.[51] Wadi Salib, it appears from the recommendations of the 1968 survey, should be demolished because it was in any case in ruins, since it had already been demolished, and because there were those who had recently destroyed it. Between 1962 and the period during which the survey was conducted in 1968, the Governmental-Municipal Haifa Slum Renewal Company cleared some 740 families, that is, 44 percent of its residents.[52] Some of the vacated buildings were totally demolished, while others were damaged or sealed. The company's preference for clearing entire buildings in one go often met with difficulties because of the refusal of the last few tenants to leave or because of what the survey termed "their inordinate demands."[53] The financial demands, "the high expectations," and the relative slowdown in the pace of clearance were attributed by the administrative bodies to "the election year."[54] The difficulty in clearing and demolishing entire continuous areas hampered the creation of sufficiently large vacant areas to facilitate the commencement of practical exploitation. Eviction of obstinate tenants by legal means was impractical, and the only hope was that when the city engineer's office checked the condition of the buildings some would be found to be dangerous structures that must be cleared by order of the regional superintendent.[55] "A picture thus emerges," the report continued, "of a neighborhood destroyed for the large part, in the remaining built-up area of which large families are dispersed, living in considerable distress."[56] A further report describes the results of the partial process as "bald."[57] The partial destruction, implies the survey's internal logic, justifies and even dictates the continuation of the demolition. "We recommend evacuating all the structures in the surveyed area," that is, not only the 87 percent of buildings that are in a shaky condition and lack adequate sanitation, but also the remainder.[58] Approximately half the forty-one stable buildings stood along the route of the road proposed in the Haifa master plan, but the renovation of the remaining twenty stable buildings was postponed owing to the cost, the need to shut down the network of existing services, and because "the stable buildings are dispersed throughout the survey area and hinder the planned construction of Wadi Salib."

"Realization of [the] assets" was far from satisfactory in the early 1970s as well. "The Shikmona strip," designated for the establishment of a precinct of government ministries, remained a bleak plot, since the prolonged negotiations with the "supreme governmental committee for housing" failed to produce a positive outcome because of a budget shortfall and the government-imposed freeze on office construction in general and on offices for government ministries in particular.[59] Construction of the Wadi Salib area likewise made no progress whatsoever. "The rapid freeway" as well as other transportation routes would pass through the remaining parts of this area, the Shikmona survey concluded, and there were as yet no continuous open areas between them available for planning and practical utilization.[60]

The city's former Jewish-Arab complexion was now, in the late 1960s, but a pale shadow flittering above the seam lines that, with the passage of time, had become a twilight zone of social marginality. Haifa Municipality took action to clear the upper Hallisa neighborhood, which had "been established in an unauthorized manner" at the time of the Mandate, had been populated during the years of "the great immigration" by Bulgarian families who had entered the buildings "of their own accord," and whose houses, once the "Bulgarians" had left, began to change hands without authorization, without a rental contract, "without any order," and without the recognition of the Israel Lands Authority. The municipality sought to clear this neighborhood whose (Arab) residents "come and go incessantly, entirely according to the availability of work in Haifa, and most of whom come from the villages of the Galilee and the surroundings."[61] In Wadi Rushmia, Mathilda Garti from Bulgaria, a piano teacher who lived on her own in an illegally constructed two-room hut, requested evacuation since all her piano students had moved house. "I am the only one left. Now live here all Arabs. Each the family have 8–9 children. They throw stones, break everything, make trouble for me, I can't go out of the house. A living there is [none] at all. I had a little money all gone."[62] Upper Hallisa and Wadi Rushmia A, home to "minorities," as they were termed in the Shikmona survey, were also proclaimed a clearance area.[63]

Like Hallisa and Rushmia, Wadi Salib remained an urban twilight zone. In 1971 it was still partially populated. Its last residents found difficulty in drawing the attention of the authorities to their sad plight. A few of the youngsters among them exploited a student demonstration in support of Soviet Jewry and Jews in Arab countries, "shouting and trying to create a commotion on the sidelines."[64] Once the police dispersed them, the mayor consented to a meeting when asked to do so by the downtown Histadrut club. Exempted from military duty, belonging to large families living in severely overcrowded conditions, they complained that "they don't allow us to work because of our past, so we have to steal in order to eat." A list of names of families with housing problems in Wadi Salib in that year indicates that only those of Moroccan origin had remained in the neighborhood.[65] Those of European origin had left the area some time previously. The remaining families were now handled in a more energetic and particular manner and were offered alternatives in the area.[66] "Interesting things emerge," related Abba Khoushy, "that large families living in very crowded conditions refuse to move out to spacious dwellings, but rather demand certain places such as the nearby Armon Cinema."[67] Some of the houses could not be demolished since they belonged to private owners and not to the Israel Lands Authority. These were Arab property owners. The Governmental-Municipal Haifa Slum Renewal Company asked the Lands Authority to expropriate these properties, and this was duly done.[68] In cases of Arab ownership of property, expropriation was the obvious solution.[69]

The municipality now found time to address those "difficult cases," that "social residue," unable to utilize the standard evacuation solutions since the apartments offered them were too small or because they preferred not to receive loans or take out a mortgage or since no guarantors could be found for them.[70] Taking note of the demands of the Black Panthers, a protest movement of second-generation immigrants from Arab countries organized in the 1970s, the municipality began to involve itself in areas outside of housing, as it sought to integrate the youngsters into the labor market by assisting them in finding work through negotiations with the army, the police, the association of artisans and small industry, and the labor bureau. The municipality had succeeded, so journalists were told, in finding jobs for twenty young men in Haifa port.[71] Their employment by the port, however, failed to develop to the satisfaction of these last residents of Wadi Salib, and their spokesman, the Neighborhoods Committee. The port management, so the committee announced in an appeal to "our dear port laborers! Dear Jews!" was delaying the employment of the Wadi Salib youngsters "by raising false accusations such as having a long criminal record and having been exempted from military service for medical reasons, and such like."[72] Upon examining the port's employment policy, the Neighborhoods Committee discovered the "sad fact" "that instead of these youngsters from the slums other people from minority groups had been accepted, some 32 of them— 27 Druze and Arabs, and only 5 Jews out of the 32 people." A list of names of all the new employees was attached to the manifesto. "We have nothing against the Druze and Muslim communities in Israel," it stated, "we seek only the good of *our sons and our youth!*"

Future

So, with which past do they threaten you? With what, in their ignorance, they call love? Do they know what love is? After all, had they known they would have spared one grove, in which we could play hide and seek. Or the undergrowth of pine trees, to which we would secretly lead the lover. Or a roof free of masts and water tanks, on which we should carve our names, in pairs, male and female, as He created them.[73]

The history of Wadi Salib is played out between two transportation routes: its birth was marked by the Hejaz railway line. Its demise, so it turned out, would be reached along a road. If Wadi Salib had an enemy, it was Haifa's urban master plan. In the heart of the neighborhood the plan proposed "an intersection of important inter-neighborhood roads, which, according to the planners, there was no way of modifying."[74] The planners determined an impersonal force majeure: "A north-west—south-east transport route will cross the area, connecting the western part of the city to the Carmel by means of the planned freeway running along the edge of Wadi Rushmia. This freeway will also facilitate further links between the centers of Hadar ha-Carmel and the downtown." Alas, "because of the intersection and the roads leading to it, the streets in the plan cover a very large area: some 38 percent of the total area surveyed." The Haifa city master plan, so it transpired, "proposes a considerable reduction in the number of residents living in Wadi Salib and its environs in the future, mainly owing to the considerable areas of land that will be required for construction of the arterial freeway and the intersections."

Sixteen local motor vehicles, most of which were commercial, were logged during the course of the survey conducted in 1968 in Wadi Salib. The survey assumed that between one to three thousand vehicles passed along the main transportation arteries on the margins of Wadi Salib each day. The planners, however, had a different vision. The main traffic artery planned to run through the heart of Wadi Salib was to serve twenty thousand vehicles per day. According to the planners' topographical concept, Wadi Salib in its present form presented "an obstacle to the smooth flow of traffic from the city to Hadar ha-Carmel and from western to eastern Haifa on the lower tier." From here it was but a small step to regarding Wadi Salib in general as an obstacle to traffic. "We should [therefore] not draw conclusions as to the importance of the area from the economic data pertaining to the current situation," the survey asserted. "On the contrary, the economic inferiority of the current residents and the businesses in the area merely underline the potential for developing the area according to modern planning based on Wadi Salib's strategic location in the urban center of the city of Haifa."

One wonders why the survey presented four alternatives when, in any case, it sought to implement only one.[75] Alternative C, which proposed classifying the entire area as a purely residential zone, was rejected since it would incur the greatest cost in financing clearance. Alternative D, which maintained flexibility between the residential and commercial components while incorporating an element of conservation, without committing itself to defining the relative weight of each component, was found to be the cheapest. Alternative A, which proposed turning the entire area to the southwest of the freeway into a residential area that would connect to the residential district on the hill above, was for some reason decreed to be the preferred one, while alternative B was not discussed separately. This last proposed rehabilitating some sixteen dunams (or four acres) of the area. "To renovate the buildings and to preserve there the atmosphere and character of the old Haifa, with its alleyways, stairways, and small stone houses." This area, according to alternative B, "will become home to artists, artisans, small cafés, and shops selling ornaments and works of art, galleries, and restaurants." In this way it would perhaps be possible to connect Wadi Salib to Hadar. "From the geographical aspect," it stated, "the place is close to the center of entertainment on Ha-nevi'im Street and could become a kind of extension of it."

The advantages of alternative A were in no way related to Wadi Salib itself and stemmed from general urban considerations. It became the preferred option by virtue of its perfect compatibility with the master plan, its perceived capacity to solve urban transportation problems, and, consequently, the promise it offered of an improved connection between the small business and industrial zone to the east of the city and the residential district to the west. Although the survey mentioned alternative solutions to the city's transportation problems, such as construction of a tunnel below part of the area for a main road or diverting most of the traffic to an upper level built on columns, these were not discussed. The proposals presented in the survey prepared in 1968 indicate that the piles of rubble were not created in a haphazard manner but were the outcome of a deliberate choice to forgo Wadi Salib's urban potential.[76] The survey's authors warned against repeating the mistakes made in renewal activities carried out in various cities in the U.S. such as Chicago and New York, where "they tried in the main to solve urban transportation problems, thereby turning the renewal districts into areas dissected by transport arteries, full of smoke and soot." The authors also noted that "Haifa city lacks a continuous entertainment and commercial center" and proposed that the possibility of designating part of the evacuated area for this purpose be examined. They believed that the renovation of one of Wadi Salib's neighborhoods as an artists' quarter might serve to attract tourists. Alongside the advantage of preserving the neighborhood's original architectural beauty—"a most precious aesthetic architectural asset"—they believed that such a step could "be one of the factors that will change the negative image of the existing area held by Haifa's population." Their acquaintance with other Israeli cities afforded them a comparative perspective and led them to observe how transportation problems in the large cities were liable to lead the middle class to prefer housing solutions within reach of their place of employment. They noted the increasing demand for new apartments in the heart of Tel Aviv as well as the renovation of dwellings in the old part of Jaffa. They thus concluded that certain strata of the middle class would prefer to purchase dwellings in areas such as Wadi Salib, "on condition that the character and image of the place changes."[77] In Haifa, however, no such development was to occur.

The various bodies continued to play with the idea of developing an artists' quarter on Wadi Salib's remaining 580 dunams well into the 1980s. Since the majority of structures of architectural value was located between Ma'aleh Ha-shihrur Street and Shivat Zion Street, the Haifa Municipality succeeded in passing the "Artists' Quarter Plan" through the various committees, declaring the area a conservation site and designating its structures "houses earmarked for conservation" several years before the Knesset passed the Conservation Law in 1991. Three bodies cooperated in implementing the initiative: the Israel Lands Authority, the Industrial Structures Company, and the Haifa Municipality. They prepared to issue a joint tender for "the establishment of an artists' quarter on the margins of Wadi Salib."[78] During work on preparation of the tender, deep divisions were exposed between the Israel Lands Authority and the Haifa Municipality or, more precisely, between the immediate real estate profit-oriented approach adopted by the authority and the municipality's somewhat belated advocacy of development and conservation. The municipality requested that the tender for sale of the plots clearly stipulate that they were designated for "retail trade in objects of art . . . art galleries, artists' workshops, and residence solely for artists whose artistic occupation required them to live there, and cafés."[79] It demanded that the general term *offices* be deleted from the tender and that its title, "Tender for Artists' and Art Precinct," be clearly and unequivocally stated. The Lands Authority, however, had no intention of strictly enforcing such usage and sought to approve a flexible formulation that would allow any form of retail trade permitted in a residential area. Given these conditions, warned the municipality's legal adviser, every entrepreneur who submitted a bid would be able to choose any usage he saw fit, including "grocery stores, for example." The sole criterion stipulated by the tender was financial in nature, and it therefore provided no legal basis for rejecting entrepreneurs with nonartistic purposes and failed to include any mechanism with the capacity to control a change in the use of the property should it change hands after the sale.[80] For this reason, the Haifa Municipality requested that the formulation of the tender booklet issued by the Israel Lands Authority be modified to stipulate clearly that only bids submitted by entrepreneurs in the area of arts and crafts would be considered. This proposal was rejected out of hand by the authority without explanation.[81] The mayor of Haifa tried to enlist the support of the agriculture minister, under whose jurisdiction the authority operated, asking him to intervene. "The authority," he wrote, "is clearly undermining the development of Wadi Salib. . . . It obstructs the establishment of the artists and arts precinct, but enables speculators and speculation to take over the place. . . . I have never come across such brazen unfairness."[82] In the end the matter of the tender was abandoned for the most prosaic of reasons: the tender issued by the Israel Lands Authority failed to take into consideration the sorry state of the area's infrastructure, which meant that any purchaser would have had to make a considerable investment in the property. In light of the exaggerated price, no taker was found for the Wadi Salib artists' quarter.

At the same time, the "Nature Preservation Society" and the "Council for Conservation of Buildings and Settlement Sites" were making a painstaking effort to conserve the little that was left of the city's Ottoman past,[83] such as the Hejaz railway station. The original station's main building, a large stone structure with a clock tower at its center, as was common in European stations, had been blown up by the Irgun (National Military Organization in the Land of Israel) in 1946. All that remained of it was its western wing. The buildings adjacent to the railway station were in poor physical condition in the early 1950s and the Amidar company, to which they were assigned, chose to seal the upper floors and let the lower floors to tenants under protected rental terms. A struggle to conserve the Haifa East Railway Station site was waged toward the end of the 1980s in the face of the municipality's intention to demolish one of the station's most beautiful buildings, the "Railway Accountant's Building," to allow for the widening of the transportation axes in Haifa's downtown. In proximity to the station building, the organizations noted, was a small Muslim cemetery in which were buried, among others, two of the city's mayors of the early twentieth century, Mustafa Pasha al-Khalil and his son Ibrahim. The conservationists had grand plans and hoped that, as part of the conservation of the historic site, "new elements will be introduced to breathe life into it," such as an artists' center, galleries, restaurants, and small businesses, alongside the development of the train museum. Its proximity to the artists' precinct, they hoped, "will lead to the creation of an entirely new and renewed area, central to the city's life."

Some measure of gratification was achieved in the mid-1990s, when a decision was made to resurrect the conservation plan alongside promotion of the "Shikmona Program" for the establishment of government buildings on the Shikmona strip. Aware of the huge investment required to renovate the properties, whose condition had deteriorated considerably, and taking care to avoid past mistakes, the Israel Lands Authority and the Haifa Municipality decided to set up a joint foundation to carry out the renewal of the area's infrastructure before its buildings and plots were put on the market. This body would then sell the properties at particularly low prices, covering only the cost of the work on the infrastructure, namely, putting the infrastructure systems in place, dismantling the stairways, and reassembling them with illumination. Of the properties, 65 percent were indeed marketed, in some cases as a package deal comprising a building site together with a structure slated for conservation. The global and local economic crisis toward the end of the 1990s and the resulting downturn in the city's local property market value led to saturation in the supply of offices and commercial space, for which there was no demand in the city. Under such circumstances, entrepreneurs were in no hurry to purchase further structures in Wadi Salib and its environs, and certainly not to conserve old buildings.

In recent years, in the wake of the construction of a complex of courts of law serving Haifa and the north on the land of the destroyed old city, law and accountancy offices have begun to purchase plots in Wadi Salib that include listed buildings at bargain prices. The status and fortunes of buildings earmarked for conservation have risen recently, as has the area's general prestige, owing to its proximity to the government precinct. The offices generally undertake the conservation work and take the opportunity to expand the buildings in accordance with the authorized plan. Initiatives for the construction of residential buildings that were envisioned by the original plan have yet to be implemented and are unlikely to materialize.

Epilogue

Iphrat Goshen and His Wife Miriam Move Into

Said's Home in Hallisa

wrote a fantastic story about return. He sat his protagonists Said and Safiyya
in a gray Fiat bearing white Jordanian license plates and sent them on their
way from Ramallah, the city in which they resided, to Haifa, the city of their
youth. This was the end of June 1967, and Said and Safiyya had been given
the opportunity of visiting their city. The purpose of the visit is clear, and
they refrain from discussing it. In the midst of the expulsion and the panic
of the flight in April 1948, Safiyya lost her son, a five-month-old infant. For
many long years, the couple has assumed with virtual certainty that Khaldun, the infant, was killed during the course of the battle. The trip home,
to the house in the Muslim neighborhood Hallisa in Haifa, was meant to
resolve the awful uncertainty that had gnawed away at them since that day.
They have come to the city in search of closure.

The steering wheel felt heavy between Said's perspiring palms. It occurred
to him to say to his wife: "I know this Haifa, but it refuses to acknowledge
me," but he thought better of it. The car had no need of a driver.[1] Said real-
izes "that he was driving the car through Haifa with the feeling that nothing
in the streets had changed." He knew them well and now feels "as though
he hadn't been away for twenty years. He was driving his car just as he used
to, as though he hadn't been absent those twenty bitter years. The [street]
names began to rain down inside his head as though a great layer of dust

had been shaken off them: Wadi Nisnas, King Faisal Street, Hanatir Square, Hallisa, Hadar" (Kanafani, pp. 151–152).

And indeed, as they approach their former home in Hallisa it seems as if time has stood still. It is the same house, a new clothesline has been strung across the balcony, on which red and white bits of washing flutter in the wind. The bell, the copper door handle, the pencil doodles on the wall, the electricity box, the fourth step broken in its center, the smooth carved balustrade which the palm slid over, the iron grillwork of the balcony guard, the wooden door. The door of Said and Safiyya's home is opened by the occupant, Miriam Goshen. "I have been expecting you for a long time," she says (p. 163). Said casts a cursory glance around the room, which reveals to him objects he had considered to be his own, "intimate and personal things he believed were sacred and private property which no one had the right to become familiar with, to touch, or even to look at" (p. 162).

But the tenant, Miriam Goshen, is living among Said's and Safiyya's possessions. She has left the photograph of Jerusalem and the small Damascene carpet hanging in the same place and has replaced three of the set of five chairs, which "seemed crude and out of harmony with the rest of the furnishings" (p. 163). The same inlaid table remained in place. The glass vase that had previously stood upon the table had been replaced by a wooden one, containing five of seven peacock feathers. Said seizes upon this small detail, seeking to establish what has become of the two missing feathers. Miriam can't remember. "Maybe Dov played with them when he was a child and lost them" (p. 165), she says. This is the turning point in the story's plot.

Kanafani stretches the human drama to its limits. He enables Said and Saffiya's child, Khaldun, to survive against all odds and to be reborn in the image and form of the boy Dov. Khaldun, the infant abandoned in the apartment in Hallisa, was passed on, so it transpires, during the fighting in the city in 1948, to Miriam, a Holocaust survivor from Poland, and to her husband Iphrat as part of a package deal in which they received Said and Safiyya's dwelling. The coincidence heightens the drama. "Thus the day was Thursday, April 29, 1948," writes Kanafani, "when Iphrat Goshen and his wife Miriam, accompanied by the chicken-faced man from the Jewish Agency carrying a five-month-old baby, entered the house of Said S. in Hallisa. As for Said and Safiyya, on that same day they were weeping together after Said had returned from the last of his endless attempts to get back into Haifa" (pp. 170–171).

Kanafani wrote "Returning to Haifa" in 1969 in Beirut.[2] At the time the story was published, the theme of "return" was not in itself a novel one within the context of post-1948 Palestinian literature.[3] But Kanafani's story, that of the Acre-born Palestinian refugee, entwines the destiny of the Palestinian refugees with that of the Jewish refugees.[4] The dialogue that develops in the apartment in the Hallisa neighborhood between the former occupants, Said and Safiyya, and the new occupants, Miriam Goshen and her son Dov, is "the first time the Palestinian and the Jew meet each other, not on the battlefield but in an ordinary room, where each of them puts forth his point of view and discusses it with the other."[5] When the story was published it was regarded as provocative. One doubts whether it would have been interpreted as such to the same extent had it appeared today.

Kanafani places two families at center stage: on the one side, Said and Safiyya and, on the other, Miriam Goshen and the memory of her dead husband Iphrat. Between them stands the intermediate link, the son, Khaldun-Dov, who enters the dwelling in Israeli army uniform as the plot unfolds. Khaldun-Dov must decide between the call of blood and loyalty to his devoted adopting parents. But the die has already been cast. Khaldun is Dov and will remain so. On the sidelines we glimpse Khalid and Khalida, Dov's siblings, the children of Said and Safiyya born after 1948, after their brother. Their names are merely derivatives of the name of the dead-live brother. When his time comes, Khalid too will be sacrificed on the altar of the Palestinian struggle, but this time voluntarily, as a heroic fighter, unlike Khaldun, abandoned in Hallisa in the midst of the panic of war, flight, and expulsion. Unlike Said and Safiyya, apart from Dov Miriam Goshen has only dead children, those from the Holocaust, those to whom she was unable to give birth, and the dead Palestinian infant, he too a Khaldun-like figure, whom she saw, as she relates, thrown down like a log of wood by Haganah soldiers during the battles of 1948 in Haifa. This dense configuration leads the actors in the drama into impossible debates. In any event, since they lack a common tongue—Arabic speakers, on the one hand, and Hebrew speakers, on the other—the storyteller rather awkwardly makes them converse in English.[6] An echo of the author Kanafani's self-criticism emerges from the reflections of his protagonist Said: "The strange sensation came over Said that he was watching a play prepared ahead of time in detail. It reminded him of cheap melodramas in trivial movies with artificial plots."[7]

The startling visit to the home that was, but is no longer, his floods Said in flashbacks, disrupting his sense of time. It is not the home of Miriam Goshen but his own home and that of his young wife Safiyya gazing out from the balcony that appears to him. The disruption of the layers of time in Hallisa, however, does not represent a rejection of a firm commitment to historical chronology. The flashbacks and streams of consciousness serve at one and the same time to undermine, contradict, and establish the chronology that underlies the narratives. Kanafani's epic work is part of a historiographic project that seeks to define the events and place them within a historical period. "Kanafani's stories," write Riley and Harlow, "are located within a specific historical context. It is a context, however, whose very determinism the stories call into question through their narrative examination of interpretation and the parameters of story-telling."[8]

The visit to the abandoned city, as portrayed in "Returning to Haifa," is a familiar literary theme. As an epoch of displacement, the twentieth century has lent it a classic stature. In an autobiographical essay titled *Visit to Hades,* the author Günther Anders depicts a visit to his hometown of Breslau in 1966. Born in Breslau, Anders pays a visit to Wroclaw, moving between the existing place and what has disappeared. "That these houses are still standing," he writes, "that even something like a section of street, almost a complete street, this is inconceivable. It is not what is absent, not the empty space, that is frightening, but, on the contrary, when one in fact expects nothing, it is that which by chance is still present."[9] Yet it is the profound expectation that all will remain as it was, that time may stand still, that pervades the pages of "Returning to Haifa." In the midst of the terrible frustration that overwhelms Said as he waits in the apartment of Miriam Goshen for her son Dov—for his son Khaldun—he relates the wondrous story of Fares al-Lubda, the neighbor from Ramalla, to his wife Safiyya.

Just like Said and Safiyya, the neighbor Fares al-Lubda went to visit his former home in Ajami in Jaffa. The door was opened by a tall, sun-tanned man wearing a white dress shirt. As al-Lubda prepared to vent his frustration on the intruding tenant it happened that he was an Arab, a resident of Manshiyya, a refugee in his own city.[10] Al-Lubda could not contain his excitement upon seeing the dwelling. "It was the same house, the same furniture and arrangement, the same color on the walls, and all the things he remembered so well."[11] His emotion grew to the point of tears when he saw that "the living room was exactly as if he'd left it that morning. It was filled with the same smell as before, the smell of the sea, which always used to stir up a maelstrom in his head of unknown worlds ready to invade and challenge."[12] The new occupants have transformed the living room into a memorial room. On the white wall opposite the entrance, exactly as on the day on which al-Lubda and his family had been driven out of Jaffa, the picture of his brother Bader was hanging, and on its right edge, as before, the wide black ribbon. On the other walls could be seen the naked nail heads that remained after Bader's mother took down the other pictures as a sign of mourning. Bader, the heroic brother, was killed in action during the fighting in Ajami in April 1948, and it now transpired that he had been adopted by the family of the intruding Palestinian occupant, who has chosen to name one of his children after him. It is of interest to note that, in contrast to the duality between Khaldun and Khaled and to the dual existence of the dead and the live Bader, Kanafani chooses to portray the scene in Jaffa in a fantastic rather than a realistic manner. He does not, for example, give a name to the new Palestinian occupant.

In describing the house in Hallisa and that in Ajami, Kanafani's writing is an act of conservation. It insists on the country's static and unchanging nature, stubbornly refusing the force of time. In attributing to Palestinian poetry a "frozen symbolism," Hanan Ashrawi has noted the limits of the power of this poetic act of conservation. This symbolism is manifested in the insoluble tension between the Palestinian yearning for the static and the rapid process of transformation of the country's appearance.[13] It would appear that Kanafani himself is aware of the futility of the stubborn resistance toward the force of time. In his narrative the victory of memory turns out to be a Pyrrhic one. After all, apart from the picture of the dead Bader, only the naked nail heads and bare walls remain. In the process of remembering, objects are diminished rather than enhanced. "[And] for us, for you and me," says Said, who succumbs to his wife Safiyya at the end of the story, "it's only a search for something buried beneath the dust of memories. And look what we found beneath the dust. Yet more dust."[14] The weakness of the aesthetics of conservation and perpetuation is revealed in its static nature; protection of the lost panorama through memory risks "hardening into a resistance to the very idea of change itself."[15] "Returning to Haifa," it now appears, is not merely a realistic novella but also a political program. Said enters through the doorway in order to complete a circle and exits through it as someone who is likely to settle an account.[16]

Kanafani was ahead of his time in confronting destiny with destiny, victim with victim. At the same time, his narrative struggles to maintain the tension between his Palestinian destiny and the refugee in the form of the Holocaust survivor Miriam Goshen whom he has courageously configured within the plot. The refugee who lives in the home of a refugee turns out to present a complex, perhaps impossible, moral challenge. A similar tension permeates the poem ". . . As He Draws Away" by the poet Mahmoud Darwish,[17] written many years after the publication of Kanafani's novella. Darwish, in fact, presents an opposing configuration to that portrayed in Kanafani's story. This time it is not the Palestinian refugee who visits his erstwhile home, but the Israeli occupant, "the stranger" or "the enemy," as he is alternately termed in the poem, who comes to the refugee's hut. Like Kanafani, Darwish addresses the difficulty inherent in the status of the enemy as a former victim. It appears, however, that the temporal distance (Darwish's poem was written in the mid-1990s, approximately a quarter of a century later than Kanafani's story), and, even more, the intimate knowledge Darwish, the former Israeli, has of "the enemy," leads him to challenge, even to confront, the tendency he attributes to "the stranger" to reap the benefit derived from his historic status as victim.[18] That "the enemy" has previously been a victim is not directly questioned, but the moral force of the victim status as an argument in the debate is weakened. In Darwish's poem this is engulfed in the totality of the enemy's generally sanctimonious position, especially in his formidable capacity to repress the position of the other. "The Enemy," so we are told in the poem, has the wonderful gift of "concealing in his hasty cough" whatever he does not wish to hear. In order to make him hear that which he refuses to listen to, Darwish sets the refugee's yearning to visit his former home against "the enemy's" actual visit to the refugee's hut.

> Say hello to our home, stranger
> Our coffee cups
> are still as they were. Can you smell
> our fingers on them? Will you tell your daughter with
> her long braid and two thick eyebrows that she has
> an absent friend
> who would like to visit her? For nothing . . .
> but to enter her mirror and see his secret:

How she follows, after him, the course of his life
In his place? Say hello to her
If time allows . . .[19]

Rather than pictures, Darwish holds up a mirror to both parties, the outstanding natural attribute of which is reflexivity. The absent occupant seeks to enter "her mirror." As a matter of course, when she looks into it she will be forced to see him and the cups of coffee he has left behind, which she has not deigned to smell. Once the girl with the braid and the dense brows allows him to peer back at her from the mirror, she will be able to see him for an instant in his civilian milieu, that which preceded his existence as a refugee. For a fraction of a second, Darwish transforms diachronic neighbors into synchronic neighbors, thereby undermining the tendency to regard the refugee as someone who by his very nature is defined as being excluded from the cosmological order.[20] For an instant, the girl with the braid and thick eyebrows will be able to see him as someone created in God's image. But he, too, will have to confront her reflection should he look into the mirror. He will have to confront his secret and see how "she follows, after him, the course of his life, in his place." The mirror will thus block the escape hatch into amnesia or nostalgia.[21] When he sees her in the mirror, he will be forced to free himself of nostalgia, since she "follows . . . the course of his life, in his place." She, on her part, confronting his image in the mirror, in the face of the coffee cups he has left behind, will free herself of amnesia.

NOTES

Prologue

1. This chapter relies entirely upon the "Minutes of the Government Commission of Inquiry Into the Events at Wadi Salib" (in Hebrew), State Archive, doc. 7253/4.

2. *Haaretz*, August 17, 1959.

3. A completely different manifesto was published in the weekly *Ha-olam ha-zeh*, stating: "Our blood will not be shed with impunity. We shall ascend to our neighbors-exploiters in Hadar ha-Carmel. We see them at night, in the lighted windows, as we search for a place to sleep in stairways and in dark cellars, and during the day wander about in pain and hunger to find a day of public work—let us rise up against them!" See S. Cohen, "Black Thursday" (in Hebrew), *Ha-olam ha-zeh* 1137, July 15, 1959, pp. 4–5.

4. Uri Avnery, "The Revolt of the Moroccans" (in Hebrew), *Ha-olam ha-zeh* 1137, July 15, 1959, p. 3.

5. Knesset Session 669, July 13, 1959, Debate on the Government's Statement on the Matter of Haifa, p. 31.

1. War

1. Peled and Shafir, *Being Israeli*, p. 28.

2. Binyamin Halfon, the Jewish Agency for Palestine, the Department for Jewish Affairs in the Middle East, *Visit to the North African Immigrants' Quarters (Haifa, End of December), Impressions and Observations of the Visit* (in Hebrew), Central Zionist Archive (hereafter CZA), S20/10/41.

3. Peled and Shafir, *Being Israeli*, p. 25.

4. Ehrlich, "A Society at War," pp. 259–263; Shenhav, *The Arab Jews*, pp. 9–10.

5. The actions taken by the Haifa Municipality against the backdrop of the intensifying national conflict have been subject to different interpretations. While Tamir Goren and Yosef Vashitz remark on the positive principles of cooperation and the constructive aspect, the scholar May Seikaly notes that the Arab representatives on the city council lacked legitimacy within their national community and were regarded as collaborators with the Jewish side. See Goren, *Cooperation in the Shadow of Confrontation*; Vashitz, "Social Changes in Haifa's Arab Society"; Seikaly, *Haifa*.

6. The terms of surrender included a demand for the disarming of all Arab forces in the city and the surrender of weapons to the British, who would hand them over to the Haganah upon their evacuation; the expulsion of all foreign Arab men of conscription age; removal of all the Arab roadblocks; arrest of all the European Nazis who had infiltrated the Arab forces; and a twenty-four-hour curfew to ensure completion of the disarming of the Arabs. In return, all Arab residents of Haifa would be allowed to continue their regular lives and live in the city as free citizens with equal rights.

7. Eshel, *Ha-Hagana Battle Over Haifa*, p. 371.

8. There are disparate data concerning the number of Jews and Arabs living in Haifa during the years 1947–1948. According to Karsh, 140,000 people were living in Haifa at the end of 1947, of whom 75,500 were Jews and 62,500–66,000 Arabs. In April 1948 the number of Arabs in the city varied between 35,000 and 40,000. Benny Morris puts the number of Arabs before the war at 65,000, and estimates that 20,000 to 30,000 had left by the beginning of April 1948. Tamir Goren quotes somewhat higher figures. He puts the number of Jews in 1946 at 74,230, while the number of Arabs in the same year is put at 70,910.

See Karsh, "Nakbat Haifa," pp. 25, 40; Morris, *The Birth of the Palestinian Refugee Problem Revisited*, pp. 186–187; Goren, "Why Did the Arab Population Leave Haifa?" 176.

9. Goren, *The Fall of Arab Haifa in 1948*, pp. 59–86.

10. Eshel, *Ha-Hagana Battle Over Haifa*, p. 318.

11. Slutsky, *History of the Hagana*, 3.2:1382.

12. Eshel, *Ha-Hagana Battle Over Haifa*, p. 327.

13. Ibid., pp. 340–342.

14. Slutsky, *History of the Hagana*, 1383.

15. Eshel, *Ha-Hagana Battle Over Haifa*, p. 303.

16. Slutsky, *History of the Hagana*, p. 1382.

17. *The Conquest of Arab and Mixed Cities*, p. 32.

18. Ibid.

19. Eshel, *Ha-Hagana Battle Over Haifa*, p. 342.

20. Ibid., p. 315.

21. Ibid., p. 314.

22. *A Survey of Activities Between April 1947 and March 1948, a Factual and Fiscal Report* (in Hebrew) (Haifa: Jewish Community in the Land of Israel, the Haifa Jewish Community Council, 1948).

23. Golani, "Watershed in Haifa," pp. 13–59.

24. See Khalidi, "The Fall of Haifa"; Morris, *The Birth of the Palestinian Refugee Problem Revisited*, pp. 186–211, 27.

25. Eshel, *Ha-Hagana Battle Over Haifa*, p. 357.

26. El-Assad, *Children of the Dew*, p. 30.

27. There are differing estimates of the number of Arabs in the city during the decisive days of April. Goren notes that British estimates put the number of Arabs in Haifa upon conclusion of the hostilities on April 24 at thirty-seven thousand, while their number on May 14, prior to the invasion of the Arab armies, was put at a mere six thousand. Morris maintains that on the night of April 21–22 there were still thirty to forty thousand Arabs living in the city, of which some fifteen thousand left during the course of the hostilities, and that their number dwindled to around four thousand on May 10, 1948. Karsh notes that when hostilities broke out there were thirty thousand Arabs in the city, that five to fifteen thousand fled during the battles, and that at the beginning of May 1948 only some three thousand remained. Khalidi reports the escape of fifty thousand Palestinians over the two days of battle.

See Goren, "Why Did the Arab Population Leave Haifa?" p. 203; Morris, *The Birth of the Palestinian Refugee Problem Revisited*, pp. 200, 206; Karsh, "Nakbat Haifa," p. 51, 59–60; Khalidi, "The Fall of Haifa," p. 22.

28. Khalidi, "The Fall of Haifa," p. 32.

29. Ibid.; Karsh, "Nakbat Haifa," p. 58.

30. Goren, "Why Did the Arab Population Leave Haifa?" p. 190.

31. Vashitz, "Social Changes in Haifa's Arab Society," p. 9.

32. Ibid., p. 12.

33. Yazbak, "Arab Migration to Haifa," pp. 77–78, 84, 86.

34. Vashitz, "Social Changes in Haifa's Arab Society," pp. 24–25.

35. Ibid., p. 16.

36. Ibid., p. 17.

37. Vashitz, "Jewish-Arab Relations in Haifa," p. 21. On this paradox in completely different contexts, see Berger, *Dionysus at Dizengof Center*, pp. 13–86.

38. Eshel, *Ha-Hagana Battle Over Haifa*, p. 305.

39. The concept of Jewish labor or conquest of labor emerged among the Jewish settlers of the second wave of immigration (1904–1914) as part of their competition with the Arab workers. It affirmed the preference for Jewish rather than Arab workers. This principle became official policy when the General Federation of Laborers

in the Land of Israel—the Histadrut—confirmed it as such after its establishment in Haifa in December 1920. The Histadrut strongly believed that control over the country would be achieved only if Jews cultivated the land themselves. However, at the same time, Ben-Gurion began to demand that the principle of Jewish labor be applied to the entire economy, and with it Labor Zionism started to promote segregation between the Jewish and Arab national communities. In 1933 the Histadrut launched its first campaign to remove Arab workers from the major cities. The forceful eviction of Arab workers ultimately precipitated the outbreak of the Arab revolt in 1936.

40. Bernstein, *Constructing Boundaries*.

41. Ibid., pp. 56, 67, 206–215.

42. Vashitz, "Social Changes in Haifa's Arab Society," pp. 20, 66.

43. Seikaly, *Haifa*, p. 2.

44. Vashitz, "Social Changes in Haifa's Arab Society," p. 79; Peled and Shafir, *Being Israeli*, pp. 80–90; Diner, *Israel in Palästina*, pp. 42–52.

45. Vashitz, "Social Changes in Haifa's Arab Society," p. 78.

46. Ibid., p. 80.

47. Written on April 27, 1948. Quoted in Goren, *From Dependence to Integration*, p. 33.

48. Morris, *The Birth of the Palestinian Refugee Problem Revisited*, p. 201.

49. Goren, *From Dependence to Integration*, p. 140–142.

50. Morris, *The Birth of the Palestinian Refugee Problem Revisited*, pp. 201–202.

51. Golda Meir, on May 6, 1948. Quoted in Morris, *The Birth of the Palestinian Refugee Problem Revisited*, p. 310.

52. Eshel, *Ha-Hagana Battle Over Haifa*, p. 377.

53. Morris, *The Birth of the Palestinian Refugee Problem Revisited*, p. 203.

54. Ibid., p. 321.

55. Eshel, *Ha-Hagana Battle Over Haifa*, p. 377.

56. Morris, *The Birth of the Palestinian Refugee Problem Revisited*, pp. 202–203.

57. Habibi, *The Secret Life of Saeed the Pessoptimist*, p. 42.

58. Goren, *From Dependence to Integration*, p. 32.

59. Morris, "Haifa's Arabs," p. 242.

60. Minutes of the Fifth Meeting of the Committee for the Affairs of Haifa Arabs, May 27, 1948, State Archive, 49/309/41.

61. Ibid.

62. Ibid.

63. Minutes of the Sixth Meeting of the Committee for the Affairs of Haifa Arabs (Together with the Committee for the Restoration of Everyday Life), June 10, 1948, at the town hall, State Archive, 49/309/41.

64. Goren, *From Dependence to Integration*, pp. 36, 136–137.

65. Morris, "Haifa's Arabs" (1990), p. 154.

66. Minutes of the Seventh Meeting of the Committee for Arab Affairs in the town hall, July 1, 1948, State Archive, 49/309/41.

67. Morris, "Haifa's Arabs" (1990), p. 156.

68. I wish to thank Motti Golani for bringing this to my notice.

69. Morris, "Haifa's Arabs" (1990), p. 157.

70. For various estimates of the number of Muslims left in Haifa, see Goren, *From Dependence to Integration*, pp. 135–136. On the assertion that the negligible number of Muslims served as the reason for Wadi Salib ceasing to be an Arab neighborhood, see Morris, *The Birth of the Palestinian Refugee Problem Revisited*, p. 210.

71. Goren, *From Dependence to Integration*, p. 204.

72. Minutes of the Eighth Meeting of the Committee for Arab Affairs, July 8, 1948, State Archive, 49/309/41.

73. Ibid.

74. Ibid., pp. 34, 65.

75. This concept was coined by Will Kymlicka to indicate the tension between the essence of citizenship and collective rights. For further reading, refer to Kymlicka, "Multicultural Citizenship," in G. Shafir, ed., *The Citizenship Debates*, pp. 167–188.

76. Minutes of the Eighth Meeting of the Committee for Arab Affairs, pp. 35–36.

77. Ibid., pp. 142.

78. Morris, *The Birth of the Palestinian Refugee Problem Revisited*, p. 344.

79. Ibid., pp. 348–349; Morris, "Yosef Weitz," pp. 530ff.; Fischbach, *Records of Dispossession*, p. 12.

80. Morris, "Yosef Weitz," pp. 532ff.; Golan, "The Transfer to Jewish Control," p. 405.

81. Goren, *From Dependence to Integration*, p. 141.

82. Goren, "The History of the Disappearance."

83. Goren, *Cooperation in the Shadow of Confrontation*, pp. 315–320.

84. Goren, *From Dependence to Integration*, p.148.

85. Morris, "Haifa's Arabs" (1988), pp. 254–257.

86. Morris, *The History of the Palestinian Refugee Problem Revisited*, p. 211.

87. Goren, *From Dependence to Integration*, p. 148.

88. Morris, "Haifa's Arabs" (1988), p. 256; Rekhess, "Initial Israeli Policy Guidelines," pp. 110–115.

89. Goren, *From Dependence to Integration*, p. 148.

90. Morris, "Haifa's Arabs" (1988), pp. 256–257.

91. Ibid.

92. Goren, *From Dependence to Integration*, p. 150.

93. Ze'ev Shoham to Mr. David Ha-Cohen, acting mayor of Haifa, June 26, 1949, Haifa City Archive, "Street Names and Numbers" file 32509.

94. Hadar ha-Carmel Council to Haifa Municipality, September 1, 1949, Haifa City Archive, file 32509; Chairman of the Municipal Committee to Hadar ha-Carmel Council, September 27, 1949, ibid.

95. Hadar ha-Carmel Council to Haifa Municipality, September 1, 1949, Haifa City Archive, file 32579.

96. Hadar ha-Carmel Council to Haifa Municipality, September 1, 1949, Haifa City Archive, "Street Names and Numbers" file 32509.

The German Colony in Haifa was the first of seven colonies established in Palestine by the Templers, an offshoot of the Protestant Church. Their situation deteriorated during the British Mandate. During the 1930s, some 30 percent of the residents of the German Colonies in Palestine joined the Nazi party. In 1939, Mandate authorities imprisoned the German settlers in camps and, approximately two years later, expelled some to Australia. Those who remained in Palestine left the country in 1948. These developments during the British Mandate transformed the population of the colony, which lost its unique German character and began to attract new residents, particularly people of means, such as senior British government employees and wealthy Palestinian and Jewish families. Following the events of 1948, Jewish families moved into the homes of the Germans who had been expelled by the British authorities during World War II and into the Arab homes in the German Colony that had been abandoned.

97. The daughters of "al-Idisi Street" to Abba Khoushy, May 1, 1951, Haifa City Archive, "Street Names and Numbers" file 32509.

98. Y. K. to the Names Committee, May 1, 1951, Haifa City Archive, "Street Names and Numbers" file 32509.

99. Iram Tsila, Israel Communist Party, Haifa branch, to the chairman of the Names Committee, April 18, 1951, Haifa City Archive, "Street Names and Numbers" file 32509. When the name was changed, shortly thereafter, to Independence Street, there were those who criticized this step as mistaken with respect to the preservation of the city's international character. "I read with interest," wrote a Mr. Hertz, that "the name of Kingsway has been changed to Haatzmaout Road. I would respectfully note that phonetically it is not an improvement and the Hebrew is difficult to transliterate. As a name for the main street of Israel's only port, its new name is not intelligible to the thousands of tourists, visitors, and foreign business firms means that come to the country. By all change the name, but, as far as the English version is concerned, it seems to me that 'Independence Way' would be more appropriate and makes the change comprehensible. I trust that you will consider this matter in light of the street's considerable significance."

100. Shimon Shreiber on behalf of the Cracow Ghetto Fighters Survivors group to Abba Khoushy, April 17, 1951, Haifa City Archive, "Street Names and Numbers" file 32509.

101. Haifa City Secretary to Mr. Shalom Silberfarb, June 26, 1949; and also Haifa City Secretary to Mr. Michael Welkind on July 27, 1950, Haifa City Archive, "Street Names and Numbers" file 32509. See also the Minutes of Meeting no. 93 of the City Committee held on Tuesday, October 19, 1948, at 10:30 a.m., paragraph 7, ibid.

102. Ben-Gurion likewise regarded the population exchange between Turkey and Greece as proof that precisely such an exchange could provide a guarantee of peaceful relations between nations. See Morris, "Notes on Zionist Historiography," pp. 51, 52–57. See also Morris, *The Birth of the Palestinian Refugee Problem Revisited*, p. 319.

103. Morris, *The Birth of the Palestinian Refugee Problem Revisited*, p. 319.

104. Minutes of Meeting of the Provisional Government, June 16, 1948, State Archive, Records of the Meetings of the Provisional Government 10/ 308–12/2/308, pp. 20–21. See also Morris, *The Birth of the Palestinian Refugee Problem Revisited*, p. 319.

105. Morris, *The Birth of the Palestinian Refugee Problem Revisited*, p. 324. The identical position was outlined by Sharett's political adviser, Leo Cohen, who asserted, "Now that the exodus of the Arabs from our country has taken place, what moral right have those who fully endorsed the expulsion of the Sudeten Germans from Czechoslovakia to demand that we readmit these Arabs?" See ibid., p. 556.

106. Ibid., pp. 326, 331.

107. Preece, "Ethnic Cleansing as an Instrument," pp. 817–842, 821.

108. Preece, "Ethnic Cleansing and the Normative Transformation."

109. Naimark, *Fires of Hatred*, p. 4.

110. Shulewitz and Israeli, "Exchanges of Populations Worldwide."

111. Morris, "Yosef Weitz," p. 523.

112. Fischbach, *Records of Dispossession*, pp. 41–43.

113. Schechtman, *European Population Transfers*.

114. Joseph Schechtman was born in 1891 in Odessa, where he completed his high school studies. Like all his Jewish contemporaries he was forced to make his way to Berlin in order to receive a university education. There he joined the organization of Jewish students, Chaver, and completed his law studies at the Friedrich-Wilhelm University in 1914. A year later he completed the state examinations for jurists at Novorasisk University in Russia and immediately turned to journalism and political activity. During the ensuing years, he busied himself with the plight of Russian Jewry, participating in local Zionist activity aimed at alleviating its suffering under the yoke of the Russian regime during the war. When Ukraine declared its independence in 1917 with German support, Schechtman became active in current affairs and was elected as a Zionist representative to the Ukrainian National Assembly. In that same year his first book on Ukrainian Jews appeared. The victory of communism in the Soviet Union led to Schechtman's first experience as a refugee. Accompanied by his wife and daughter, he crossed the Dniester in 1920, fled

initially to Romania, where he stayed for a while, and then on to Berlin. Here for some two years he edited Jewish Yiddish- and Russian-language journals and was active in the central committee of the Russian Zionist organization in the city. In 1924 he moved with his family to Riga and stayed there for two years while working as a regular journalist on the Yiddish and Russian Jewish press. In 1926 he moved to Paris in his new capacity as general secretary of the executive of the Revisionist movement and a member of the editorial committee of its Russian language organ *Rassviet.* In 1936 Schechtman was elected president of the Revisionist movement in Warsaw, to which he moved with his second wife, whom he had married in 1930 upon becoming a widower with a daughter and baby. In Warsaw Schechtman was active in support of the organization of Eastern European Jewry in a political struggle against the prevalent anti-Jewish policy and, alongside Jabotinsky, assumed leadership of the struggle for the program of evacuation of Poland's Jews. Following the dissolution of the presidency of the Revisionist movement in Warsaw, Schechtman remained in Poland and continued to promote the evacuation program in the countries of Eastern Europe. Upon the outbreak of war, in 1939, he escaped with his family to France and, after France's surrender, he escaped to the U.S., becoming a refugee for the second time in his life. During this time, he was forced to learn English. In 1941 he personally initiated the establishment of an organization for the study of population movement. Owing to his familiarity with European contexts, he was made a member of the United States Office of Strategic Services (OSS) in Washington in 1944–1945. This summary is based on I. Benari, *Joseph Schechtman in Memoriam, 1970,* Archive of the Revisionist Movement, P-1/1/227. See also Schlögel, "Tragödie der Vertreibungen," p. 80; Mazower, *No Enchanted Place,* pp. 115ff.

115. Schechtman, *European Population Transfers,* p. 454.

116. Ibid., p. 468.

117. Ibid.

118. Ibid., p. 467.

119. Goren, *Material Pertaining to Issues of Transfer and Exchange of Populations Between Countries* (in Hebrew), CZA, A457/113.

Ezra Danin was the person who introduced Schechtman's book to the committee. He was given the task of writing the section on the recent international history of populations transfer and found Schechtman's book on the subject "invaluable." Fischbach, *Records of Dispossession,* p. 41.

120. In light of the circumstances under which Schechtman composed his book, there is no little irony in the fact that it became the ideological platform of the Israeli transfer committee. The misunderstandings that arose at a meeting of the Institute for Jewish Affairs, which funded Schechtman's research, indicate just how innovative this study was at the time. During the course of a discussion among the

institute's members as to whether to support the project, one of them raised the naive question "Where does colonization stop and forceful transfer begin?" And indeed, in 1941, when Schechtman began his work, the perspective necessary to distinguish between migration and forced migration was still lacking. When the funding of Schechtman's research project was discussed by the Institute for Jewish Affairs in 1941, some of the participants sought clarifications regarding its "Jewish aspect," particularly in view of the tension between the institute's limited financial means and its primary commitment to a Jewish research agenda. An altercation over priorities took place between the head of the institute, Dr. Jacob Robinson, and Dr. Theodor H. Gaster. "Do you consider Jews in Romania more important than evacuation of population?" asked Robinson. "Yes, I do," replied Gaster, "The League of Nations have other experts to whom they will turn on question of transfer, etc., and not to us; but for Jewish problems they have no other authorities, and we must be prepared to supply all Jewish information." The speed at which it would transpire that Schechtman's research could indeed provide necessary information on burning Jewish issues was certainly not foreseen at the time. See Minutes of the Meeting of the Institute of Jewish Affairs, held on Thursday, October 3, 1941, American Jewish Archives, Cincinnati, Ohio, World Jewish Congress Collection, series C, box 4, file 8 (AJA, WJC, C4/8). My thanks to Omri Kaplan-Feuereisen for making this document available to me.

121. Goren, *Material Pertaining to Issues of Transfer and Exchange*, p. 2.

122. Ibid., p. 3.

123. Ibid., p. 4.

124. The summary included the Bulgarian-Romanian precedent, the transfer of Germans from Lithuania, the transfer of the Sudeten Germans, the population exchange between Czechoslovakia and Hungary, and the population exchange between Hindus and Muslims. See Joseph Schechtman to Ezra Danin, December 6, 1948, Revisionist Movement Archive, P-2/10/227.

125. Joseph Schechtman to Moshe Sharett, December 4, 1950, Revisionist Movement Archive, P-2/10/227. See also Schechtman, *The Arab Refugee Problem*, p. 105.

126. Goren, *Material Pertaining to Issues of Transfer and Exchange*, p. 15.

127. Ibid., p. 4.

128. Memorandum on the Settlement of Arab Refugees submitted to the Head of Israel's Provisional Government by Yosef Weitz, Ezra Danin, and Zalman Lifshitz, Tel Aviv, October 31, 1948, CZA, A246/140. The authors of the memorandum begin by noting numerous cases of population deportation in the twentieth century and, as they put it, "mass migrations of peoples from one country to another"—about which they had learned from Schechtman's book: the flight of the Assyrians from Turkey to Armenia in 1915, from Armenia to Iraq in 1918, and from Iraq to Syria in

1933; the flight of the Armenians from Turkey; the migration of the Greeks from Turkey and Bulgaria between 1915 and 1922; migration between the countries of Europe during the period between the two world wars and both during and after the Second World War; the migration between India and Pakistan; and, finally, the migration of 3.5 million Germans from Czechoslovakia, Romania, Yugoslavia, and Hungary or, as this period of history is referred to in the report, "deliberate deportation by virtue of victory in war." On the transfer committee, see Morris, "Yosef Weitz"; for a critique of Benny Morris's approach, see Masalha, "A Critique on Benny Morris."

129. Morris insists that the motive for the long list of "migrations of peoples" was tactical and apologetic; namely, to present the list of crimes committed in this sphere to the nations liable to criticize Israel's policy so as to neutralize such criticism. See Morris, "Yosef Weitz," p. 549.

130. Memorandum on the Settlement of Arab Refugees, p. 2.

131. Goren, *Material Pertaining to Issues of Transfer and Exchange,* p. 14.

132. Memorandum on the Settlement of Arab Refugees, p. 6.

133. Reichman, "Partition and Transfer," p. 327.

134. Schechtman, *The Arab Refugee Problem,* pp. 31–32.

135. Schechtman enumerates the Turks and the Greeks; the Greeks and the Bulgarians; the Germans from Czechoslovakia, from Poland, from Hungary, and from Yugoslavia; the Poles, the Ukrainians, the Ruthenians, the Russians, and the Lithuanians; the Indians and the Pakistanis. See ibid., 32.

136. Nonreturn was Schechtman's first resolute conclusion drawn from the many historical examples with which he was more familiar than others. Adherence to the principle of compensation was his second conclusion. The transfer committee adopted both these recommendations. The government of Israel, which received the report in October 1948, soon lost interest in the second conclusion. See Morris, "Yosef Weitz," pp. 552–553.

137. Memorandum on the Settlement of Arab Refugees, p. 11.

138. Kanafani, "The Land of Sad Oranges," pp. 75–80, quote from p. 77.

139. Golan, "Jewish Refugees," "Redistribution and Resistance."

140. Regarding these processes in Jerusalem, see Golan, *Wartime Spatial Changes.*

141. Morris, *The Birth of the Palestinian Refugee Problem Revisited,* pp. 383–384. On the prevention of the return of refugees to Haifa, see Goren, *From Dependence to Integration,* p. 139.

142. Morris, *The Birth of the Palestinian Refugee Problem Revisited,* pp. 383–384.

143. Ibid.; Ben-Artzi and Goren, "Molding the Urban Space."

144. Yablonka, *Survivors of the Holocaust,* pp. 19–20.

145. For a rare mention of Holocaust survivors taking over Palestinians' homes in Haifa and elsewhere, see Fischbach, *Records of Dispossession*, p. 9.

146. During the entire period of the British Mandate in Palestine, the number of Jewish immigrants from Morocco and Tunisia remained minute—some one thousand people who made up 0.002 percent of all Jewish immigrants during this period. In 1937 the Jews of North Africa constituted 2.2 percent of world Jewry. In the early 1950s they comprised 4.35 percent of all the Jews. See Feuerstein and Rishel, *Children of the Mellah*, p. 55; Schechtman, *On the Wings of Eagles*, p. 288.

147. Tsur, *A Torn Community*, p. 253. Slightly different data appear in Dominitz, "Immigration and Absorption of Jews from Arab Countries," p. 158. Dominitz notes that the number of immigrants from Morocco in the years 1948–1951—the years of mass immigration—was very small. Out of the approximately 700,000 immigrants who arrived during those years, there were only some 14,000 of Moroccan origin, which is likewise only a small proportion of the total of 260,000 immigrants from Arab countries during this period.

148. The migration of Jews from Arab countries gave rise to a new type of demographic anxiety, no longer directed at the delicate balance between Jews and Arabs. This was rather an internal anxiety, focusing upon three distinct but interconnected aspects: the numerical balance between Ashkenazi Jews and Mizrahi Jews, the cultural orientation of the state currently under construction, and its future political regime. This anxiety explains the paradox between the actual data—which indicate relatively low numbers—on Moroccan immigrants and the collective memory regarding their immigration. Yaron Tsur notes that the Moroccans were well suited "to represent the new triangular threat, both because of the realistic kernel for the creation of their negative stereotype and owing to their high proportion among the oriental immigration of that period." See Tsur, *A Torn Community*, pp. 271, 326.

149. Ibid., pp. 403–404.

150. Laskier, *The Jews of the Maghreb*, pp. 74–75.

151. Laskier, *North African Jewry*, pp. 92–94; Laskier, *Israel and the Maghreb*, pp. 48–50.

152. Tsur, *A Torn Community*, p. 83.

153. Oujda, located close to Algeria, served as a main transit station at which potential candidates for clandestine immigration congregated in order to cross the border on their way to the ports of Algeria. The large accumulation of Jewish refugees in Oujda over a relatively short period and the involvement of Arab residents in the clandestine border crossings brought the Israeli-Palestinian conflict to the attention of the locals. These developments were politically inflamed and led to hostile reactions and a boycott of Jewish businesses. On May 23, 1948, Moroccan sultan Mohammed V made a speech expressing firm solidarity with the Palestinians and support

for the position of the Arab League, on the one hand, while making a distinction between Zionism and the local Jews who were loyal to Morocco, on the other. This speech could obviously not have had a moderating effect. It contained internal contradictions between an expression of patronage and threat and its content was deliberately distorted in the ensuing days. The speech failed to prevent the Israeli-Palestinian conflict from boiling over in Morocco and led to the outbreak, two weeks later, of violent incidents during which forty Jews were killed. This outbreak of violence evoked differing interpretations: from the French perspective, it proved that Morocco was not yet ripe for independence and was unable to adequately protect the safety of its citizens. From the viewpoint of the Moroccan nationalists, the events showed that it was France that was unable to guarantee the safety of the residents. On the part of the Jews, these events symbolized the dangers lying in wait for them during the process of Morocco's liberation. See Sa'adon, "'The Palestinian Element,'" pp. 106ff; Laskier, *North African Jewry*, pp. 91–102; Laskier, *Israel and the Maghreb*, pp. 52–53.

154. There are differing estimates of the number of migrants from Morocco in the years 1948–1949. Schechtman, for example, puts it at eight thousand. See Schechtman, *On the Wings of Eagles*, p. 288.

155. Morris, *1948*, p. 415.

156. Goren, *From Dependence to Integration*, p. 62.

157. It is of interest to note that in March 1949 the minister, Bekhor Shitrit, was the first among Israeli government ministers to raise the issue of the distress suffered by Iraqi Jews. Out of concern for their safety following prohibition of the activities of the Zionist movement in Iraq, Shitrit proposed holding the property of Israeli Arabs as a guarantee of the property of Iraq's Jews. This proposal was rejected by Israel's foreign ministry at the time and later as well. In September 1949 Shitrit once again raised the situation of the Jews in Arab countries at a cabinet meeting, floating the possibility of transferring the Jews and their property under United Nations' supervision. Foreign Minister Moshe Sharett rejected these proposals out of hand. Given the lack of a peace treaty with Iraq, he considered any attempt to discuss these issues with the Iraqi government naive.

158. Morris, *The Birth of the Palestinian Refugee Problem Revisited*, p. 323.

159. Morris, "Yosef Weitz," p. 530.

160. Memorandum on the Settlement of Arab Refugees, p. 32. See also Masalha, *Expulsion of the Palestinians*, p. 30. This type of linkage was proposed already in the 1930s, ibid., pp. 73–74.

161. On the linkage between Palestinian and Jewish property, see Fischbach, *Records of Dispossession*, pp. 164–187, and *Jewish Property Claims Against Arab Countries*, pp. 52–67; Shenhav, *The Arab Jews*, pp. 110–135, and "The Jews of Iraq"; Schechtman, "The Case for Arab-Jewish Exchange of Population."

162. Ben-Artzi and Goren, "Molding the Urban Space," p. 21; Golan, "From Arab Towns to Israeli Cities," p. 271.

163. Gonen, *Between City and Suburb*, p. 47.

164. Ibid., p. 46.

165. A. Nesher, "The Travails of Wadi Salib" (in Hebrew), *Haaretz*, July 17, 1959.

2. Commotion

1. The Commission of Inquiry Into the Events at Wadi Salib, evidence given by David Ben-Harush, July 26, 1959, State Archive, vol. 7253/1.

2. Regarding the decision to set up the commission and for an appraisal of its activity, see Dahan-Kalev, "'Self-Organizing Systems,'" pp. 121–122, 128–130.

3. On the development of the alcoholism stereotype applied to Moroccan immigrants, see Tsur, *A Torn Community*, p. 312.

4. On Mapai's method of promoting "artificial leadership" among immigrants of Asian-African origin and thereby blocking the emergence of an internal leadership, see Bernstein, "Immigrant Transit Camps," pp. 36–37. See also the distinction between "positive leaders" and "negative leaders" in Bernstein, "Immigrants and Society," pp. 252–253.

5. The Commission of Inquiry Into the Events at Wadi Salib, evidence given by David Ben-Harush, July 26, 1959, State Archive, 7253/1:11.

6. For example, the sum of 730 liras given to Ben-Harush in return for a written announcement that he published in which he gave an assurance that the Union of North African Immigrants did not support any political party. See *Haaretz*, September 2, 1959.

7. Dahan-Kalev, "The Wadi Salib Riots."

8. Marinsky and Lichtman, *In Light and in Darkness*, pp. 41–74; *Haaretz*, September 7, 1959, September 8, 1959.

9. *Haaretz*, September 9, 1959, September 13, 1959.

10. *Al Hamishmar*, August 25, 1959. This spelling is a prevalent corruption of the name of the second Muslim caliph, 'Umar ibn al-Khattăb.

11. *Al Hamishmar*, August 26, 1959.

12. Marinsky and Lichtman, *In Light and in Darkness*, p. 50.

13. *Haaretz*, August 14, 1959.

14. *Al Hamishmar*, September 4, 1959.

15. *Haaretz*, August 11, 1959, August 14, 1959, August 16, 1959; *Al Hamishmar*, August 11, 1959, August 15, 1959, August 16, 1959.

16. *Haaretz*, August 17, 1959; *Al Hamishmar*, August 17, 1959.

17. Marinsky and Lichtman, *In Light and in Darkness*, p. 57.

18. *Haaretz*, August 26, 1959; *Al Hamishmar*, August 26, 1959.

19. Marinsky and Lichtman, *In Light and in Darkness*, p. 55.

20. Sami Shalom Chetrit notes that, in any case, the proceedings failed to adhere to "any claim that this was a fair trial," since "[the Commission for the Investigation of the Wadi A-Salib Events . . . finished its investigation and the composition of its report on August 10, 1959, before the trial itself had ended. All of the commission's work was coverd in the media, and that the exposure may have influenced the court, which concluded its sessions only on September 28—providing the judges with enough time to read the commission's report and its conclusions carefully before giving their verdict." See Chetrit, *Intra-Jewish Conflict in Israel*, p. 68.

21. *Haaretz*, August 26, 1959.

22. *Haaretz*, August 31, 1959.

23. *Haaretz*, September 2, 1959.

24. *Al Hamishmar*, September 2, 1959.

25. *Haaretz*, September 6, 1959; Herzog, *Political Ethnicity*, pp. 143–144.

26. Marinsky and Lichtman, *In Light and in Darkness*, p. 63.

27. *Haaretz*, September 3, 1959.

28. Prison sentences were handed down to other detainees as well, but these were shorter and did not receive the same public exposure; see *Haaretz*, September 4, 1959.

29. *Haaretz*, September 23, 1959.

30. Dahan-Kalev, "The Wadi Salib Riots," 153.

31. Meeting of the minister of defense with young North African students, Ben-Gurion Archive in the Negev, file pertaining to Wadi Salib, North African immigrants, 1959–1960, 5–18–5.

32. See the Commission of Inquiry Into the Events at Wadi Salib, evidence given by Avigdor Eshet, morning session, August 4, 1959, State Archive, 7253/3:9.

33. Hannah Herzog refers in this context to "the existence, side by side, of two contradictory tendencies. On the one hand, the tendency to categorize the population and to mobilize it on an ethnic basis, and on the other hand, the tendency to reject the legitimacy of the ethnic basis in the name of the 'melting pot' ideology." See Herzog, *Political Ethnicity*, 175.

34. Report of the Public Commission of Inquiry into the July 9, 1959 Riots in Wadi Salib, submitted to the government on August 17, 1959, p. 13.

35. Calvino, *Invisible Cities*, p. 17.

36. Rubinstein, "In Memoriam," pp. 401–407.

37. Knesset Israel, *Biographies of Members of Israel's Knesset*.

38. Elnekaveh, *The Book of Our Rabbi*.

39. Shils, "S.N. Eisenstadt."

40. The Commission of Inquiry Into the Matter of Wadi Salib (memorandum), submitted to the members of the Government Commission of Inquiry Into the Dis-

turbances at Wadi Salib by Zvi Barzilay, deputy mayor of Haifa, July 29, 1959, State Archive, vol. 7252/3.

41. Gonen, *Between City and Suburb*, p. 101.

42. On the reflection of this contrast on the development of Zionist architecture see Nitzan-Shiftan, "Contested Zionism," p. 27. See also Kunda and Oxman, "The Flight of the Camel," pp. 57–58.

43. Home comments that "the Haifa plan, awaiting the High Commissioner's approval, was partially destroyed in the attack on the King David Hotel in Jerusalem in 1946, and never came into force, although its remains are preserved as a historical document. See Home, "Town Planning and Garden Cities," p. 32.

44. Seikaly notes that certain exceptions to this administrative principle were made with regard to issues that served the interests of the Jewish sector. See Seikaly, *Haifa*, p. 59.

45. Vashitz, "Social Changes in Haifa's Arab Society," p. 50.

46. Seikaly emphasizes that the Jewish institutions showed greater interest in and understanding of the urban master plan and exerted greater influence on it, and thereby ensured that the Jewish sectarian interest would be preserved as far as possible within the framework of urban development. See Seikaly, *Haifa*, 63. For further reading on the advantages held by the Jewish economic sector over the Arab one within the informal imperialism in Palestine, see Smith, *The Roots of Separatism in Palestine*, 4–9.

47. Vashitz, "Rural Migration to Haifa," p. 114.

48. Additional factors propelling the Arab fellah from village to city were the following: the deterioration in the position of the Arab fellah; a surplus annual workforce in an economy burdened by heavy debt; high taxation and payment of high rental for land; the reduction in the area of land remaining at the disposal of the peasants in the wake of takeovers by large landowners and the sale of land to Jewish companies and individuals; the contraction of local rural crafts in the Galilee owing to the inability to compete with imports; saving in manpower owing to advanced technologies of plowing and harvesting, and drought management. See Gilbar, "Trends in the Demographic Development," p. 52; Vashitz, "Rural Migration to Haifa," pp. 115–116.

49. Yazbak, "Arab Migration to Haifa," pp. 49, 54–55. Yazbak recounts how a resident of Nazareth was encouraged by his mother to move to Haifa, "to the city full of people" (*ilay baled al-naas*), to find a livelihood. Ibid., p. 65.

50. On the tension between economic cooperation and nationalist enmity in conditions of geographic proximity, see Reichman, *From Foothold to a Settled Territory*, p. 85.

51. Aharonowitz, *Hadar ha-Carmel*, p. 35. Faced with refusal on the part of the municipality to connect the neighborhood to Rotenberg's electricity company, in

1925 the Hadar ha-Carmel Committee concluded a direct and independent agreement with the company. Once Hadar ha-Carmel's streets began to be lit by electric lighting in 1925, the municipality began to install electric illumination throughout the city. See Goren, *Cooperation in the Shadow of Confrontation*, pp. 70–72.

52. Since most of the architects who took part in the planning and construction of Hadar ha-Carmel had been trained in Germany, the neighborhood was inspired both by the original English model and by the German adaptation of the English garden city model. In that respect it is difficult to determine categorically whether Hadar ha-Carmel was planned as a "garden city" or as a "garden suburb," two different approaches prevalent in the period. In the official progress report written in English, the neighborhood is referred to as a garden suburb, whereas in German, in the internal correspondence between the neighborhood committee and the architect Richard Kaufmann, it is referred to as a *Gartenstadt*, or "garden city." See Herbert and Sosnovsky, *The Garden City as Paradigm*.

53. Aharonowitz, *Hadar ha-Carmel*, p. 41.

54. Ibid., p. 59; Herbert and Sosnovsky, *The Garden City as Paradigm*, p. 22.

In the 1930s and 1940s the garden was regarded as the most attractive public site in the country. The British architect and town planner Patrick Geddes, who at the time was engaged on various projects in Bombay in India and who in 1919 was asked by the settlement institutions to express an opinion on several construction projects in Palestine, was enchanted by the garden, and the shady olive trees planted there, and reported it to be "unusually attractive and promising."

Home remarks that Geddes's plan for Haifa, which was prepared in cooperation with the military governor Stanton, was considered by the Mandate administration to be too grandiose. Home, *Of Planting and Planning*, p. 157.

55. Aharonowitz, *Hadar ha-Carmel*, p. 78.

56. Ibid., p. 58. On occasion this insistence on uniformity led to tension, such as the "window dispute," when homeowners rejected the window design stipulated by the architect Richard Kaufmann, representing the "Hakhsharat ha-yishuv Company."

57. Luke, *Cook's Traveler's Handbook*, p. 270.

58. Schwartz, *Glimpses of Palestine*, p. 64.

59. Lumby, *Cook's Traveler's Handbook for Palestine and Syria*, 248.

60. Seikaly, *Haifa*, pp. 128–129.

61. Vashitz, "Rural Migration to Haifa," pp. 118–119; Yazbak, "Arab Migration to Haifa," pp. 144–146; Goren, *Cooperation in the Shadow of Confrontation*, pp. 299–308; Seikaly, *Haifa*, p. 50.

62. Vashitz, "Social Changes in Haifa's Arab Society," p. 57.

63. Seikaly, *Haifa*, p. 8.

64. Vashitz, "Social Changes in Haifa's Arab Society," pp. 125, 130.

65. Aharonowitz, *Hadar ha-Carmel*, pp. 104–107. In his book about the troubled relations between Jaffa and Tel Aviv, Mark LeVine explains that, because Jaffa had undergone a transformation into the center of an urban region whose power and economy were expanding, "the fathers of Tel Aviv had the luxury of designing their city as a Garden Suburb, without an industrial or commercial district." LeVine, *Overthrowing Geography*, p. 175.

66. The Technion is the first institution of higher learning in Palestine and was initiated by the German-Jewish Organization Ezrah and opened as a school of engineering and sciences in 1924. The Hebrew language Reali School in Haifa was founded prior to the beginning of World War I and moved in 1923 to a building on the old Technion campus that had served until then as a British military hospital.

67. We may perhaps borrow from Amiram Gonen's work on the beginnings of Tel Aviv: "The character of the garden suburb of Ahuzat Bayit on the outskirts of Jaffa was a mere episode that should be viewed within the context of Jewish-Arab relations rather than as an expression of a preference for suburban living on the part of the new Jewish middle class." See Gonen, *Between City and Suburb*, p. 34.

68. Aharonowitz, *Hadar ha-Carmel*, pp. 106–110.

69. These developments compounded the considerable ambivalence surrounding Hadar ha-Carmel's urban planning. Already in its early years, and independent of the increasingly violent dimension of the Jewish-Arab conflict, the projects initiated and the infrastructure constructed in Haifa were in stark contrast to the limited nature of its urban planning. The founding of the Technion, a national institute of learning, as well as the welfare, health, cultural, and religious infrastructures indicated the wish to transform Hadar ha-Carmel into "the Tel-Aviv of Haifa." The indecisiveness of Richard Kaufmann's plan was manifested in the lack of clear boundaries for the neighborhood, and these remained undefined.

70. Herbert and Sosnovsky, *The Garden City as Paradigm*, p. 32.

71. Gonen, *Between City and Suburb*, p. 35.

72. Seikaly, *Haifa*, p. 66.

73. Vashitz, "Social Changes in Haifa's Arab Society," pp. 67, 70. The weakness of Arab society and its lack of communal patterns meant that the collective national interest was always subordinated to individual-economic interests, even in these circumstances of an acute lack of housing. See ibid., p. 163; and also Gonen, *Between City and Suburb*, p. 37.

74. Seikaly, *Haifa*, p. 66.

75. Goren, "Was There Really Discrimination?" p. 123.

76. The Commission of Inquiry Into the Events at Wadi Salib, evidence given by David Ben-Harush, July 26, 1959, State Archive, doc. 7253/1, p. 16.

77. For further details on the supervisor of Arab property in the northern district and director Naftali Lifshits, see Fischbach, *Records of Dispossession*, p. 16.

78. Benny Morris views the act of concentration in a favorable manner, noting that it enabled the Haganah to protect Haifa's Arabs more efficiently from attack by such extremist Jewish paramilitary groups as the Irgun or the Lehi while facilitating the regular flow of produce to the city and enabling the remaining Arabs to find work. See Morris, "Haifa's Arabs," pp. 243–244.

79. Segev, *1949*, pp. 53–55.

80. Goren, *From Dependence to Integration*, p. 40.

81. Minutes of the Eighth Meeting of the Committee for Arab Affairs in Haifa, July 8, 1948, State Archive, 49/309/41.

82. Gonen, *Between City and Suburb*, 51.

83. On the life style of the upper-class Arab bourgeoisie in upper Wadi Salib, see Kanafani, *Sha'ara el-Bourge 15*.

84. Peleg, *Survey on Preservation of a Building*.

85. This description of the House of Arches relies on documentation compiled by the Haifa Municipality's Department for Long-term Planning. I thank Mr. Waleed Karkabi for his help.

86. On the migration of the rich to Haifa following the reform of the property laws in 1858, see Bernstein, *Constructing Boundaries*, pp. 50–51.

87. On the central space house, see Fuchs, "The Arab Residential Home," pp. 71–77.

88. The first signs of European influence became apparent both in the internal appearance and facades of the buildings constructed at the time. Thus, for example, the appearance of the openings changed, with the arches making way for rectangular windows. Glass windows likewise became more prevalent during the 1870s. Certain changes in lifestyle made their mark as later additions to buildings. Service rooms, such as kitchens, washrooms, and toilets, had not been part of the original central space house since these activities generally took place outside the house or at the basement level. The service wing was a later addition, and its nature indicates that it had previously been conceived as external to the structure.

89. Aleph, *Haifa Municipality*.

90. Habibi, *The Secret Life of Saeed the Pessoptimist*, p. 45.

91. Minutes of the Ninth Meeting of the Committee for Arab Affairs in Haifa, July 22, 1948, State Archive, 49/309/41. See also Goren, *From Dependence to Integration*, p. 64.

92. Goren, *From Dependence to Integration*, pp. 40–42.

93. Minorities Ministry, Haifa branch to the commander of Haifa district, December 19, 1948, State Archive, 49/309/68.

94. Ibid.

95. These data are taken from Ben-Artzi and Goren, "Molding the Urban Space," p. 18.

96. Minorities Ministry, Haifa branch to the commander of Haifa district, December 13, 1948, State Archive, 49/309/68.

97. Minorities Ministry, Haifa branch to the commander of Haifa city, August 31, 1948, ibid. See also Goren, *From Dependence to Integration*, pp. 66–67.

98. Commander of Haifa district to Minorities Ministry in Haifa, September 13, 1948, State Archive, 49/1323/10.

99. The Provisional Arab Committee to the director of the Minorities Ministry, November 14, 1948, ibid. See also Goren, *From Dependence to Integration*, p. 67.

100. Morris, *The Birth of the Palestinian Refugee Problem Revisited*, pp. 389–390.

101. Haifa District Military Police to the Minorities Ministry, Re: Number 40 Abbas Street Haifa. Your letter MAH/PSB1299/1/, December 10, 1948, State Archive, 49/309/83.

102. Minorities Ministry, Haifa branch to the commander of Haifa district, September 3, 1948, State Archive, 49/309/68.

103. Ibid.

104. Report on Organized Incursions by Soldiers Into Arab Houses, State Archive, 49/1323/10.

105. Minutes of meeting in the mayor's office, Tuesday, ibid.

106. Ibid.

107. Ibid.

108. Ibid. The problem of the invading war invalids was in the end resolved by Archbishop Hakim, who placed at their disposal without charge a seven-room building in the Wadi Jamal neighborhood. See Goren, *From Dependence to Integration*, p. 72.

109. The Provisional Arab Committee to the director of the Minorities Ministry, September 8, 1948, State Archive, 49/1323/10.

110. Shihadeh Salah of Haifa Municipality to the director of the Minorities Ministry, Haifa branch, January 16, 1949, ibid.

111. On the authorization for the unification of Salah's family, see Goren, *From Dependence to Integration*, pp. 175, 178.

112. The Jewish Agency, Section for Handling of Immigrants to the Minorities Ministry in Haifa, November 7, 1948, State Archive, 49/1322/2.

113. Szymborska, "Census," in *Sounds, Feelings, Thoughts*, p. 77.

114. Weiss, "Ethnic Cleansing, Memory, and Property."

115. Szelenyi, "Housing Inequalities and Occupational Segregation."

116. Ibid., 2. For a different standpoint, see Musil, "Housing Policy," p. 31.

117. Hoffnung, *Israel*, pp. 164–166.

118. Ibid., p. 165.

119. Commission of Inquiry Into the Wadi Salib Events, the evidence of David Ben-Harush, July 26, 1959, State Archive, doc. 7253/1, p. 4.

120. Ibid., p. 6.

121. Ibid.

122. Ibid., p. 7.

123. See also the evidence of Shlomo Rosenblum, Commission of Inquiry Into the Wadi Salib Events, July 29, 1959, State Archive, doc. 7253/1, p. 15.

124. Commission of Inquiry Into the Wadi Salib Events, the evidence of Heinrich First, July 27, 1959, ibid., p. 18–19.

125. Ibid., pp. 19–24.

126. This information appears also in the evidence given by the director of the Housing Department of the Development Authority.

127. Hoffnung, *Israel*, 160.

128. Ibid., 161; Forman and Kedar, "From Arab Land to 'Israel Land.'"

129. Liskovsky, "'Resident Absentees' in Israel," p. 187; Forman and Kedar, "From Arab Land to 'Israel Land,'" p. 814; Fischbach, *Records of Dispossession*, pp. 19–23.

130. Forman and Kedar, "From Arab Land to 'Israel Land,'" p. 815.

131. Forman and Kedar stress that the Pakistani law served as Lifshitz's main model. Ibid., pp. 810, 816.

132. Y. Shimoni, director of the Asia Department, Foreign Ministry, to Joseph Schechtman, August 31, 1950, Revisionist Movement Archive, P-1/1/227.

133. Joseph Schechtman to Yehuda Eilat, September 10, 1951, ibid.

134. Ibid.

135. Abba Eban to Joseph Schechtman, March 18, 1952, Revisionist Movement Archive, P-2/10/227.

136. Forman and Kedar, "From Arab Land to 'Israel Land,'" p. 817.

137. Kretzmer, *The Legal Status of the Arabs in Israel*, pp. 56–57.

138. Fischbach, *Records of Dispossession*, pp. 22ff.

139. Kedar, "On the Legal Geography of Ethnocratic Settler States"; Forman and Kedar, "From Arab Land to 'Israel Land,'" pp. 817–818; Dumper, *Islam and Israel*, p. 33; Fischbach, *Records of Dispossession*, pp. 53–57.

140. Kretzmer notes that the property of the Muslim waqf was also transferred to the Development Authority; it was later partially returned to Muslim communities in cities in which trust committees were established. See Kretzmer, *The Legal Status of the Arabs in Israel*, p. 58.

141. Geremy Forman demonstrates "how a national government concerned with domestic inter-ethnic power relations made strategic use of its legal advantages to reshape socio-spatial relations." In Forman, "Law and the Historical Geography of the Galilee," p. 813. For more on the limitations and constraints on Palestinian Israeli citizens litigating against the State of Israel see ibid., pp. 805–811.

142. The law stipulated that the property be sold for its calculated worth for tax purposes in the years 1947–1948, while consideration should be given to reducing the price owing to damage that limited its use. Considering the extent of inflation of the Israeli currency in the years 1947–1953, the absentees' property was sold at a price far below its original worth.

143. Forman and Kedar, "From Arab Land to 'Israel Land,'" p. 822.

144. Hoffnung, *Israel*, p. 174.

145. Yitshak Fonti, director of the Development Authority's Housing Department, morning meeting, August 5, 1959, evidence given before the commission (vol. 3), State Archive, doc. 7253/1, file 3, pp. 15–18.

146. Eng. B. A. Friedjung, Office for Preparation of a Master Plan, to the mayor, September 6, 1953, Haifa City Archive, "Housing of Evacuees from Dangerous Structures" file, 032543.

147. See R. Bar to Ehrlich (undated), Haifa City Archive, file 054626. See also the municipal engineer to the secretary of Tel Aviv Municipality, January 28, 1953, "Sanitary Services of Abandoned Property," ibid.

148. Notes taken at a meeting held in the inspector's office, January 23, 1952, ibid.

149. Memorandum of Attorney Zvi Barzilay, deputy mayor of Haifa, July 29, 1959, evidence given before the commission (vol. 3), State Archive, doc. 7252/1, file 3, p. 6. A similar assertion was made in evidence given by city councilor Z. Iram. See Commission of Inquiry Into the Wadi Salib Events, State Archive, doc. 7253/1, p. 3. See also Fischbach, *Records of Dispossession*, p. 32; Zweig, "Restitution of Property and Refugee Rehabilitation," pp. 56–64.

150. Commission of Inquiry Into the Wadi Salib Events, July 26, 1959, evidence given by David Ben-Harush, Commission of Inquiry Into the Wadi Salib Events, State Archive, doc. 7253/1, p. 16.

151. Meeting of the defense minister with young students from North Africa, Ben-Gurion Archive in the Negev, file on the topic of Wadi Salib, North African immigrants, 1959–1960, 5–18–5.

152. Tsur, *A Torn Community*, p. 322. Not only did Israel apply a policy of preferential treatment of one Diaspora against another concerning migration, but it also subsidized an improvement of living standards for the veteran population by building special condominiums at a time when a substantial part of the immigrant population was still living in transit camps and tent camps. See Gonen, *Between City and Suburb*, p. 74. Contrary to accepted opinion, Ben-Gurion was partially in favor of selective migration: while he was not in favor of placing a limit on the numbers of immigrants, he did favor exercising choice with regard to their quality. His attitude toward Moroccan Jews was, according to Avi Picard, particularly negative. See Picard, "The Beginnings of the Selective Immigration."

153. *Mellah* was the name given to the Jewish quarters in Morocco from the fourteenth century on, when the first separate Jewish quarter was established in the city of Fez on a salt swamp known as Mellah. See Brown, "Mellah and Medina," p. 39.

154. Tsur, *A Torn Community*, p. 265.

155. Ibid., pp. 267–269.

156. Ibid., p. 287; Picard, "The Beginnings of Selective Immigration."

157. Tsur, *A Torn Community*, pp. 281ff, 315.

158. Ibid., p. 405; Laskier, *North African Jewry*, p. 121.

159. Ibid., p. 138.

160. Ibid., pp. 169–170, 176–177, 187–191; Laskier, *Israel and the Maghreb*, p. 72.

161. Schechtman, *On the Wings of Eagles*, p. 291.

162. Ibid., p. 296.

163. Dominitz, "Immigration and Absorption of Jews from Arab Countries," p. 156.

164. Malka, *Selection in the Immigration of Moroccan Jews*; Schechtman, *On the Wings of Eagles*, pp. 271–310.

165. On this matter it is of interest to note Deborah Bernstein's comment. As early as 1980 she pointed out the disparity between the application of selection and the principle of the Law of Return, commenting that "it is therefore striking that no mention is made of this policy [the policy of selection] in the sociological literature, and that no attempt is made to study its effect on the attitude of those immigrants who did get through the selection." See Bernstein, "Immigrants and Society," p. 259.

166. *Haaretz*, 24.8.1955.

167. Schechtman, *On the Wings of Eagles*, pp. 295–296.

168. Laskier, *North African Jewry*, pp. 192–194, 195–197; Laskier, *Israel and the Maghreb*, pp. 68–69.

169. Schechtman, *On the Wings of Eagles*, p. 305.

170. Laskier, *Israel and the Maghreb*, pp. 47ff.

171. Torpey, "Making Whole What Has Been Smashed."

172. Diner, "Restitution and Memory."

173. Barkan, *The Guilt of Nations*, p. 24.

174. Goschler, "Return of Property," pp. 440–443; Frei, Brunner, and Goschler, *Die Praxis der Wiedergutmachung*, p. 47.

175. Barkan. *The Guilt of Nations*, pp. 308ff.

176. Maier, "Overcoming the Past?" p. 297.

177. Weitz, "A Rival Banner," p. 457. On the Herut movement's stand against the reparation agreement, see also Weitz, "Herut Party Against the Reparations Agreement," pp. 188–189.

178. These data are drawn from Teitelbaum, "Individual Compensation."

179. Landesberger, *The Influence of Individual Compensation Payments*, pp. 46–48. See also Teitelbaum, "Individual Compensation"; Gonen, *Between City and Suburb*, 99.

180. Elmelekh and Levin-Epstein, "Migration and Housing in Israel," pp. 245–246.

181. Khazzoom, "Did the Israeli State Engineer Segregation?"

182. Evidence given by David Ben-Harush (unconnected to the protagonist Ben-Harush), afternoon session of August 10, 1959, given before the commission (vol. 3), State Archive, doc. 7253/1, file 3, p. 1.

183. Barkan, "Restitution and Amending Historical Injustices." See also the use made by Michael Feige of the concept of "undeserving poor," coined by George Bernard Shaw, in Feige, "Dionysus in the Center," p. 217.

184. Malkki, *Purity and Exile*, p. 9.

185. Baruch Kimmerling speaks of the Holocaust survivors' "symbolic property." See Kimmerling, *Immigrants, Settlers, Natives*, p. 300.

3. Evacuation

1. Hacohen, *Immigrants in Turmoil*, pp. 80–81.

2. *The Abba Khoushy Book* (in Hebrew), part 2, chapter 22, "Slum Rehabilitation," as it appears in the Haifa City Archive, file 47136.

3. Abitbul, "Processes of Modernization and Development," pp. 382–386.

4. Feuerstein and Rishel, *Children of the Mellah*, p. 57.

5. Abu-Lughod, *Rabat*, pp. 203ff. Schechtman provides the following figures for the number of Jews living in Morocco's cities in 1947: Casablanca 86,375, Marrakech 18,750, Fes 18,020, Meknes 15,842, Rabat 14,250. See Schechtman, *On the Wings of Eagles*, p. 273.

6. Abitbul, "Processes of Modernization and Development," pp. 382–386.

7. Schechtman, *On the Wings of Eagles*, p. 273.

8. Feuerstein and Rishel, *Children of the Mellah*, p. 57.

9. Malka, *Selection in the Immigration of Moroccan Jews*, p. 29.

10. Schechtman, *On the Wings of Eagles*, p. 273.

11. Canetti, *The Voices of Marrakesh*, p. 45.

12. Picard, "The Beginnings of Selective Immigration," p. 359.

13. Feuerstein and Rishel, *Children of the Mellah*, p. 61.

14. Ibid., p. 80.

15. Schechtman, *On the Wings of Eagles*, p. 274.

16. See Conrad, "Doppelte Marginalisierung, p. 156; Golan, "Jewish Nationalism, European Colonialism, and Modernity," p. 488; Rabinow, "Colonialism, Modernity," pp. 170ff.; Abu-Lughod, *Rabat*, p.147.

17. Schechtman, *On the Wings of Eagles*, pp. 273–275.

18. Feuerstein and Rishel, *Children of the Mellah*, p. 80.

19. Tsur, *A Torn Community*, p. 362.

20. Ibid., p. 363.

21. Ibid., p. 370.

22. Laskier, *North African Jewry*, pp. 121–123.

23. Tsur, *A Torn Community*, p. 376.

24. Picard, "The Beginning of Selective Immigration," p. 363.

25. Tsur, *A Torn Community*, pp. 389–390.

26. Efrat, "Mold," pp. 81–82; Cohen, *The City in Zionist Ideology*, p. 4. A somewhat different interpretation is offered by Iris Graicer, who asserts that "on the one hand the labor movement and all its parties regarded the village as the ideal blueprint for a healthy society in the Land of Israel, and agricultural activity as the essence of the labor movement's spiritual, moral, and cultural potential, but, on the other hand, quietly and almost unnoticed, a clear standpoint began to crystallize, according to which, without a parallel development of the urban sector, Zionist ideology had no chance at all." SeeGraicer, "The Ideological Basis of the Labor Movement," p. 137.

27. Whereas in focusing on the village the Zionist settlement utopia was no different from other modern utopias, the latter proposed alternative rural models within an existing urban tapestry. Zionist settlement, on the contrary, was an attempt to establish a modern, progressive society solely upon a foundation of agricultural settlement. An additional aspect that distinguishes this branch of Zionism's attitude toward agriculture is derived from the fact that agricultural endeavor alone, as opposed to urban settlement, was able to establish the Zionist movement's exclusive ownership of the purchased tracts of land by virtue of its continual presence. See Diner, *Israel in Palästina*, pp. 41, 49. Moreover, private ownership and the exchange structure that characterizes the urban economy interfered with the pioneering effort to take over the land and stood in the way of the "stages" strategy designed to isolate the Jewish element from the general local social context. Ibid., pp. 54–56.

28. Troen, *Imagining Zion*, p. 179.

29. Ruppin, *The Jews' Struggle for Existence*. In Europe it was the city, claimed Ruppin, that led to the decline in birth rate, contributed to a negative Jewish demography, and, as though this were not enough, it led the Jews to enlightenment and success and in so doing enhanced animosity on the part of gentile competitors toward them.

30. Vashitz, *Social Changes in Haifa's Arab Society*, p. 9.

31. De Vries, "Abba Khoushy," 236.

32. Golan, "Jewish Settlements in Former Arab Towns," p. 150.

33. Reichman, *From Foothold to Settled Territory*, p. 81.

34. Ibid., pp. 96–103; Golan, "Jewish Settlements in Former Arab Towns," pp. 153–154.

35. Sharon, "'To Build and Be Built'"; Troen, *Imagining Zion*, p. 191.

36. Troen, *Imagining Zion*, p. 195.

37. Sharon, *Physical Planning in Israel*.

38. Akzin and Dror, *Israel*, pp. 60–63; see also Troen, *Imagining Zion*, pp. 184–187.

39. Sharon, *Physical Planning in Israel*, p. 6.

40. Efrat, "Mold," 81–82. For a different appraisal, see Troen: "Directing immigrants to new towns may have been the only possible way of bringing substantial populations to distant and underpopulated or even vacant areas. . . . Israel's planners operated within a framework that gave primacy to collective needs. In so doing they continued a tradition originating with the first Zionist agricultural colonies, whose location was perceived in terms of national requirements rather than benefits for individuals." Troen, *Imagining Zion*, p. 207.

41. Hacohen, *Immigrants in Turmoil*, pp. 124–129; Kark, "Planning, Housing, and Land Policy," pp. 487.

42. Morris, *The Birth of the Palestinian Refugee Problem Revisited*, p. 394.

43. *Katrielibka* is the derisory name for a fictional, archetypal *shtetl*. Hacohen, *Immigrants in Turmoil*, p. 141.

44. Ruppin, "Die Landarbeiterfrage in Palästina," pp. 74–75.

45. The Commission of Inquiry Into the Wadi Salib Events, evidence given by Dr. Ra'anan Weitz, August 9, 1959, State Archive, doc. 7252/3, file 3, pp.12–17.

46. Kemp, "'Migration of Nations,'" p. 38.

47. Ibid., p. 44.

48. Ibid. See also Dominitz, "Immigration and Absorption of Jews from Arab Countries," pp. 173–175.

49. Efrat, "Mold," p. 82.

50. Kemp, "Migration of Nations."

51. Cohen, *The City in Zionist Ideology*, p. 54.

52. Kemp, "Migration of Nations."

53. Ibid., p. 57.

54. Ibid.

55. Hacohen, *Immigrants in Turmoil*, pp. 291–296.

56. Kemp, "Migration of Nations," pp. 53–55.

57. Ibid., pp. 61–64.

58. The Commission of Inquiry Into the Wadi Salib Events, evidence given by Mr. Kalman Levy, August 4, 1959, State Archive, doc. 7252/3, file 3, pp. 1–13. See also Tsur, *A Torn Community*, p. 387.

59. For more on "from the ship to the settlement" see: Laskier, *North African Jewry*, 130.

60. The Commission of Inquiry Into the Wadi Salib Events, evidence given by Dr. Ra'anan Weitz, State Archive, doc. 7252/3, file 3.

61. The Commission of Inquiry into the Wadi Salib Events, evidence given by Mr. Kalman Levy, August 4, 1959, ibid.

62. Brinbaum, *The Children of Wadi Salib*, p. 11.

63. Kemp, "Migration of Nations," p. 64.

64. Report of the Public Commission of Inquiry into the July 9, 1959 Disturbances in Wadi Salib, submitted to the cabinet on August 17, 1959, p. 13.

65. Goren, "The Vision of 'a Greater Jewish Haifa,'" "Plans and Proposals for Augmenting the Jewish Community."

66. See *Notes on the Development of Haifa*, August 1938, CZA, S25/5110.

67. Ibid.

68. Ben-Artzi, "On the History of Haifa Street Names"; Azaryahu, "A Tale of Two Cities," "The Purge of Bismarck and Saladin"; Azaryahu and Kook, "Mapping the Nation."

69. Y. Proshenski, Minutes of Meeting of a Session of the Committee on General Affairs and Street Names, March 12, 1951, Haifa City Archive, "Street Names and Numbers" file, 32509.

70. Ibid.

71. The City Secretary to the *Haganah* Members Organization, February 12, 1951, Haifa City Archive, file 32507. See also previous submissions: Minutes of an extraordinary meeting of the Municipal Committee that took place in the municipality on January 3, 1949 at 10 a.m., section 3, ibid.; Minutes of Meeting no. 99 of the Municipal Committee, which took place on Tuesday, August 30, 1949 at 9:30 a.m., section 20, ibid.

72. The Haganah Members Committee in Greater Haifa to A. Halfon, April 16, 1951, Haifa City Archive, "Street Names and Numbers" file 32509.

73. Ibid.

74. Minutes of Meeting of the Committee on General Affairs and Street Names, April 16, 1951, ibid.

75. The city secretary to Mr. Yosef Daniel, March 29, 1951, ibid.

76. Minutes of Meeting of the Committee on General Affairs and Street Names, March 12, 1951, ibid.

77. Notes from a meeting of the Names Subcommittee, January 28, 1953, Haifa City Archive, file 32507.

78. The City Secretary to the Language Council in Jerusalem, February 1953, ibid.

79. Minutes of Meeting of a session of the Scientific Committee for Advice on Names, December10, 1953, Haifa State Archive, file 82579.

80. Ben-Artzi, "Wadi Salib and Its Place."

81. Haifa Municipality, February 4, 1954, List of the names of the neighborhoods and city areas with Arabic and foreign names to be changed to Hebrew names (handwritten list), Haifa City Archive, file 82579.

82. Minutes of Meeting of the Scientific Committee, February 18, 1954, Haifa City Archive, file 82579.

83. Ibid.

84. Minutes of Meeting of a session of the Scientific Committee, April 29, 1954, ibid.

85. Ibid.

86. The mayor to the Names Committee affiliated with the Culture Committee on November 3, 1953, Haifa City Archive, file 32579.

87. Mansour, *Haifa Arab Streets.* I thank Dr. Johnny Mansour for our conversation.

88. Boneh, *Haifa Street Lexicon.*

89. Habibi, *Ikhtayyeh,* pp. 116–117.

90. Report of the Public Commission of Inquiry Into the July 9, 1959 Disturbances in Wadi Salib, submitted to the cabinet on August 17, 1959, p. 15.

91. Lu-Yon and Kalush, *Housing in Israel,* p. 40.

92. Hague, "Renegotiating Places," pp. 154–157.

93. Ibid., p. 157.

94. Sawicki, *Soviet Land and Housing Law,* pp. 142–144.

95. Thus, for example, in Warsaw, in which only 7 percent of residential buildings were left in decent shape at the end of the war. See Perényi, *Die Moderne Stadt,* pp. 64–66.

96. Szelenyi, "Housing Inequalities," p. 7.

97. Ibid.

98. The Slums Clearance Act, State Archive, 109/3496/8.

99. Memorandum of lawyer Zvi Barzilay, deputy mayor of Haifa, July 29, 1959, evidence presented to the commission (volume 3), State Archive, doc. 7252/1, file 3.

100. Abba Khoushy, the morning session of August 5, 1959, ibid.

101. Bernstein, *Constructing Boundaries,* p. 57.

102. H. Hochwald, director of the Welfare Department to the mayor, March 19, 1953, Haifa City Archive, "Evacuee Housing Dangerous Structures," file 032543.

103. The city engineer to the acting mayor, December 16, 1955, ibid.; Memorandum of a meeting on the matter of Ard Ramel held on Thursday, January 5, 1956, ibid.

104. Treasurer of Tel Aviv Municipality to Mr. Zvi Barzilay, October 3, 1957, ibid.

105. Survey of the Shemen neighborhood residents, ibid.

106. M. Rofeh, city secretary, to the Shemen Neighborhood Committee in Haifa, September 30, 1956, Haifa City Archive, "Evacuee Housing Dangerous Structures," file 032543.

107. To the residents of Shemen neighborhood from Mayor Abba Khoushy, May 24, 1959, ibid.

108. Ben-Zion Milman, director of the Housing Projects Department, to Abba Khoushy, mayor of Haifa, August 6, 1959, ibid.

109. Placard, ibid.

110. On the structuring of dependence as a method, see Bernstein, "Immigrant Transit Camps."

111. The Governmental-Municipal Haifa Slum Renewal Company, concise survey (up to April 1966) in preparation for the visit by the minister of housing on May 19, 1966, Haifa City Archive, file 47136. See also attorney Yehiel Simhon to Abba Khoushy, June 25, 1967, Haifa City Archive, file 032553; M. Rofeh, Haifa City secretary, to attorney Simhon, July 3, 1967.

112. The Slums Clearance Act, State Archive, 109/3496/8.

113. Proposal for the foundation of a joint company of the government and Haifa Municipality, memorandum drafted and concluded between the government of Israel on behalf of the State of Israel represented by the Housing Department Administration, hereafter (the government) and Haifa Municipality, August 21, 1960, Haifa City Archive, file 032575.

114. Minutes of the First Meeting of the Provisional Directorate of the Governmental-Municipal Haifa Slum Renewal Company, held on March 23, 1961, in Haifa, ibid.

115. Haifa Municipality estimated it to be even lower, at only around 18.1 percent. See the Slum Law, State Archive, 109/3496/8.

116. Ibid.

117. Yehuda Baharav, director of the Haifa Slum Renewal Company to Mr. Bruner, Property Department, April 12, 1961, Haifa State Archive, file 032575: Minutes of the Second Meeting of the Provisional Directorate of the Governmental-Municipal Haifa Slum Renewal Company, held on May 8, 1961, in the Haifa Town Hall, ibid.

118. Yehuda Baharav to Mr. Shafek, Inspectorate Department, April 9, 1961, ibid.; Yehuda Baharav, director of the Haifa Slum Renewal Company to Y. Drori, director of the central region of Amidar Company, January 5, 1962, ibid.

119. Hannah and Haleb Naim to the mayor of Haifa, October 14, 1960, ibid.

120. Simmel Brish to Abba Khoushy, October 26, 1960, ibid.

121. Z. Cohen to Abba Khoushy, July 21, 1961, ibid.

122. Mazal Cohen to Abba Khoushy, October 12, 1962, ibid.

123. Rachel Yosefson to Abba Khoushy, December 12, 1962, ibid.

124. The Governmental-Municipal Haifa Slum Renewal Company to Y. Drori, director of the central region of Amidar Company Ltd., July 8, 1962, ibid.

125. Heinrich First to the mayor of Haifa, October 24, 1962, ibid.

126. The Governmental-Municipal Haifa Slum Renewal Company to M. Rofeh, city secretary, November 2, 1962, ibid.; M. Rofeh to Heinrich First, November 7, 1962, ibid.

127. Shikmona, the Governmental-Municipal Haifa Slum Renewal Company, to David Ben-Harush, November 9, 1972, Haifa City Archive, file 032548.

128. Minutes of the Ninth Meeting of the Directorate of the Governmental-Municipal Haifa Slum Renewal Company held on Wednesday, September 5, 1962, in the Haifa Town Hall, Haifa City Archive, file 032575.

129. Minutes of the Twelfth Meeting of the Directorate of the Governmental-Municipal Haifa Slum Renewal Company held on Wednesday, April 1, 1963, in Haifa Town Hall, Haifa City Archive, file 032559.

130. Proposal for decisions on slum evacuations submitted to a meeting of the city council on March 24, 1963, ibid.; Minutes of the Thirteenth Meeting of the Directorate of the Governmental-Municipal Haifa Slum Renewal Company held on Wednesday, June 19, 1963, in Haifa Town Hall, ibid.; Minutes of the Fourteenth Meeting of the Directorate of the Governmental-Municipal Haifa Slum Renewal Company held on Wednesday, September 23, 1963, in Haifa Town Hall, ibid.; The plots that were purchased included block 10852, which had been included in the area confined within ÐUmar ibn al-KhattÐb Street to the west, Nuzhah and Ekron Streets and Miller Steps to the east, Afghani Street to the south, and Kibbutz Galuyot Street to the north. Block 10852 included Miller Steps to the west, Shukri Steps to the east, Naftali Imber Street to the south, and Kibbutz Galuyot Street to the north. See the Governmental-Municipal Haifa Slum Renewal Company Ltd. to the director of the Ownership and Registration Department of the Israel Lands Administration, September 26, 1963, ibid.

131. M. Fleaman, deputy mayor, to the Haifa Workers Council, Housing Committee, August 29, 1963, ibid.

132. M. Fleaman, deputy mayor, to the Housing Committee, Haifa Workers Council, November 6, 1963, ibid.

133. Yehuda Baharav, the Governmental-Municipal Haifa Slum Renewal Company Ltd., to the director of the central region of Amidar, August 1, 1963, ibid.

134. The Governmental-Municipal Slum Renewal Company to Y. Drori, director of the central region of Amidar Ltd., July 8, 1962, Haifa City Archive, file 032575.

135. The Slum Law, State Archive, 109/3496/81.

136. The Governmental-Municipal Haifa Slum Renewal Company Ltd., General Report for 1963/64, State Archive, doc. 3711/19.

137. Agreement between the Israel Lands Administration and the Governmental-Municipal Haifa Slum Renewal Company Ltd., ibid.

138. List of the buildings and plots under private ownership in the area adjacent to Wadi Salib called Shikmona in Haifa, Haifa City Archive, file 032575.

139. Minutes of Meeting of the Board of Directors of the Governmental-Municipal Haifa Slum Renewal Company Ltd., held on Monday, January 20, 1964, in Haifa Town Hall, State Archive, doc. 3711/19.

140. Ibid. On the strategies that the Israeli state used for dispossessing the *waqf* of its property see Dumper, *Islam and Israel*, pp. 32–37.

141. Dumper claims that there was "preferential treatment for the Christians"; ibid., p. 40.

142. The only one to oppose this move was Mr. Kaminka, who felt that "it is unjust to place a burden of additional cost on the price of apartments for those being rehoused"; ibid.

143. Baharav, *Survey and General Report*.

144. Kolka, "Wadi Salib," p. 29.

145. Ibid., p. 30. See also Meeting of the Directorate on October 25, 1964, at the Housing Ministry, Haifa, the Governmental-Municipal Haifa Slum Renewal Company, State Archive, doc. 3711/19.

146. Kolka, "Wadi Salib," p. 30.

147. Outlines for Activation of a Family Adoption Program, Haifa City Archive, file 032557.

148. Baharav, *Survey and General Report*, p. 1.

149. Ibid.

150. Mr. Ben-Zion Milman, agent representing the shares held by the government, Minutes of the Annual General Meeting and the Meeting of the Board of Directors of the Governmental-Municipal Haifa Slum Renewal Company Ltd., held on Wednesday, October 7, 1964, in Haifa Town Hall, State Archive, doc. 3711/19.

151. Kolka, "Wadi Salib," p. 30.

152. Ravit Gadot to Abba Khoushy, December 3, 1963, Haifa City Archive, file 032559.

153. Jacobsen, *After the Clearance*, p. 10.

154. A. Nesher, "The Suffering of Wadi Salib" (in Hebrew). *Haaretz*, July 17, 1959.

155. A. B. Friedjung, Town Planning Section to the deputy mayor, July 1964, Haifa City Archive, file 032557.

156. Concise Minutes of the Directorate Meeting held on November 15, 1964, the Governmental-Municipal Haifa Slum Renewal Company, State Archive, doc. 3711/19.

157. The Governmental-Municipal Haifa Slum Renewal Company, Directorate Meeting held on March 16, 1965, in the Town Hall, Concise Minutes, Haifa City Archive, file 032557.

158. Application by the representatives of nineteen grocery store owners in the Wadi Salib neighborhood to the director of the Slum Clearance Company, August 27, 1964, ibid.

159. Albert Algrisy to Abba Khoushy, August 6, 1968, Haifa City Archive, file 032553.

160. M. Rofeh, city secretary, to Albert Algrisy, August 9, 1968, ibid.

161. Kolka, "Wadi Salib," p. 30.

162. Jacobsen, *After the Clearance*, p. 28.

163. Ibid., p. 11; Rabbi Maimon Gedalya Committee to the Neveh Sha'anan Communal Association Ltd. Committee, August 17, 1971, Haifa City Archive, file 032550. Several years thereafter, Shikmona would be required to enlarge the evacuees' apartments it had built on Rabbi Maimon Street. See Shikmona Directorate Meeting, May 21, 1973, Haifa City Archive, file 032548.

164. Jacobsen, *After the Clearance*, p. 28.

165. Ibid., p. 29.

166. Ibid., pp. 29–30.

167. Letter from David Ben-Gurion to B. Shitrit and E. Sasson, Sdeh Boker, October 11, 1962, Ben-Gurion Archive in the Negev, file on Wadi Salib, North African Immigrants, 1959–1960, 5–18–5: "And the main thing—this is not an 'ethnic' problem, but rather a central Israeli problem, and the entire country and entire people must make an effort to solve the problem wherever it appears, and every ministry must play its part since the Orientals are the same as all the children of Israel."

168. Ben-Gurion, October 15, 1962, ibid.

169. A. Nesher, "Rotten Fruit in Wadi Salib: Thieves at Age Seven—Burglars at Age Eight" (in Hebrew), *Haaretz*, December 21, 1962, p. 9.

170. Minutes of the Sixteenth Meeting of the Board of Directors of the Governmental-Municipal Haifa Slum Renewal Company Ltd., held on Monday, June 1, 1964 in Haifa Town Hall, The State Archive, doc. 3711/19.

171. Jacobsen, *After the Clearance*, pp. 28, 34.

172. Graicer, "Shekhunat Ha-Ovdim," pp. 30–32; Troen, *Imagining Zion*, pp. 106–109.

173. Blau, *The Architecture of Red Vienna*; Gonen, *Between City and Suburb*, p. 36.

174. Gold, *The Experience of Modernism*, pp. 51–52.

175. Blau, *The Architecture of Red Vienna*, p. 154.

176. Ibid., pp. 156–157. On the negative effect of suburban housing on the quality of life of the Israeli woman, see Carmi, "Human Values in Urban Architecture."

177. Both of these, incidentally, were deliberately characterized by low-rise construction, thereby aiding the attempts of the Jewish National Fund to restrain the meteoric rise in the price of urban land, which threatened to generate an upheaval

in the market price of land in general and to obstruct the overall purchases of the Jewish National Fund. See Diner, *Israel in Palästina*, pp. 57–58.

178. Efrat, *The Israeli Project*, p. 956.

179. Ibid.

180. Gonen, *Between City and Suburb*, p. 41.

181. Efrat, *The Israeli Project*, p. 956.

182. Ibid., p. 958.

183. Diner, *Israel in Palästina*, pp. 58–59.

184. Graicer, "Ideological Conflicts as Factors," pp. 195–196, 200–201; Kolodney, "The Politics of the Landscape," pp. 149–154.

185. Efrat, *Urbanization in Israel*, pp. 85–86. A similar assertion as to the kibbutz-like character of the planning department's concept of the city after 1948 is made by Zvi Efrat in Efrat, "Mold," p. 86.

186. Gonen, *Between City and Suburb*, pp. 43–44.

187. On the positive orientation of Austria's social democracy toward the urban experience, see Blau, *The Architecture of Red Vienna*, pp. 158–159.

188. Efrat, "Mold," p. 82.

189. Gonen, *Between City and Suburb*, p. 106.

190. Jacobsen, *After the Clearance*, p. 31

191. Baruch Baram, director of the Community Work Bureau, to Mr. Sahnin, deputy mayor, October 20, 1964, Haifa City Archive, file 032557.

192. Jacobsen, *After the Clearance*, p. 40.

193. Ibid., p. 15.

194. Hazani and Ilan, *Social Consequences of Urban Renewal*, pp. 14–15.

195. Ibid., p. 19.

196. Ibid., p. 15

197. Geertz, "Thick Description," p. 14.

198. Hazani and Ilan, *Social Consequences of Urban Renewal*, p. 52.

199. The Governmental-Municipal Haifa Slum Renewal Company Ltd., Second Management Meeting, April 20, 1964, State Archive, doc. 3711/19.

200. Abba Khoushy, morning session on August 5, 1959, Evidence before the Commission (vol. 3), State Archive, doc. 7253/1, file 3.

201. The Governmental-Municipal Haifa Slum Renewal Company Ltd., Management Meeting, May 9, 1965, Concise Minutes of Meeting, State Archive, doc. 3711/19.

202. Ibid., pp. 39–40.

203. Kohn, *Western Civilization in the Near East*, pp. 69–70.

204. Minutes of the Twenty Fourth Meeting of the Board of Directors of the Governmental-Municipal Haifa Slum Rehabilitation Company, held on Wednesday, April 5, 1967, in Haifa Town Hall, Haifa City Archive, file 032553.

205. Minutes of the Thirtieth Meeting of the Board of Directors of the Governmental-Municipal Haifa Slum Rehabilitation Company, held on Sunday, February 23, 1969, ibid.

206. Ibid. The tendency to prefer exchange apartments grew stronger as the years passed. In 1968/69, the Wadi Salib evacuees chose 144 exchange apartments compared to only 24 dwellings in housing projects. See the Governmental-Municipal Slum Rehabilitation Company, Concise Survey of Company Activities in 1968/69, ibid.

207. Jacobsen, *After the Clearance*, p. 12.

208. Ibid.

209. Ibid., pp. 12–13.

210. Jacobs, *The Death and Life of Great American Cities*, p. 7.

211. Topalov, "Social Policies from Below," p. 261.

212. On the tendency of new neighborhoods for residents of cleared neighborhoods to become slums, see Jacobs's groundbreaking book, *The Death and Life of Great American Cities*, pp. 4, 270.

213. Jacobsen, *After the Clearance*, p. 28.

214. Ibid., p. 29.

215. In the years 1961/62 and 1963/64, 218 evacuees chose to move to a housing project and 445 chose exchange apartments. The Governmental-Municipal Haifa Slum Renewal Company Ltd., Concise Report on the Company's Activities; Minutes of Meeting of the Annual General Meeting and Meeting of the Board of Directors of the Governmental-Municipal Haifa Slum Renewal Company Ltd., held on Wednesday, October 7, 1964, in Haifa Town Hall; Minutes of the Sixteenth Meeting of the Board of Directors of the Governmental-Municipal Haifa Slum Rehabilitation Company, held on Monday, June 1, 1964, in Haifa Town Hall, State Archive, doc. 3711/19.

216. Ibid.

217. Harvey, *Social Justice and the City*.

218. Ibid., p. 24.

219. LeVine, "Locating Home."

220. Lu-Yon and Kalush, *Housing in Israel*, p. 27.

221. Weber, *The City*.

222. Isin, "Historical Sociology of the City," pp. 312–325.

223. Young, "Residential Segregation and Differentiated Citizenship."

224. Ibid.

225. Richard Ford makes a similar argument, contending that "we must not forget that in order to reject segregation, we need not unreservedly accept integration; indeed, especially for racial minorities, some degree of separatism may represent the best or only avenue of empowerment and fulfillment." Ford, "The Boundaries of Race," p. 99.

226. Young, "Residential Segregation," p. 243.

227. Ibid., p. 245.

228. Ibid., p. 242.

229. Bickford, "Constructing Inequality."

230. Ibid., p. 363.

231. Ford, "The Boundaries of Race" (1994), "The Boundaries of Race" (2001).

232. Ford, "The Boundaries of Race" (2001), p. 87.

233. Gonen, *Between City and Suburb*, p. 80.

234. Ibid., p. 82.

4. *Khirbeh*

Khirbeh is an Arabic word colloquially adopted by Hebrew speakers to denote a dilapidated structure or ruin, frequently found in abandoned Arab villages and neighborhoods.

1. Bambus, *Palästina*, p. 108.

2. Ibid., p. 109.

3. Ruete, *Reisen in Syrien und Palästina*, pp. 244–245.

4. Baedeker, *Palästina und Syrien*, p. 258.

5. Bambus, *Palästina*, p. 110.

6. Herzl, *Old-New Land*.

7. Ibid., p. 42.

8. Ibid., pp. 81–82. Toward the end of the 1920s, Palestine could indeed boast one of the best developed railway systems in the Middle East. See Biger, "A Geographical Analysis of Imperial Rule."

9. Trietsch, *Palästina Handbuch*, pp. 114–115.

10. Ibid., p. 175.

11. Carmel, *The History of Haifa in the Days of the Turks*, pp. 149–159; Pik, "Meissner Pasha"; Schiller, "Haifa in the Nineteenth Century"; Yazbak, *Haifa in the Nineteenth Century*; Karkar, *Railway Development in the Ottoman Empire*, pp. 64–88; Rothschild, "Meissner Pasha."

12. *Kurze militärgeographische Beschreibung*, p. 54.

13. Trietsch, *Palästina Handbuch*, 175; See also Efrat, *Urbanization in Israel*, p. 80.

14. Among the Jews living in Haifa in the nineteenth century, those of Moroccan origin formed the majority: Efrat, *Urbanization in Israel*, 78; see also Bernstein, *Constructing Boundaries*, p. 52.

15. *Kurze militärgeographische Beschreibung*, p. 37.

16. Meissner nevertheless did erect a sturdy wharf for mooring boats and barges, which he equipped with cranes that unloaded the equipment and materials required

for further construction. Two wharves lay at the disposal of the city: "Lloyd" wharf belonged to the Austrian shipping company, which ran most of the maritime traffic to and from Haifa by means of steamships, and the railway wharf. A third German pier opposite the German colony was designated for bathing purposes only.

17. Press, *Palästina und Südsyrien Reisehandbuch*, p. 250.

18. On the relations between city, empire, railway, and modernity, see Thom, "City, Region, and Nation," pp. 193–194.

19. Vashitz, "Social Changes in Haifa's Arab Society," p. 24; Seikaly, *Haifa*, p. 33.

20. Ben-Artzi, "Wadi Salib and Its Place in the Development of Haifa"; Bernstein, *Constructing Boundaries*, pp. 51, 57; Efrat, *Urbanization in Israel*, p. 7.

21. Seikaly, *Haifa*, pp. 16–17.

22. Press, *Palästina und Südsyrien Reisehandbuch*, p. 250. To the Western eyes of the guide's author, and indeed of all the guides' authors, the German colony, as a neighborhood of villas, appeared to be the most attractive of Haifa's neighborhoods. At the outbreak of World War I, Haifa's German colony comprised one-quarter of the city's area. See Efrat, *Urbanization in Israel*, p. 78.

23. Wilson, "Haifa."

24. Baedeker, *Palestine and Syria*, p. 229.

25. Press, *Palästina und Südsyrien Reisehandbuch*, p. 249.

26. Baedeker, *Palästina und Syrien*, p. 257.

27. H. Bonne, "Haifa: Seine Gegenwart und Zukunft," Palästina. Touristen-Nummer 1927–1928, *Mischar W'taasia. Handel und Industrie. Halbmonatsschrift für Palästinawirtschaft* 5, nos. 15–16 (1927): 276.

28. Press, *Palästina und Südsyrien Reisehandbuch*, p. 248. In the 1920s the train journey from the Suez Canal to Haifa took nine and a half hours. See Bonne, *Haifa*, p. 275. This was a daily service. See Luke, *The Traveler's Handbook for Palestine and Syria*, p. 257.

29. Fein, "British Policy," pp. 129–130.

30. Ibid., p. 131.

31. Stern, "The Dispute Concerning the Construction of Haifa Port," pp. 173, 180.

32. See Sluglett, "Formal and Informal Empire in the Middle East"; Balfour-Paul, "Britain's Informal Empire." See also Mejcher, *Imperial Quest for Oil*; Seikaly, *Haifa*, p. 3.

33. Fein, "British Policy," p. 135; Vashitz, "Social Changes in Haifa's Arab Society," pp. 45–47.

34. See Palestine Government, *Opening of Haifa Harbour*, October 31, 1933, n.p.

35. Moneta, *Port of Haifa Authority*, p. 10; Troen, *Imagining Zion*, p. 121.

36. Lumby, *Cook's Traveler's Handbook for Palestine and Syria*, p. 246.

37. Quoted in Seikaly, *Haifa*, p. 171; See also Bernstein, *Constructing Boundaries*, p. 53.

38. In his book *Israel in Palästina*, Dan Diner notes the transformation from land as "terra," namely as ground, to "territory," in the sense of control, within a framework disguised as a private market economy in which the Zionist purchase of land took place. See Diner, *Israel in Palästina*, pp. 22–25.

39. Granovsky, "Die Bodenpolitische Bedeutung der Haifa-Bay."

40. M. P. Kenworthy, "Haifa Harbour and the British Empire."

41. Bonne, *Haifa*, p. 276.

42. Granovsky, "Haifa Bay Land Policy," p. 75.

43. The quotation "Haifa lacks any singular architectural or historical character" is from Yehuda Baharav, senior engineer with the Haifa Municipality and director of the Governmental-Municipal Haifa Slum Renewal Company, in an interview with Gila Kolka. See Kolka, "Wadi Salib."

44. Amiran and Shahar, "The Towns of Israel."

45. Ibid., pp. 360–363. See also Troen, *Imagining Zion*, p. 127.

46. Ilan Troen spells this out clearly: "For all the advantages that Haifa enjoyed, Tel Aviv benefited more from the energies and opportunities generated by the Zionist movement." Ibid., p. 127.

47. Amiran and Shahar, "The Towns of Israel," p. 356.

48. *The Wadi Salib Survey*, prepared for the Physical Planning Department of the Ministry of Housing for submission to the Construction and Clearance of Renewal Areas Authority, Industrial Development Company Ltd. (Haifa, 1968), p. 9.

49. Ibid., pp. 20–21.

50. Ibid., p. 23.

51. Jacobs, *The Death and Life of Great American Cities*, p. 27.

52. Ibid., p. 30.

53. Governmental-Municipal Haifa Slum Renewal Company Ltd., General Report for 1963/64, document 3711/19.

54. Meir Hare'uveni, "Rapid Renewal of Slums," discussion with Haifa deputy mayor Avraham Sahnin (in Hebrew), *Lamerhav*, June 24, 1965.

55. Minutes of Meeting of the Board of Directors of the Governmental-Municipal Haifa Slum Renewal Company, held on Monday, January 20, 1964, in Haifa Municipality, State Archive, doc. 3711/19. See also Minutes of Meeting no. 20 of the Board of Directors of the Governmental-Municipal Haifa Slum Renewal Company, held on Wednesday, September 1, 1965, in Haifa Municipality, ibid.

56. Minutes of Meeting no. 16 of the Board of Directors of the Governmental-Municipal Haifa Slum Renewal Company, held on Monday, June 1, 1964, in Haifa Municipality, ibid.

57. Minutes of Meeting no. 15 of the Board of Directors of the Governmental-Municipal Haifa Slum Renewal Company, held on Monday, January 20, 1964, in Haifa Municipality, ibid.

58. *The Wadi Salib Survey,* p. 12.

59. Baharav, *Survey and General Report,* p. 22.

60. Ibid.

61. M. Rofeh, city secretary, to Danny Agmon, aide to the deputy prime minister, Deputy Prime Minister's Office, August 6, 1970, Haifa City Archive, file 032550.

62. Garti Mathilda to Felman, May 13, 1971, ibid.

63. Baharav, *Survey and General Report,* p. 1.

64. The city secretary to the mayor, May 4, 1971, Haifa City Archive, file 032550.

65. List of Large Families, Housing Problems in Wadi Salib, first list, ibid.

66. Notes from a meeting held in the office of the city secretary on June 17, 1971, at 8:00 am with large families from slum neighborhoods, ibid.

67. The city secretary to the mayor regarding a program for solution of the housing problem of large families, July 5, 1971, ibid.

68. Yehuda Baharav to Mr. D. Hoffman, Israel Lands Authority, October 20, 1969, ibid.; Y. Baharav to Mr. Moshe Sitbon, January 31, 1971, ibid.; city secretary to the municipal engineer, municipal treasurer, municipal secretary regarding expropriation of private houses and land in the slum clearance area of Wadi Salib, ibid.

69. Office memorandum from the city secretary to the mayor regarding the handling of problems of poverty and distress, May 24, 1971, ibid.

70. Background material for a press conference with the mayor, December 28, 1971, ibid.

71. Ibid.

72. Zohar Gedalyahu, Neighborhoods Committee, January 12, 1972, ibid.

73. Habibi, *Ikhtayyeh,* p. 11.

74. *The Wadi Salib Survey,* p. 28.

75. Ibid., pp. 14, 105.

76. "Wadi Salib Haifa," sent by S. Shaked, deputy manager of planning, Ministry of Housing, to the minister of housing, M. Bentov, March 3, 1968, State Archive, doc. 3432/3.

77. Ibid.

78. "Development of an Artists' Quarter in Wadi Salib Haifa" file, Haifa City Archive, file 40474.

79. Ze'ev Rivlin, legal adviser, to City Engineer A. Yanovitch, July 1, 1986, ibid.

80. Ibid.

81. The legal adviser to Mr. Moshe Gat, deputy director of the Israel Lands Authority, November 4, 1986, ibid.; Moshe Gat, deputy director of the Israel Lands

Authority and director of the Urban Department, to Ze'ev Rivlin, legal adviser—
Haifa Municipality, November 10, 1986, ibid.; Ze'ev Rivlin to Moshe Gat, November
13, 1986, ibid.

82. Aryeh Gurel, mayor of Haifa, to A. Nehemkin, minister of housing, November 14, 1986, ibid.

83. Keshet, *Haifa East Railway Station*.

Epilogue

1. Kanafani, "Returning to Haifa," p. 150.

2. The third of the six children of his lawyer father, Kanafani was born in Acre
in 1936 and grew up in comfortable circumstances. As was the custom among the
upper middle class, he was sent to study at the French mission school in Jaffa. Upon
the fall of Acre in 1948, his family fled to a small village in southern Lebanon, then
on to a mountainous region outside Damascus, and finally to a refugee neighborhood on the outskirts of Damascus. It was then that he, in effect, began to learn
Arabic, since his spoken Arabic was insufficient to gain command of the literary
language. At the age of sixteen he began to contribute to the family's livelihood by
working as a teacher in the city's refugee camp. At this time he also began studying
Arabic literature at Damascus University, where he made the initial contact with
George Habash and his organization. At the age of twenty he joined his family in
Kuwait, where he began working as a teacher in a government school. In the sum-
mer of 1960 he was invited by Habash to join the editorial staff of the *al-Hurriyya*
(Independence) journal, and this took him to Beirut. A year later he married a
Danish woman, went underground since he was stateless, and in 1962 published
his first story, "Men in the Sun," which brought him wide recognition and acclaim
in literary circles. In 1963 he became editor of the Nasserist daily *al-Muharrir* (The
Liberator) and the biweekly *Filastin* (Palestine), which appeared as a supplement
to the daily. In 1967 he became editor of the daily *al-Anwar* (The Lights). In 1969
he joined the Popular Front for the Liberation of Palestine, editing its mouthpiece
and becoming its chief spokesman. In July 1972 his short life came to an end when
his car was booby-trapped and exploded in front of his home as he was seated in
it together with his niece. See Karen E. Riley and Barbara Harlow, "Introduction,"
in Kanafani, *Palestine's Children*, pp. 1–12; Flores, "Gassan Kanafanis politisches
Engagement."

3. Tibawi, "Visions of Return."

4. Some have noted that this is the first attempt in Arab literature to portray a Jew
as a human figure rather than as a caricature of the enemy. See Riley and Harlow,
"Introduction." Shimon Balas claims: "In all the stories that touch on the Israeli-
Arab conflict it is difficult, perhaps impossible, to find a single objective description

of an Israeli." See Balas, *Palestinian Stories*, p. 17. Balas holds Kanafani up as a clear example in support of this claim.

5. Riley and Harlow, "Introduction," p. 25.

6. Balas, *Arabic Literature Under the Shadow of War*, p. 130.

7. Kanafani, "Returning to Haifa," p. 179.

8. Riley and Harlow, "Introduction," pp. 17–18. The reading of Kanafani by Riley and Harlow shows a similarity on this point with the reading of Cleary, who observes the paradox that "the felt need for the 'big' social, realistic novel is often strongest precisely in those colonized and peripheral areas of the world where social conditions make it most difficult to realize. To put it another way, the same social conditions that create the pressure towards social realism can also frustrate its realization." See Cleary, *Literature, Partition, and the Nation-State*, p. 194.

9. Anders, *Besuch im Hades*, p. 53.

10. On Manshiyya, see Rothbard, *White City Black City*; Golan, "Politics of Wartime Demolition," pp. 438–443.

11. Kanafani, "Returning to Haifa," p. 174.

12. Ibid.

13. Slyomovics, *The Object of Memory*, p. 179. A similar metaphor is employed by Salim Tamari: "Among the earlier generation of exiles there is a dominant tendency to 'freeze' the homeland into frames of pastoral, idyllic, paradise lost." Tamari, "Bourgeois Nostalgia and the Abandoned City," p. 179.

14. Kanafani, "Returning to Haifa," p. 187.

15. Cleary, *Literature, Partition, and the Nation-State*, p. 204.

16. For a different reading, see Yahav, "Yearning for the Homeland," p. 13. Yitzhak Laor's reading is more accurate. He asserts: "Said repeatedly emphasizes that the solution is to be found only in war. This, if you will, is the political credo of the novel. Something in the structure of the plot leads toward that in which Kanafani has believed from the outset. And nevertheless, what Said, or Kanafani, has to say may explain why his prediction of war comes to pass." See Laor, "We Have Not Come to Say," p. 13.

17. Darwish, ". . . As He Draws Away," in Darwish, *Why Have You Left the Horse Alone?* pp. 192–196.

18. In this context, the change is apparent in the position of Darwish himself, who, in the mid-1980s, wrote: "We are the victims of he who has appropriated the monopoly over the role of victim, and an occurrence in which he was the victim gave him the right to become our murderer, who is exempt from trial." See Darwish and al-Qasim, *Two Halves of the Orange*, p. 104.

19. Darwish, ". . . As He Draws Away," pp. 192–196.

20. Malkki, *Purity and Exile*, p. 9.

21. Sennet, "The Foreigner," p. 224.

BIBLIOGRAPHY

Abitbol, Michel. "Processes of Modernization and Development in the Modern Age" (in Hebrew). In *The History of the Jews in the Moslem Lands,* part 2, *From the Middle of the Nineteenth Century to the Middle of the Twentieth Century,* pp. 363–468. Jerusalem: Zalman Shazar Center, 1986.

Abu-Lughod, Janet L. *Rabat: Urban Apartheid in Morocco.* Princeton: Princeton University Press, 1980.

Aharonowitz, Haim. *Hadar ha-Carmel: A Saga of Labor and Creation by the Generation of Founders and Builders* (in Hebrew). Haifa: Hadar ha-Carmel Committee, 1958.

Akzin, Benjamin, and Yehezkel Dror. *Israel: High-Pressure Planning.* New York: Syracuse University Press, 1966.

Aleph, Yael, ed. *Haifa Municipality, the Department of Long-Term Planning, the House of Arches: Wadi Salib, Haifa* (in Hebrew). Physical Survey by Eng. Edward Kollick, Antiquities Authority. Jerusalem: May 1995.

Amiran, David H. K., and Arie Shahar. "The Towns of Israel: The Principles of Their Urban Geography." *Geographical Review* 51 (1961): 348–369.

Anders, Günther. *Besuch im Hades: Auschwitz und Breslau 1966; Nach "Holocaust" 1979.* Munich: Beck, 1996.

Azaryahu, Maoz. "A Tale of Two Cities: Commemorating the Israeli War of Independence in Tel Aviv and Haifa" (in Hebrew). *Cathedra* 68 (1993): 98–125.

——— "The Purge of Bismarck and Saladin: The Renaming of Streets in East Berlin and Haifa, a Comparative Study in Culture Planning." *Poetics Today* 13, no. 2 (1992): 351–367.

Azaryahu, Maoz, and Rebekka Kook. "Mapping the Nation: Street Names and Arab-Palestinian Identity: Three Case Studies." *Nations and Nationalism* 8, no. 2 (2002): 195–213.

Baedeker, Karl. *Palestine and Syria: With Routes Through Mesopotamia and Babylonia and the Island of Cyprus—Handbook for Travelers.* Leipzig: Karl Baedeker, 1912.

——— *Palästina und Syrien: Handbuch für Reisende.* Leipzig: Karl Baedeker, 1897.

Baharav, Yehuda. *Survey and General Report for the Years 1962–1972* (in Hebrew). Shikmona, the Governmental-Municipal Haifa Slum Renewal Company, Haifa, 1972.

Balas, Shimon. *Arabic Literature Under the Shadow of War* (in Hebrew). Tel Aviv: Am Oved, 1978.

——— *Palestinian Stories* (in Hebrew). Tel Aviv: Eked, 1970.

Balfour-Paul, Glen. "Britain's Informal Empire in the Middle East," In Judith M. Brown and William Roger Louis, eds., *The Oxford History of the British Empire*, 4:490–514. Oxford: Oxford University Press, 1999.

Bambus, Willy. *Palästina: Land und Leute.* Berlin: Siegfried Cronbach, 1898.

Barkan, Elazar. "Restitution and Amending Historical Injustices in International Morality: The Eastern European and Swiss Cases." In Dan Diner and Gotthard Wunberg, eds., *Restitution and Memory: Material Restoration in Europe*, pp. 255–272. New York: Berghahn, 2007.

——— *The Guilt of Nations: Restitution and Negotiating Historical Injustices.* New York: Norton, 2000.

Ben-Artzi, Yossi. "On the History of Haifa Street Names" (in Hebrew). *Jewish Language Review* 7 (1987): 16–28.

——— "Wadi Salib and Its Place in the Development of Haifa" (in Hebrew). *Mivnim* 76 (January 1989): 36–37.

Ben-Artzi, Yossi, and Tamir Goren. "Molding the Urban Space of Haifa Arabs in 1948" (in Hebrew). *Studies in the Geography of Israel* 15 (1998): 19–23.

Benjamin, Walter, and Asja Lacis. "Naples." In *Walter Benjamin Selected Writings*, 1:415–416. Trans. Edmund Jephcott. Cambridge: Harvard University Press, 1996.

Berger, Tamar. *Dionysus at Dizengof Center* (in Hebrew). Tel Aviv: Ha-kibbutz Hame'uhad, 1998.

Bernstein, Deborah. *Constructing Boundaries: Jewish and Arab Workers in Mandatory Palestine.* Albany: State University of New York Press, 2000.

——— "Immigrant Transit Camps: The Formation of Dependent Relations in Israeli Society." *Ethnic and Racial Studies* 4, no. 1 (January 1981): 26–43.

——— "Immigrants and Society: A Critical View of the Dominant School of Israeli Sociology." *British Journal of Sociology* 31, no. 2 (June 1980): 246–264.

Bickford, Susan. "Constructing Inequality: City Spaces and the Architecture of Citizenship." *Political Theory* 28, no. 3 (2000): 355–376.

Biger, Gideon. "A Geographical Analysis of Imperial Rule: British Regime in Eretz-Israel (Palestine) 1917–1929" (in Hebrew). *Eretz Israel: Archaeological, Historical, and Geographical Studies* 22 (1991): 27–35.

Blau, Eva. *The Architecture of Red Vienna, 1919–1934.* Cambridge: MIT Press, 1999.

Boneh, Eliezer. *Haifa Street Lexicon* (in Hebrew). Haifa: Haifa Municipality, Department of Development and Tourism, 1974.

Bonne, H. "Haifa: Seine Gegenwart und Zukunft." Palästina. Touristen-Nummer 1927–1928, *Mischar W'taasia. Handel und Industrie. Halbmonatsschrift für Palästina-wirtschaft* 5, no. 15–16 (1927): 275.

Brinbaum, Lea. *The Children of Wadi Salib* (in Hebrew). Tel Aviv: Am Oved, 1975.

Brown, Kenneth L. "Mellah and Medina. The Moroccan City and Its Jewish Quarter (Sala, ca. 1880–1930)" (in Hebrew). *Pe'amim: Studies in the Cultural Heritage of Oriental Jewry* 4 (1980): 39–59.

Calvino, Italo. *Invisible Cities.* Trans. William Weaver. San Diego: Harcourt, 1974.

Canetti, Elias. *The Voices of Marrakesh: A Record of a Visit.* London: Marion Boyars, 1993.

Carmel, Alex. *The History of Haifa in the Days of the Turks* (in Hebrew). Haifa: Haifa University Institute, 1969.

Carmi, Ram. "Human Values in Urban Architecture." In Soen Dan, ed., *New Trends in Urban Planning: Studies in Housing, Urban Design, and Planning,* pp. 159–175. Oxford: Pergamon, 1979.

Chetrit, Sami Shalom. *Intra-Jewish Conflict in Israel: White Jews, Black Jews,* London: Routledge, 2010

——— *The Mizrachi Struggle in Israel: Between Oppression and Liberation, Between Identification and Alternative, 1948–2003* (in Hebrew). Tel Aviv: Am Oved, 2004.

Cleary, Josef. *Literature, Partition, and the Nation-State.* Cambridge: Cambridge University Press, 2002.

Cohen, Eric. *The City in Zionist Ideology.* Jerusalem: Institute for Urban Studies, 1970.

The Conquest of Arab and Mixed Cities in the War of Independence (in Hebrew). Symposium booklet 8. Ramat Efal: Yad Tabenkin, Center for the History of the Defense Force—the Haganah, 1989.

Conrad, Sebastian. "Doppelte Marginalisierung: Plädoyer für Eine Transnationale Perspektive auf die Deutsche Geschichte." *Geschichte und Gesellschaft* 28, no. 1 (2002): 145–169.

Dahan-Kalev, Henriette. "'Self-Organizing Systems': Wadi Salib and the 'Black Panthers'—Implications on the Israeli Society" (in Hebrew). Ph.D. diss., Hebrew University of Jerusalem, 1991.

———— "The Wadi Salib Riots" (in Hebrew). In Adi Ophir, ed., *Fifty to Forty-Eight: Critical Moments in the History of the State of Israel,* pp. 149–157. Jerusalem and Tel Aviv: Van Leer Institute and Ha-kibbutz ha-me'uhad, 1999.

Darwish, Mahmoud. *Why Have You Left the Horse Alone?* New York: Archipelago, 1995.

Darwish, Mahmoud, and Samih al-Qasim. *Two Halves of the Orange* (in Hebrew). Tel Aviv: Mifras, 1991.

De Vries, David. "Abba Khoushy and the Labor Hegemony in Haifa in the Late 20s" (in Hebrew). *Contemporary Jewry* 14 (2001): 225–261.

Diner, Dan. *Israel in Palästina: Über Tausch und Gewalt im Vorderen Orient*. Athenäum: Königstein/Ts, 1980.

———— "Restitution and Memory: The Holocaust in European Political Cultures." *New German Critique* 90 (2003): 36–44.

Dominitz, Yehuda. "Immigration and Absorption of Jews from Arab Countries." In Malka Hillel Shulewitz, ed., *The Forgotten Million: The Modern Jewish Exodus from Arab Lands,* pp. 155–184. New York: Cassel, 1999.

Dumper, Michael. *Islam and Israel: Muslim Religious Endowments and the Jewish State.* Washington, DC: Institute for Palestine Studies, 1994.

Efrat, Elisha. *Urbanization in Israel.* New York: St. Martin's, 1984.

Efrat, Zvi. "Mold." In Haim Yacobi, ed., *Constructing a Sense of Place: Architecture and the Zionist Discourse,* pp. 76–88. Aldershot: Ashgate, 2004.

———— *The Israeli Project: Building and Architecture, 1948–1973* (in Hebrew). Vol. 2. Tel Aviv: Tel Aviv Museum of Art, 2005.

Ehrlich, Avishai. "A Society at War: The National Dispute and the Social Structure" (in Hebrew). In Uri Ram, ed., *Israeli Society: Critical Perspectives,* pp. 253–274. Tel Aviv: Breirot, 1993.

El-Assad, Mohamad. *Children of the Dew: A Novella* (Hebrew translation from Arabic). Tel Aviv: Pardes, 2005.

Elmelekh, Yuval, and Noach Levin-Epstein. "Migration and Housing in Israel: Another Look at Ethnic Inequality" (in Hebrew). *Megamot* 39, no. 3 (1999): 243–269.

Elnekaveh, Yosef. *The Book of Our Rabbi Ya'akov Avihatsira* (in Hebrew). Jerusalem: Ner Yitshak Yeshiva, 1990.

Eshel, Zadok. *The Ha-Hagana Battle Over Haifa* (in Hebrew). Organization of Haganah Members in Haifa. Tel Aviv: Ministry of Defense, 1978.

Feige, Michael. "Dionysus in the Center and a Different Look at Israeli Historiography" (in Hebrew). *Theory and Criticism* 26 (Spring 2005): 201–234.

Fein, Jonathan. "British Policy Toward the Development of Haifa Harbor, 1906–1924: Strategic Considerations" (in Hebrew). *Cathedra* 89 (1998): 127–154.

Feuerstein, Reuven, and Mark Rishel. *Children of the Mellah: Cultural Retardation Among Moroccan Children and its Educational Significance* (in Hebrew). Jerusalem:

Department of Children's and Youngsters' Immigration, the Jewish Agency, and the Szold Institute for Children and Youngsters, 1963.

Fischbach, Michael R. *Jewish Property Claims Against Arab Countries.* New York: Columbia University Press, 2008.

——— *Records of Dispossession. Palestinian Refugee Property and the Arab-Israeli Conflict.* New York: Columbia University Press, 2003.

Flores, Alexander. "Gassan Kanafanis politisches Engagement." In Wolfdietrich Fischer, ed., *Männer unter tödlicher Sonne*, pp. 11–19. Würtzburg: Ergon, 1995.

Ford, Richard T. "The Boundaries of Race: Political Geography in Legal Analysis." In Nicholas Blomley, David Delaney, and Richard T. Ford, eds., *The Legal Geographies Reader: Law, Power and Space*, pp. 87–104. Oxford: Blackwell, 2001.

——— "The Boundaries of Race: Political Geography in Legal Analysis." *Harvard Law Review* 107, no. 8 (1994):1843–1921.

Forman, Geremy. "Law and the Historical Geography of the Galilee: Israel's Litigatory Advantages During the Special Operation of Land Settlement." *Journal of Historical Geography* 32 (2006): 796–817.

Forman, Geremy, and Alexandre (Sandy) Kedar. "From Arab Land to 'Israel Land': The Legal Dispossession of the Palestinians Displaced by Israel in the Wake of 1948." *Society and Space* 22, no. 6 (2004): 809–830.

Frei, Norbert, José Brunner, and Constantin Goschler. *Die Praxis der Wiedergutmachung. Geschichte, Erfahrung und Wirkung in Deutschland und Israel.* Göttingen: Wallstein, 2009.

Fuchs, Ron. "The Arab Residential Home in Ottoman Haifa: Architectural Documentation" (in Hebrew). In Yossi Ben-Artzi, ed., *Haifa: Local History*, pp. 63–104. Haifa: Haifa University Press, 1998.

Geertz, Clifford. "Thick Description: Toward an Interpretive Theory of Culture." *The Interpretation of Cultures.* New York: Basic Books, 1973.

Gilbar, Gad. "Trends in the Demographic Development of the Palestinian Arabs, 1870–1948" (in Hebrew). *Cathedra* 45 (1988): 43–56.

Golan, Arnon. "From Arab Towns to Israeli Cities: Lod and Ramleh in the War of Independence and Thereafter" (in Hebrew). *Contemporary Jewry* 14 (2001): 263–289.

——— "Jewish Nationalism, European Colonialism, and Modernity: The Origins of the Israeli Public Housing System." *Housing Studies* 13, no. 4 (1998): 487–505.

——— "Jewish Refugees in Eretz Israel During the War of Independence" (in Hebrew). *Contemporary Jewry* 8 (1993): 217–242.

——— "Jewish Settlements in Former Arab Towns and Their Incorporation Into the Israeli Urban System (1948–1950)." *Israeli Affairs* 9, no. 1–2 (2003): 149–164.

——— "Politics of Wartime Demolition and Human Landscape Transformation." *War in History* 9, no. 4 (2002): 431–445.

———— "Redistribution and Resistance: Urban Conflicts During and Following the 1948 War." *Journal of Modern Jewish Studies* 1, no. 2 (2002): 117–130.

———— "The Transfer to Jewish Control of Abandoned Jewish Lands During the War of Independence." In Ilan S. Troen and Noah Lucas, eds., *Israel: The First Decade of Independence*, pp. 403–440. Albany: State University of New York Press, 1995.

———— *Wartime Spatial Changes: Former Arab Territories Within the State of Israel, 1948–1950* (in Hebrew). Ben-Gurion Research Center: Ben-Gurion University of the Negev, 2001.

Golani, Motti. "Watershed in Haifa: Britain and the Civil War in Palestine, December 1947–May 1948." In Anita Shapira, ed., *A State in the Making: Israeli Society in the First Decades* (in Hebrew), pp. 13–59. Jerusalem: Zalman Shazar Center, 2001.

Gold, John Robert. *The Experience of Modernism: Modern Architects and the Future City, 1928–1953*. London: Spon, 1997.

Gonen, Amiram. *Between City and Suburb: Urban Residential Patterns and Processes in Israel*. Avebury: Aldershot, 1995.

Goren, Tamir. *Cooperation in the Shadow of Confrontation: Arabs and Jews in Local Government in Haifa During the British Mandate* (in Hebrew). Ramat Gan: Bar Ilan University Press, 2008.

———— *From Dependence to Integration: Israeli Rule and the Arabs of Haifa, 1948–1950: A Historical and Geographical Analysis* (in Hebrew). Haifa: Haifa University, Jewish-Arab Center, 1996.

———— "Plans and Proposals for Augmenting the Jewish Community in Haifa During the British Period" (in Hebrew). *Horizons in Geography* 54 (2002): 5–27.

———— *The Fall of Arab Haifa in 1948* (in Hebrew). Beersheba: Ben-Gurion University of the Negev, Ministry of Defense, 2006.

———— "The History of the Disappearance of the 'Old City' from the Perspective of Haifa, 1948–1951" (in Hebrew). *Horizons in Geography* 40–41 (1994): 57–81.

———— "The Vision of 'A Greater Jewish Haifa': The Annexation of Neighborhoods for Demographic Benefits During the British Mandate" (in Hebrew). *Studies in Zionism, the Yishuv, and the State of Israel* 11 (2001): 230–260.

———— "Was There Really Discrimination? Municipal Policy and the Division of Resources Between Jews and Arabs in Haifa, 1940–1947" (in Hebrew). *Cathedra* 113 (2004): 113–142.

———— "Why Did the Arab Population Leave Haifa?" (in Hebrew). *Cathedra* 80 (1996): 175–208.

Goschler, Constantin. "Return of Property and Competition for Memory" (in Hebrew). In Yfaat Weiss and Gilad Margalit, eds., *Memory and Amnesia: The Holocaust in Germany*, pp. 440–443. Tel Aviv: Ha-kibbutz ha-me'uhad, 2005.

Graicer, Iris. "Ideological Conflicts as Factors Shaping the Map of Local Government in Mandatory Palestine" (in Hebrew). *Studies in the Geography of the Land of Israel* 14 (1993): 186–224.

———— "Shekhunat Ha-Ovdim (Workers Estates): Socio-Ideological Experimentation in Shaping the Urban Scene in Palestine During the British Mandate" (in Hebrew). Ph.D. diss., Hebrew University of Jerusalem, 1982.

———— "The Ideological Basis of the Labor Movement Toward Urban Settlement in Palestine, 1905–1930" (in Hebrew). *Studies in the Geography of Israel* 12 (1985): 186–224.

Granovsky, Abraham. "Haifa Bay Land Policy." In *Palestine and Near East Economic Magazine* 4 (1929): 4–5.

———— "Die bodenpolitische Bedeutung der Haifa-Bay." In *Haifa Vergangenheit Gegenwart Zukunft: Anlässlich des Erwerbs der Boden der Haifa-Bay*, pp. 34–35. Jerusalem: Keren Kayemeth LeIsrael, 1929.

Habibi, Emile. *Ikhtayyeh* (in Hebrew). Tel Aviv: Am Oved, 1988.

———— *The Sacred Life of Saeed the Pessoptimist*. Trans. Salma Khadra Jayyusi and Trevor LeGassick. London: Zed, 1985.

Hacohen, Devora. *Immigrants in Turmoil: The Great Wave of Immigration to Israel and Its Absorption, 1948–1953* (in Hebrew). Jerusalem: Ben-Zvi Institute, 1994.

Hague, Cliff. "Renegotiating Places: The Experience of Low-Demand Housing in Salford, England." In M. Carley, P. Jenkins, and H. Smith, eds., *Urban Development and Civil Society: The Role of Communities in Sustainable Cities*, pp. 154–172. London: Earthcan, 2001.

Harlow, Barbara, and Karen E. Riley. "Introduction." In Ghassan Kanafani, *Palestine's Children: Returning to Haifa and Other Stories*, 1–12. London: Lynne Rienner, 2000.

Harvey, David. *Social Justice and the City*. Baltimore: Johns Hopkins University Press, 1973.

Hazani, Moshe, and Ilan Yeshayahu. *Social Consequences of Urban Renewal: The Ethnic Synagogues in Wadi Salib and Their Social Role* (in Hebrew). Ramat Gan: Bar-Ilan University, Local Government Institute, 1970.

Herbert, Gilbert, and Silvina Sosnovsky. *The Garden City as Paradigm: Planning on the Carmel, 1919–1923*. Haifa: Technion, 1986.

Herbert, Zbigniew. *"The Abandoned": Selected Poems*. Oxford: Oxford University Press, 1977.

Herzl, Theodor. *Old-New Land (Altneuland)*. New York: Bloch, 1960.

Herzog, Hannah. *Political Ethnicity: The Image and the Reality* (in Hebrew). Tel Aviv: Yad Tabenkin, Institute for the Study of Zionism and Pioneering in Oriental Countries, Ha-kibbutz ha-me'uhad, 1986.

Hoffnung, Menahem. *Israel: Security Needs Versus the Rule of Law* (in Hebrew). Jerusalem: Nevo, 1991.

Home, Robert K. *Of Planting and Planning: The Making of British Colonial Cities.* London: Routledge, 1996.

———— "Town Planning and Garden Cities in the British Colonial Empire, 1910–1940." *Planning Perspectives* 5 (1990): 23–37.

Isin, Engin F. "Historical Sociology of the City." In Gerard Delanty and Engin F. Isin, eds., *Handbook of Historical Sociology,* pp. 312–325. London: Saga, 2003.

Jacobs, Jane. *The Death and Life of Great American Cities.* New York: Vintage, 1961.

Jacobsen, Hanoch. *After the Clearance: The Wadi Salib Residents in Their New Environment—Concluding Report of the Follow-up Study on the Wadi Salib Evacuees* (in Hebrew). Haifa: Technion Research and Development Institution, Center for Research on People at Work, Center for Research on the City and Its Environs, 1975.

Kanafani, Abd el-Latif. *Sha'ara el-Bourge 15: Haifa* (in Arabic). Beirut: Bisan, 1996.

Kanafani, Ghassan. "Returning to Haifa." In *Palestine's Children: Returning to Haifa and Other Stories,* pp. 149–196. Trans. Barbara Harlow and Karen E. Riley. London: Lynne Rienner, 2000.

———— "The Land of Sad Oranges." In *Men in the Sun and Other Palestinian Stories,* pp. 75–80. Trans. Hilary Kilpatrick. London: Lynne Rienner, 1999.

Kark, Ruth. "Planning, Housing, and Land Policy, 1948–1952: The Formation of Concepts and Governmental Frameworks." In Ilan S. Troen and Noah Lucas, eds., *Israel: The First Decade of Independence,* pp. 461–494. Albany: State University of New York Press, 1995.

Karkar, Yaqub N. *Railway Development in the Ottoman Empire, 1856–1914.* New York: Vintage, 1972.

Karsh, Efraim. "Nakbat Haifa: Collapse and Dispersion of a Major Palestinian Community." *Middle Eastern Studies* 37, no. 4, (2001): 25–70.

Kedar, Alexandre (Sandy). "On the Legal Geography of Ethnocratic Settler States: Notes Towards a Research Agenda." *Current Legal Issues,* no. 5 (2003): 401–441.

Kemp, Adriana. "'Migration of Nations' or 'The Great Conflagration': State Control and Resistance in the Israeli Border Land" (in Hebrew). In Hanan Hever, Yehuda Shenhav, and Pnina Motzafi-Haller, eds., *Mizrahim in Israel: A Critical Observation Into Israel's Ethnicity,* pp. 36–67. Tel Aviv: Ha-kibbutz ha-me'uhad, 2002.

Kenworthy, M. P. "Haifa Harbour and the British Empire." *Palestine and Near East Economic Magazine* 4, no. 4–5 (1929): 64–65.

Keshet, B. *Haifa East Railway Station, the Train Museum Plaza, Conservation Survey* (in Hebrew). Haifa: Haifa Municipality, Department for Long-term Planning, June 1998.

Khalidi, Walid. "The Fall of Haifa." *Middle East Forum* 35 (December 1959): 22–32.

Khazzoom, Aziza. "Did the Israeli State Engineer Segregation? On the Placement of Jewish Immigrants in Development Towns in the 1950s." *Social Forces* 84, no. 1 (2005): 115–134.

Kimmerling, Baruch. *Immigrants, Settlers, Natives: The Israeli State and Society, Between Cultural Pluralism and Culture War* (in Hebrew). Tel Aviv: Alma and Am Oved, 2004.

Kiš, Danilo. *A Tomb for Boris Davidovich.* New York: Harcourt Brace Jovanovich, 1978.

Kohn, Hans. *Western Civilization in the Near East.* New York: AMS, 1966.

Kolka, Gila. "Wadi Salib: The Story of an Evacuation" (in Hebrew). *Mivnim* 76 (January 1989): 29–32.

Kolodney, Ziva. "The Politics of the Landscape: Landscape Production in Transition Between Mandate and Sovereign Haifa." Ph.D. diss., Haifa: Technion Department of Architecture and Town Planning, 2010.

Knesset Israel. *Biographies of Members of Israel's Knesset from the First Knesset, 1948, to the Twelfth Knesset, 1992* (in Hebrew). Jerusalem: Knesset, 1993.

Kretzmer, David. *The Legal Status of the Arabs in Israel.* Boulder: Westview, 1990.

Kunda, Sigal Davidi, and Robert Oxman. "The Flight of the Camel: The Levant Fair of 1934 and the Creation of a Situated Modernism." In Haim Yacobi, ed., *Constructing a Sense of Place: Architecture and the Zionist Discourse,* pp. 52–75. Aldershot: Ashgate, 2004.

Kurze militärgeographische Beschreibung von Palästina. Berlin: Kartographische Abteilung der Kgl. Preussischer Landesaufnahme, 1917.

Kymlicka, Will. "Multicultural Citizenship." In Gershon Shafir, ed., *The Citizenship Debates. A Reader,* pp. 167–188. Minneapolis: University of Minnesota Press, 1998.

Landesberger, Michael. *The Influence of Individual Compensation Payments on Consumption and Savings in Israel and Some Discussions on the Function of Consumption* (in Hebrew). Jerusalem: Bank of Israel Research Department, 1969.

Laor, Yitzhak. "We Have Not Come to Say: Get Out of Here; That Would Take a War" (in Hebrew). *Haaretz Cultural and Literary Supplement,* May 18, 2001, p. 13.

Laskier, Michael M. *Israel and the Maghreb: From Statehood to Oslo.* Gainesville: University Press of Florida, 2004.

——— *North African Jewry in the Twentieth Century: The Jews of Morocco, Tunisia, and Algeria.* New York: New York University Press, 1994.

——— *The Jews of the Maghreb in the Shadow of Vichy and the Swastika* (in Hebrew). Tel Aviv: Tel Aviv: Diaspora Research Institute, 1992.

LeVine, Mark. "Locating Home: Overthrowing Geography, Misreading Modernity, and Other Adventures in the Search for the Routes That Divide Us." In Ron Robin and Bo Stråth, eds., *Homelands: Poetic Power and the Politics of Space,* pp. 165–188. Bruxelles: P.I.E.–Peter Lang, 2003.

——— *Overthrowing Geography: Jaffa, Tel Aviv, and the Struggle for Palestine, 1880–1948.* Berkeley: University of California Press, 2005.

Liskovsky, Aharon. "'Resident Absentees' in Israel" (in Hebrew). *New East* 3 (1960): 186–192.

Luke, Harry Charles. *Cook's Traveler's Handbook for Palestine and Syria*. London: Simpkin, Marshall, 1929.

——— *The Traveler's Handbook for Palestine and Syria*. London: Simpkin, Marshall, Hamilton, Kent, 1924.

Lumby, Christopher. *Cook's Traveler's Handbook for Palestine and Syria*. London: Simpkin, Marshall, Hamilton, Kent, 1934.

Lu-Yon, Yubert, and Rachel Kalush. *Housing in Israel: Policy and Inequality* (in Hebrew). Tel Aviv: Edva Center, 1994.

Maier, Charles S. "Overcoming the Past? Narrative and Negotiation, Remembering, and Reparation: Issues at the Interface of History and the Law." In John Torpey, ed., *Politics and the Past: On Repairing Historical Injustices*, pp. 295–304. Maryland: Rowman and Littlefield, 2003.

Malka, Haim. *Selection in the Immigration of Moroccan Jews in 1948–1956* (in Hebrew). Haim Malka, 1998.

Malkki, Liisa H. *Purity and Exile: Violence, Memory, and National Cosmology Among Hutu Refugees in Tanzania*. Chicago: University of Chicago Press, 1995.

Mansour, Johnny. *Haifa Arab Street* (in Arabic). Haifa: Sdc, 1999.

Marinsky, Arie, and Moshe Lichtman. *In Light and in Darkness* (in Hebrew). Jerusalem: Idanim, 1992.

Masalha, Nur. "A Critique on Benny Morris." In Ilan Pappe, ed., *The Israel Palestine Question*, pp. 211–220. London: Routledge, 1999.

——— *Expulsion of the Palestinians: The Concept of "Transfer" in Zionist Political Thought, 1882–1948*. Washington, D.C., Institute for Palestine Studies, 1992.

Mazower, Mark. *No Enchanted Place: The End of Empire and the Ideological Origins of the United Nations*. Princeton: Princeton University Press, 2009.

Mejcher, Helmut. *Imperial Quest for Oil: Iraq, 1910–1928*. London: Ithaca, 1976.

Moneta, J., ed. *Port of Haifa Authority, Research Section [Mit Hafenplan u. Statistiken]: 25 Years Port of Haifa, 1933–1958*. Haifa, 1958.

Morris, Benny. "Haifa's Arabs: Displacement and Concentration, July 1948." *Middle East Journal* 42, no. 2 (1988): 241–259.

——— "Haifa's Arabs: Displacement and Concentration, July 1948." In *1948 and After: Israel and the Palestinians*, pp. 149–171. Oxford: Clarendon, 1990.

——— *1948: The First Arab-Israeli War*. New Haven: Yale University Press, 2008.

——— "Notes on Zionist Historiography and the Idea of Transfer 1937–1944." In *Jews and Arabs in Palestine / Israel 1936–1956*, 42–57 (in Hebrew). Tel Aviv: Am Oved, 2000.

——— *The Birth of the Palestinian Refugee Problem Revisited*. Cambridge: Cambridge University Press, 2004.

——— "Yosef Weitz and the Transfer Committees, 1948–1949." *Middle Eastern Studies* 22, no. 4 (1986): 522–561.

Musil, Jirzí. "Housing Policy and the Sociospatial Structure of Cities in a Socialist Country: The Example of Prague." *International Journal of Urban and Regional Research* 11, no. 1 (1987): 27–36.

Naimark, Norman M. *Fires of Hatred: Ethnic Cleansing in Twentieth-Century Europe.* Cambridge: Harvard University Press, 2001.

Nitzan-Shiftan, Alona. "Contested Zionism: Alternative Modernism—Erich Mendelssohn and the Tel Aviv Chug in Mandate Palestine." In Haim Yacobi, ed., *Constructing a Sense of Place: Architecture and the Zionist Discourse*, pp. 17–51. Aldershot: Ashgate, 2004.

Palestine Government. *Opening of Haifa Harbour*, October 31, 1933.

Peled, Yoav, and Gershon Shafir. *Being Israeli: The Dynamics of Multiple Citizenship.* Cambridge: Cambridge University Press, 2002.

Peleg, D. *Survey on Preservation of a Building on Hatam Sofer Street, Book 2* (in Hebrew). Haifa Municipality, Department of Long-term Planning, Haifa, 1999.

Perényi, Imre. *Die Moderne Stadt: Gedanken über die Vergangenheit und Zukunft der Städteplanung.* Budapest: Akadémiai Kiadó, 1970.

Picard, Avi. "The Beginnings of the Selective Immigration in the 1950s" (in Hebrew). *Studies in Zionism, the Yishuv, and the State of Israel* 9 (1999): 338–394.

Pik, Pinchas. "Meissner Pasha: The Pioneer of Railways in Palestine, the Man, His Railways, and Their Fortunes" (in Hebrew). *Cathedra* 10 (1979): 102–128.

Preece, Jennifer J. "Ethnic Cleansing and the Normative Transformation of International Society." Conference Paper in *Failed States III: Globalization and the Failed State.* Florence, Italy. http://www.comm.ucsb.edu/research/mstohl/failed_states/2000/papers/jacksonpreece.html

——— "Ethnic Cleansing as an Instrument of Nation-State Creation: Changing State Practices and Evolving Norms." *Human Rights Quarterly* 20 (1998): 817–842.

Press, Jesaia. *Palästina und Südsyrien Reisehandbuch.* Jerusalem: Im Auftrage des Palestine Express Comp., Benjamin Hary, 1921.

Rabinow, Paul. "Colonialism, Modernity: The French in Morocco." In Nezar Al-Sayyad, ed., *Forms of Dominance: On the Architecture and Urbanism of the Colonial Enterprise*, pp. 167–182. Avebury: Aldershot, 1992.

Reichman, Shalom. *From Foothold to Settled Territory: The Jewish Settlement, 1918–1948—a Geographical Interpretation and Documentation* (in Hebrew). Jerusalem: Ben-Zvi Institute, 1979.

——— "Partition and Transfer: Crystallization of the Settlement Map of Israel Following the War of Independence, 1948–1949." In Ruth Kark, ed., *The Land That Became Israel. Studies in Historical Geography*, pp. 320–330. Jerusalem: Magnes, 1989.

Rekhess, Eli. "Initial Israeli Policy Guidelines Towards the Arab Minority, 1948–1949." In Laurence J. Silberstein, ed., *New Perspectives on Israeli History*, pp. 103–123. New York: New York University Press, 1991.

Rothbard, Sharon. *White City Black City* (in Hebrew). Tel Aviv: Bavel, 2005.

Rothschild, Walter. "Meissner Pasha: German Railway Construction in the Ottoman Empire." In Haim Goren, ed., *Germany and the Middle East: Past, Present, and Future*, pp. 225–242. Jerusalem: Magnes, 2003.

Rubinstein, Elyakim. "In Memoriam of Judge Moshe Etzyoni: Law, Wisdom and Love of Men and People" (in Hebrew). *Law and Government in Israel* 5 (1999/2000): 401–407.

Ruete, Said. *Reisen in Syrien und Palästina mit Besonderer Berücksichtung der Dortigen Templergemeinden.* Berlin: Verlag von Dietrich Reimer, 1898.

Ruppin, Arthur. "Die Landarbeiterfrage in Palästina." *Palästina* 3–4 (1912): 64–75.

——— *The Jews' Struggle for Existence* (in Hebrew). Tel Aviv: Bialik Institute, 1940.

Sa'adon, Hayim. "'The Palestinian Element' in Violent Eruptions Between Jews and Moslems in Moslem Countries" (in Hebrew). *Pe'amim* 63 (1995): 86–131.

Sawicki, Stanislaw J. *Soviet Land and Housing Law: A Historical and Comparative Study.* New York: Praeger, 1977.

Schechtman, Joseph B. *European Population Transfers, 1939–1945.* New York: Oxford University Press, 1946.

——— *On the Wings of Eagles: The Plight, Exodus and Homecoming of Oriental Jews.* New York: Thomas Yoseloff, 1961.

——— *The Arab Refugee Problem.* New York: Philosophical Library, 1952.

——— "The Case for Arab-Jewish Exchange of Population." In Joseph B. Schechtman, ed., *Population Transfers in Asia*, pp. 84–141. New York: Hallsby, 1949.

Schiller, Elli, ed. "Haifa in the Nineteenth Century" (in Hebrew). In *Haifa and Its Sites*, pp. 73–74. Jerusalem: Ariel, 1985.

Schlögel, Karl. "Tragödie der Vertreibungen: Über das Erfordernis, ein europäisches Ereignis neu zu erzählen." *Lettre* 79 (2003): 78–83.

Schwartz, Julius. *Glimpses of Palestine.* New York: Ashland, 1927.

Segev, Tom. *1949: The First Israelis.* New York: Free Press, 1986.

Seikaly, May. *Haifa: Transformation of a Palestinian Arab Society, 1918–1939.* London: I. B. Tauris, 1995.

Sennet, Richard. "The Foreigner." In Angelika Poferl and Natan Sznaider, eds., *Ulrich Becks kosmopolitisches Projekt: Auf dem Weg in eine andere Soziologie*, pp. 218–227. Baden-Baden: Nomos, 2004.

Sharon, Arie. *Physical Planning in Israel* (in Hebrew). Jerusalem: Government Printer, 1952.

Sharon, Smadar. "'To Build and Be Built': Planning the National Space in the First Years of Israeli Statehood" (in Hebrew). Master's thesis, Tel Aviv University, 2004.

Shenhav, Yehouda. *The Arab Jews: A Postcolonial Reading of Nationalism, Religion, and Ethnicity.* Palo Alto, CA: Stanford University Press, 2006.

——— "The Jews of Iraq, Zionist Ideology, and the Property of the Palestinian Refugees of 1948: An Anomaly of National Accounting." *International Journal of Middle East Studies* 31 (1999): 605–630.

Shils, Edward. "S. N. Eisenstadt: Some Personal Observations." In Erik Cohen, Moshe Lissak, and Uri Almagor, eds., *Comparative Social Dynamics: Essays in Honor of S. N. Eisenstadt,* pp. 1–8. Boulder: Westview, 1985.

Shulewitz, Malka Hillel, and Raphael Israeli. "Exchanges of Populations Worldwide: The First World War to the 1990s." In Malka Hillel Shulewitz, ed., *The Forgotten Million: The Modern Jewish Exodus from Arab Lands,* pp. 126–141. New York: Cassel, 1999.

Sluglett, Peter. "Formal and Informal Empire in the Middle East." In Robin W. Winks and William R. Louis, eds., *The Oxford History of the British Empire,* 5:416–436. Oxford: Oxford University Press, 1999.

Slutsky, Yehuda. *History of the Hagana: From Resistance to War* (in Hebrew). Ed. Ben-Zion Dinur. Vol. 3, part 2. Tel Aviv: Am Oved, 1972.

Slyomovics, Susan. *The Object of Memory: Arab and Jew Narrate the Palestinian Village.* Philadelphia: University of Pennsylvania Press, 1998.

Smith, Barbara Jean. *The Roots of Separatism in Palestine: British Economic Policy, 1920–1929.* London: I. B. Tauris, 1993.

Stern, Shimon. "The Dispute Concerning the Construction of Haifa Port During the Period of the British Mandate" (in Hebrew). *Cathedra* 21 (1981): 171–186.

Survey of Activities Between April 1947 and March 1948, a Factual and Fiscal Report (in Hebrew). Haifa: Jewish Community in the Land of Israel, Haifa Jewish Community Council, 1948.

Szelenyi, Ivan. "Housing Inequalities and Occupational Segregation in State Socialist Cities: Commentary to the Special Issue of IJURR on East European Cities." *International Journal of Urban and Regional Research* 11, no. 1 (1987): 1–8.

Szymborska, Wislawa. *Sounds, Feelings, Thoughts: Seventy Poems.* Trans. Magnus J. Krynski and Robert A. Maguire. Princeton: Princeton University Press, 1981.

Tamari, Salim. "Bourgeois Nostalgia and the Abandoned City." *Comparative Studies of South Asia, Africa and the Middle East* 23, nos. 1 and 2 (2003): 173–180.

Teitelbaum, Raul. "Individual Compensation for the Holocaust Survivors and Social Stratification in Israel" (in Hebrew). *Theory and Criticism* 27 (Autumn 2005): 71–101.

Thom, Martin. "City, Region, and Nation: Carlo Cattaneo and the Making of Italy." *Citizenship Studies* 3, no. 2 (1999): 187–201.

Tibawi, Abd al-Latif. "Visions of Return: The Palestine Arab Refugees in Arabic Poetry and Art." *Middle East Journal* 17 (1963): 507–526.

Topalov, Christian. "Social Policies from Below: A Call for Comparative Historical Studies." *International Journal of Urban and Regional Research* 9, no. 2 (1985): 254–271.

Torpey, John. "Making Whole What Has Been Smashed: Reflections on Reparations." *Journal of Modern History* 73 (2001): 333–358.

Trietsch, Davis. *Palästina Handbuch* . Berlin: Jüdischer Verlag, 1912.

Troen, Ilan S. *Imagining Zion: Dreams, Designs, and Realities in a Century of Jewish Settlement.* New Haven: Yale University Press, 2003.

Tsur, Yaron. *A Torn Community: The Jews of Morocco and Nationalism, 1943–1954* (in Hebrew). Tel Aviv: Am Oved, 2001.

Vashitz, Yosef. "Jewish-Arab Relations in Haifa, 1940–1948" (in Hebrew). In Yosef Nevo and Yoram Nimrod, eds., *The Arabs Facing the Zionist Movement and Jewish Community, 1946–1950*, pp. 21–37. Kiryat Tivon: Oranim, 1987.

——— "Rural Migration to Haifa During the Mandate Period: A Process of Urbanization?" (in Hebrew). *Cathedra* 45 (1987): 113–130.

——— "Social Changes in Haifa's Arab Society Under the British Mandate" (in Hebrew). Ph.D. diss., Hebrew University of Jerusalem, 1993.

Weber, Max. *The City.* Ed. and trans. Don Martindale and Gertrud Neuwirth. New York: Free Press, 1958.

Weiss, Yfaat. "Ethnic Cleansing, Memory, and Property—Europe, Israel/Palestine, 1944–1948." In Raphael Gross and Yfaat Weiss, eds., *Jüdische Geschichte als allgemeine Geschichte. Dan Diner zum 60. Geburtstag*, pp. 158–188. Göttingen: Vandenhoeck and Ruprecht, 2006.

Weitz, Yehiam. "A Rival Banner: The Herut Movement and Israel's Relations with Germany." (in Hebrew). *Zion* 67 (2002): 435–464.

——— "Herut Party Against the Reparations Agreement" (in Hebrew). In Adi Ophir, ed., *Fifty to Forty-Eight: Critical Moments in the History of the State of Israel*, pp. 99–112. Jerusalem and Tel Aviv: Van Leer Institute of Jerusalem and Ha-kibbutz ha-me'uhad, 1999.

——— *The First Step to Power: The Herut Movement, 1949–1955* (in Hebrew). Jerusalem: Yad Ben-Zvi, 2007.

Wilson, Sir Charles William. "Haifa," 29:206. *Encyclopaedia Britannica.* Ed. Donald Mackenzie Wallace and Hugh Chisholm. 10th ed. Edinburgh: Black, 1902.

Yablonka, Hannah. *Survivors of the Holocaust: Israel After the War.* New York: New York University Press, 1999.

Yahav, Dan. "Yearning for the Homeland" (in Hebrew). *Iton 77* 257, no. 25 (2001): 13.

Yazbak, Mahmoud. "Arab Migration to Haifa: A Quantitative Analysis Based on Arab Sources" (in Hebrew). *Cathedra* 45 (1987): 131–146.

——— "Arab Migration to Haifa, 1933–1948" (in Hebrew). Master's thesis, Haifa University, 1986.

——— *Haifa in the Nineteenth Century: A History of the City and Society* (in Hebrew). Haifa: Haifa University, 1998.

Young, Iris Marion. "Residential Segregation and Differentiated Citizenship." *Citizenship Studies* 3, no. 2 (1999): 237–252.

Zweig, Ronald W. "Restitution of Property and Refugee Rehabilitation: Two Case Studies." *Journal of Refugee Studies* 6, no. 1/4 (1993): 56–64.

INDEX